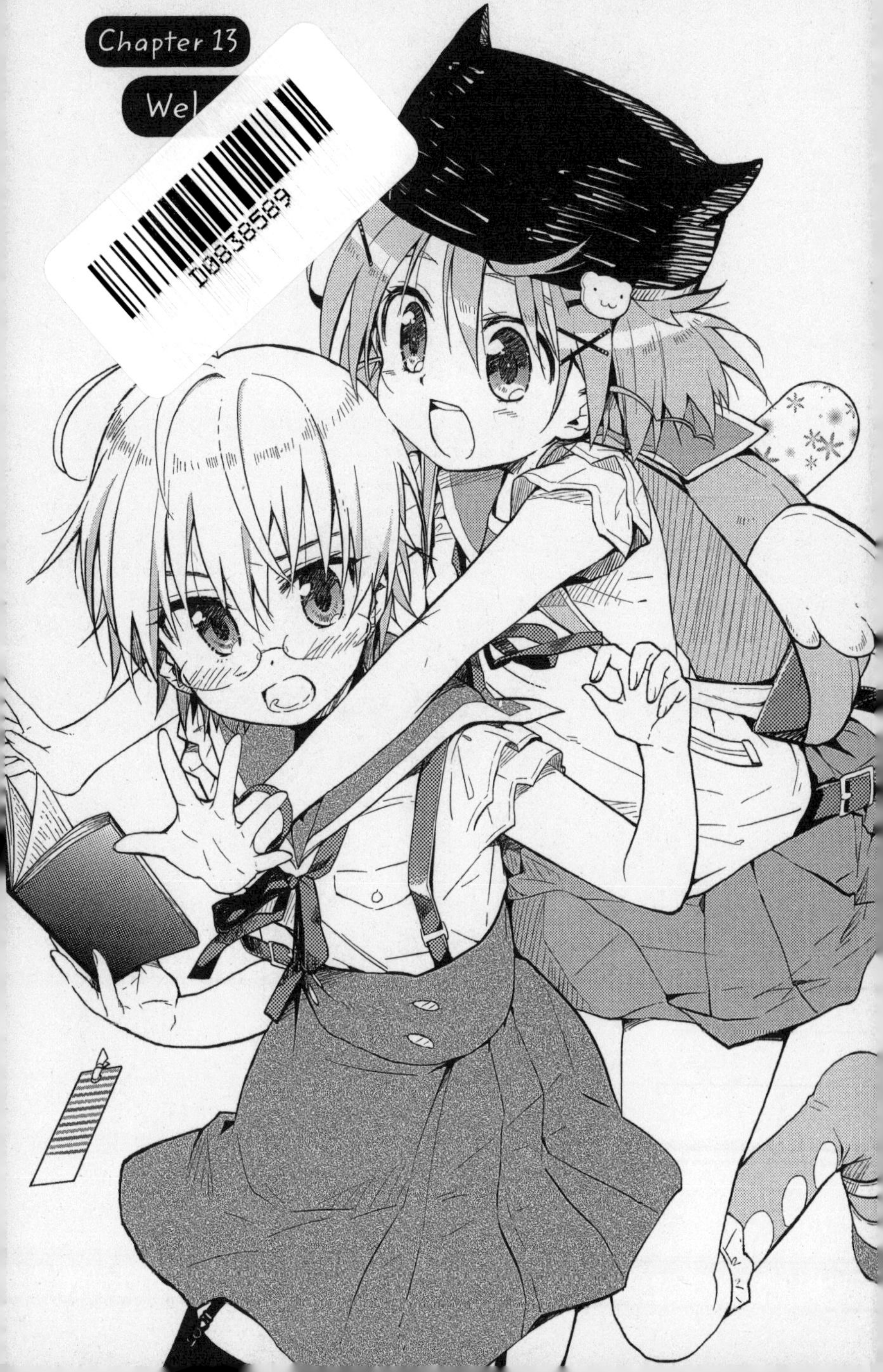
Chapter 13
Wel

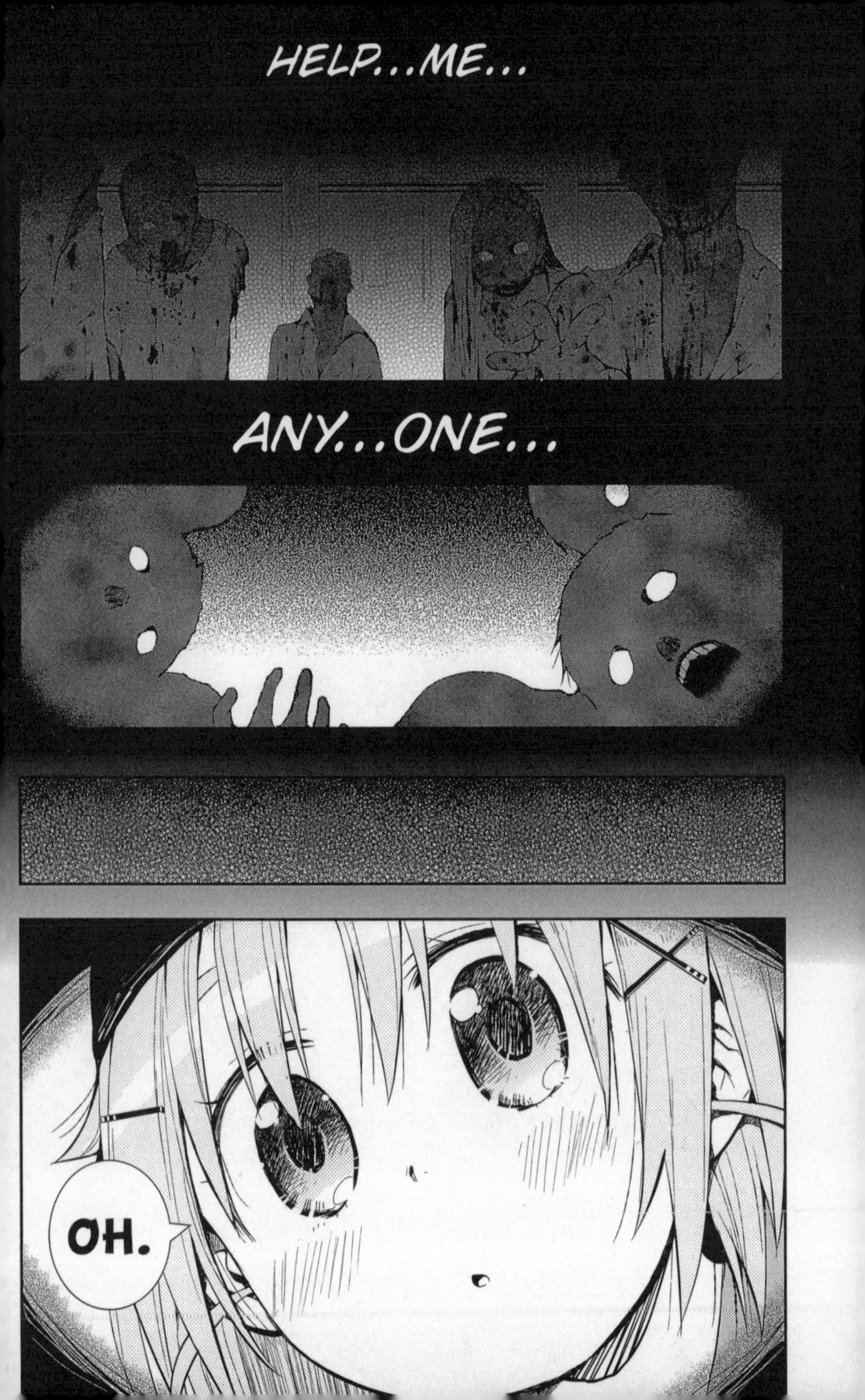
HELP...ME...
ANY...ONE...
OH.

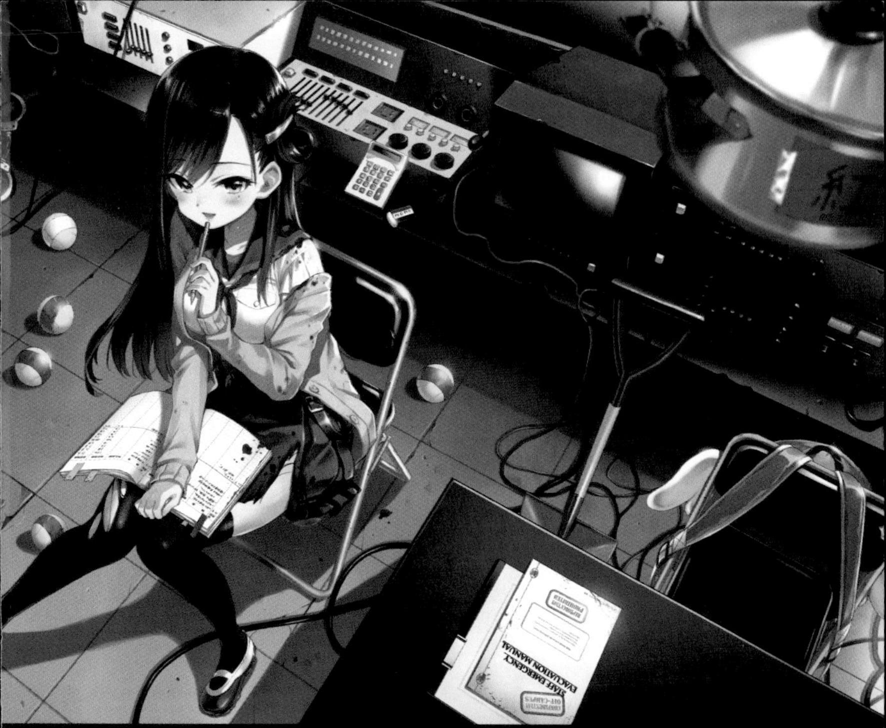

ART BY SADORU CHIBA
STORY BY NORIMITSU KAIHOU (NITROPLUS)
VOLUME 3

SCHOOL-LIVE!

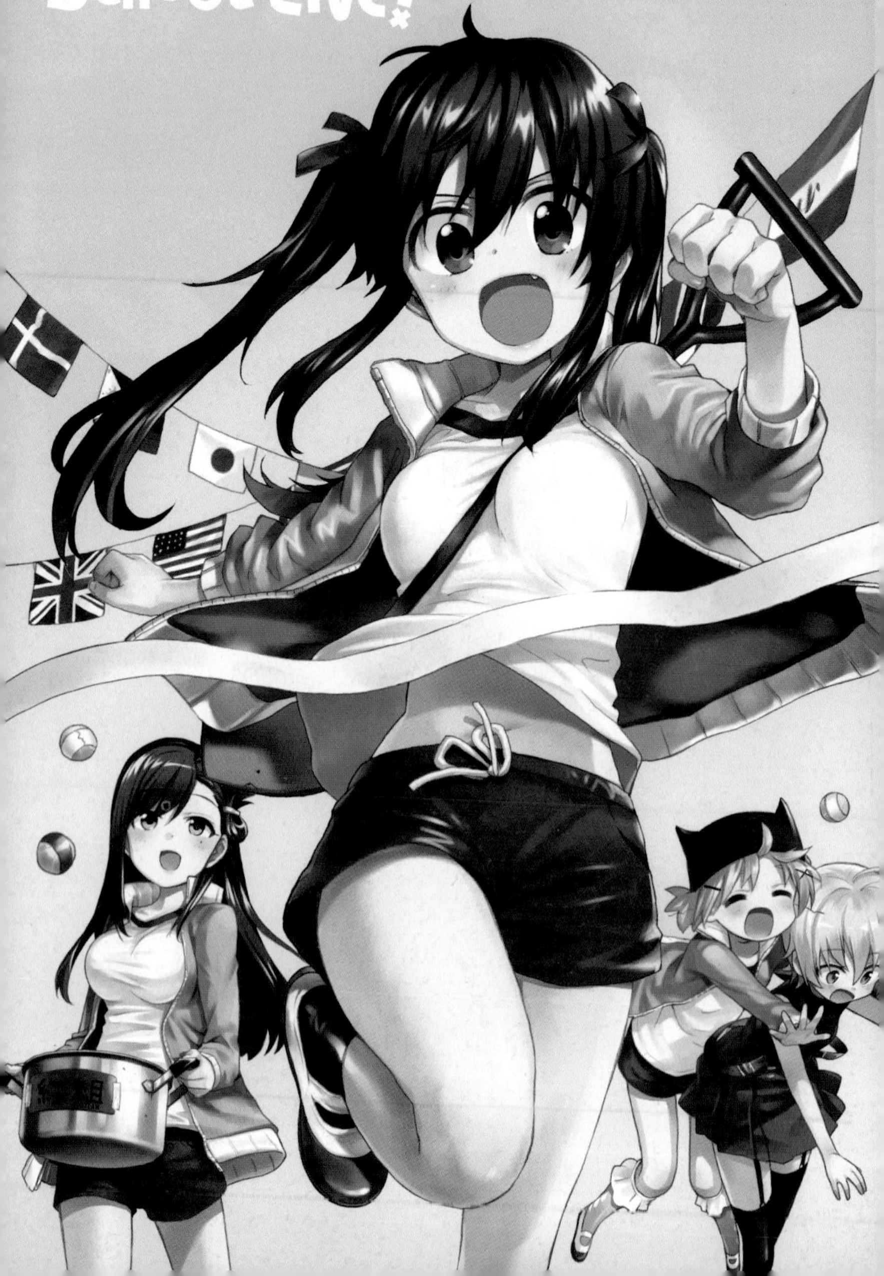

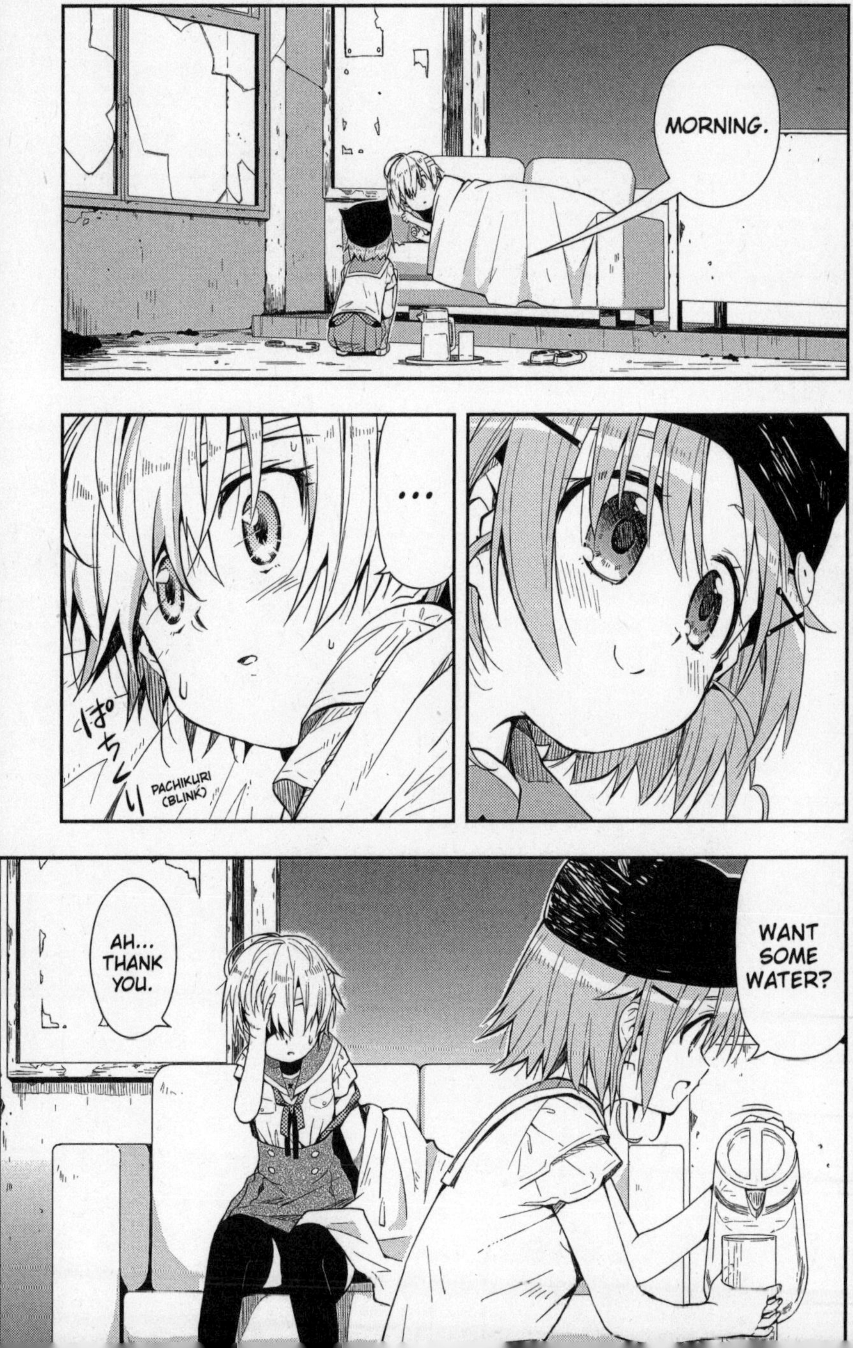
MORNING.
...
ぱちくり
PACHIKURI (BLINK)
WANT SOME WATER?
AH... THANK YOU.

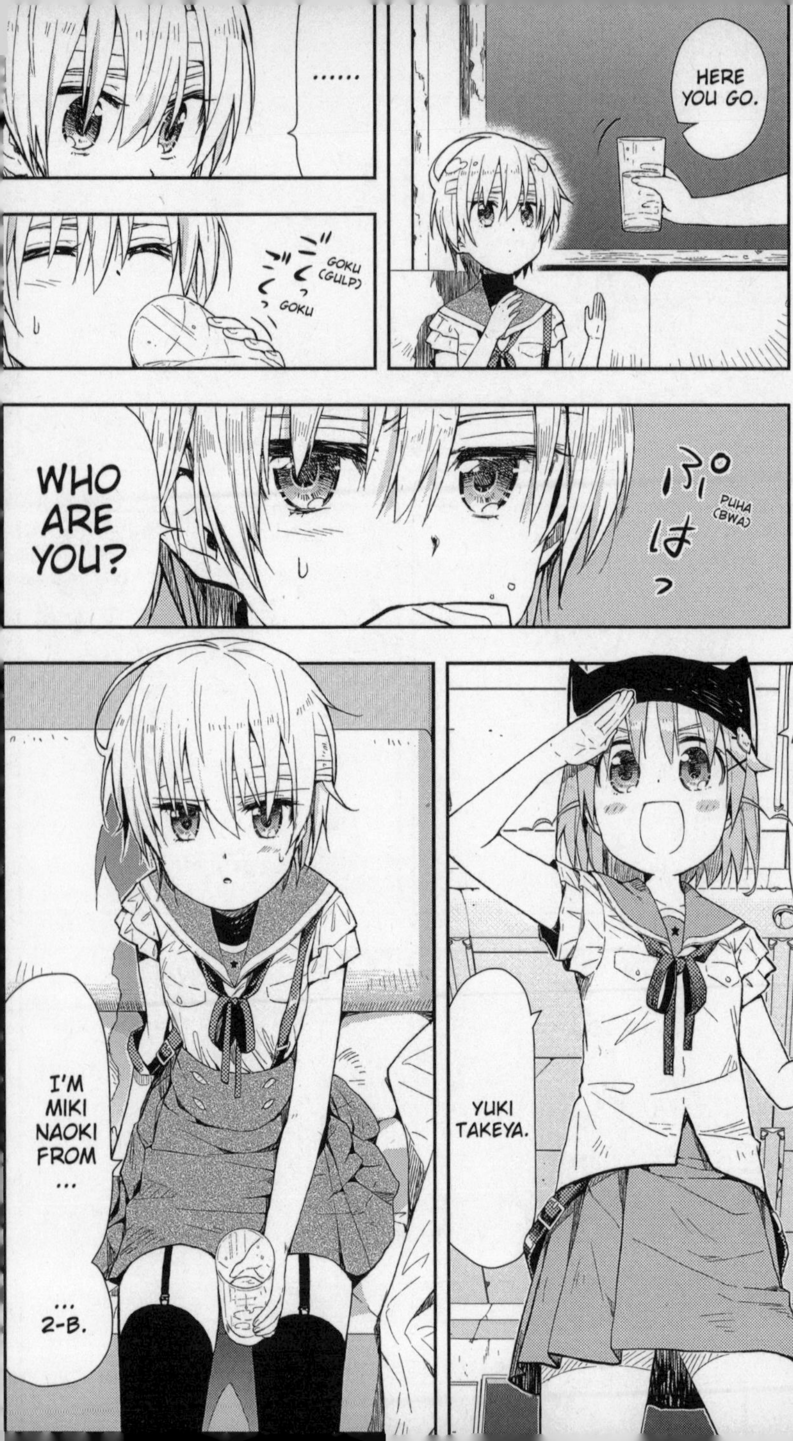
HERE YOU GO.
......
GOKU (GULP)
GOKU
ぷはっ
PUHA (BWA)
WHO ARE YOU?
MEGURI-GAOKA HIGH SCHOOL YEAR 3, CLASS C.
YUKI TAKEYA.
I'M MIKI NAOKI FROM ...
... 2-B.

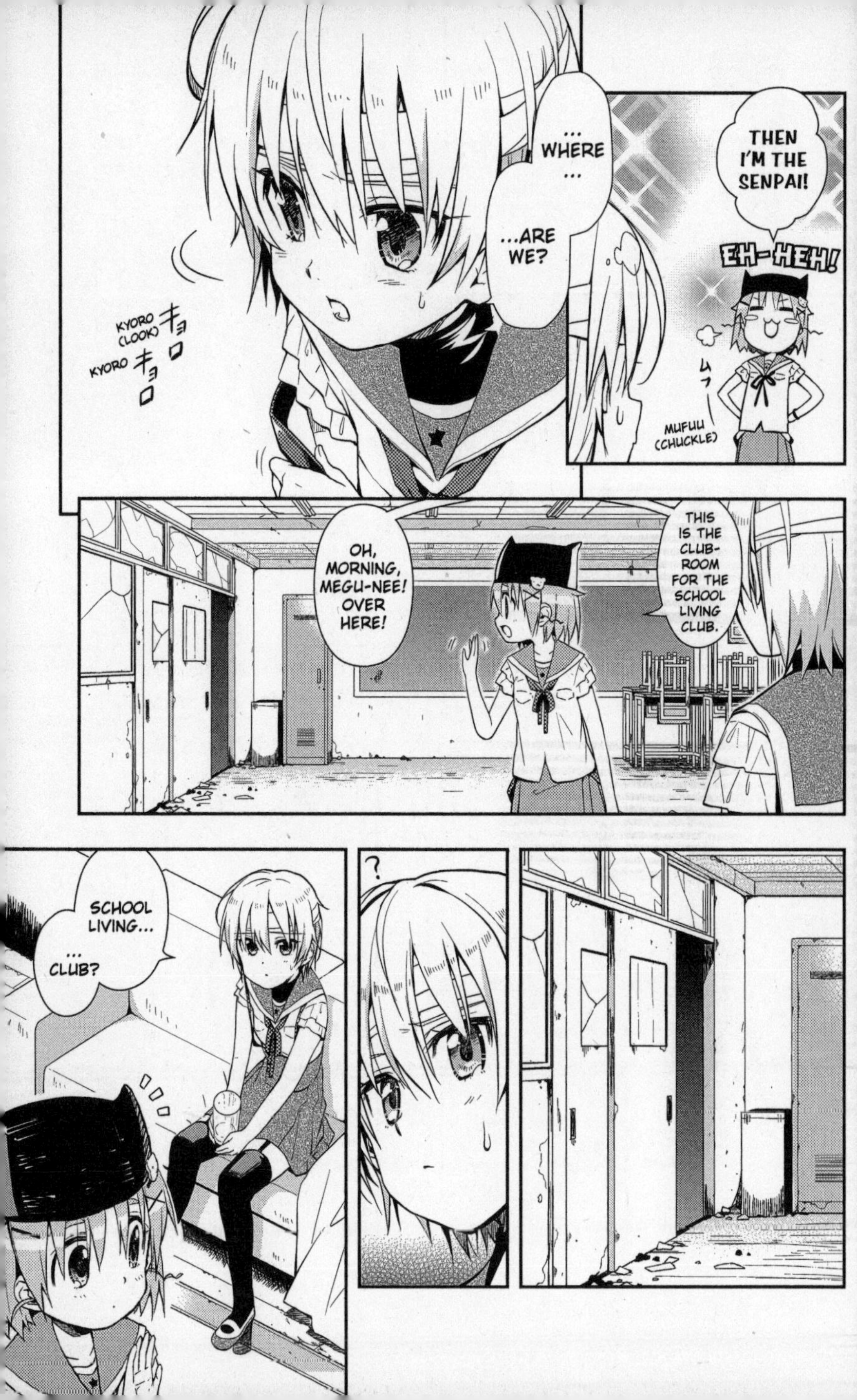
THEN I'M THE SENPAI!
EH-HEH!
ムフー
MUFUU (CHUCKLE)
... WHERE ...
...ARE WE?
キョロキョロ
KYORO (LOOK) KYORO
THIS IS THE CLUB-ROOM FOR THE SCHOOL LIVING CLUB.
OH, MORNING, MEGU-NEE! OVER HERE!
?
SCHOOL LIVING... ...CLUB?

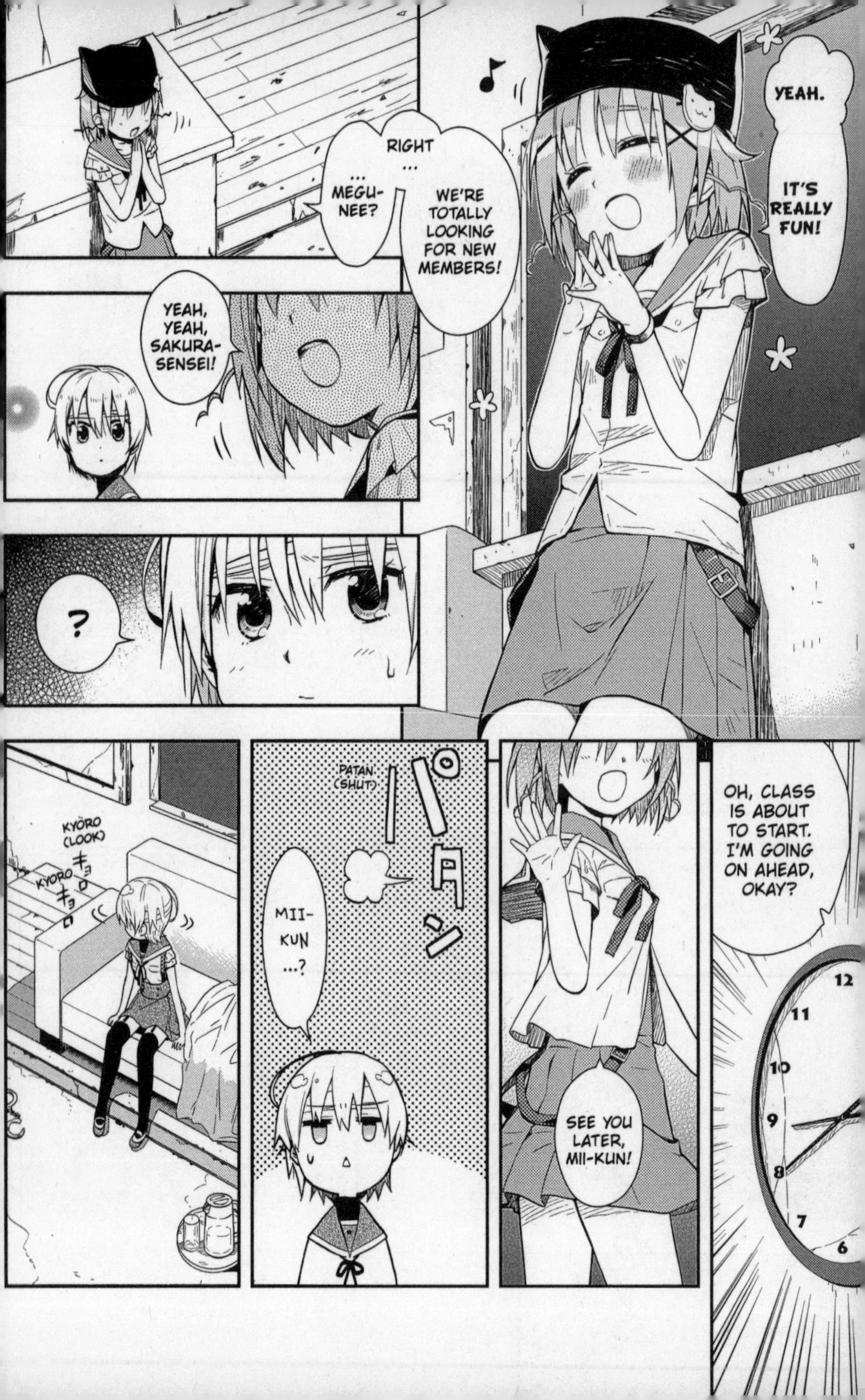
YEAH.
IT'S REALLY FUN!
WE'RE TOTALLY LOOKING FOR NEW MEMBERS!
RIGHT ... ...MEGU-NEE?
YEAH, YEAH, SAKURA-SENSEI!
?
OH, CLASS IS ABOUT TO START. I'M GOING ON AHEAD, OKAY?
SEE YOU LATER, MII-KUN!
PATAN (SHUT)
MII-KUN ...?
KYORO (LOOK)
KYORO

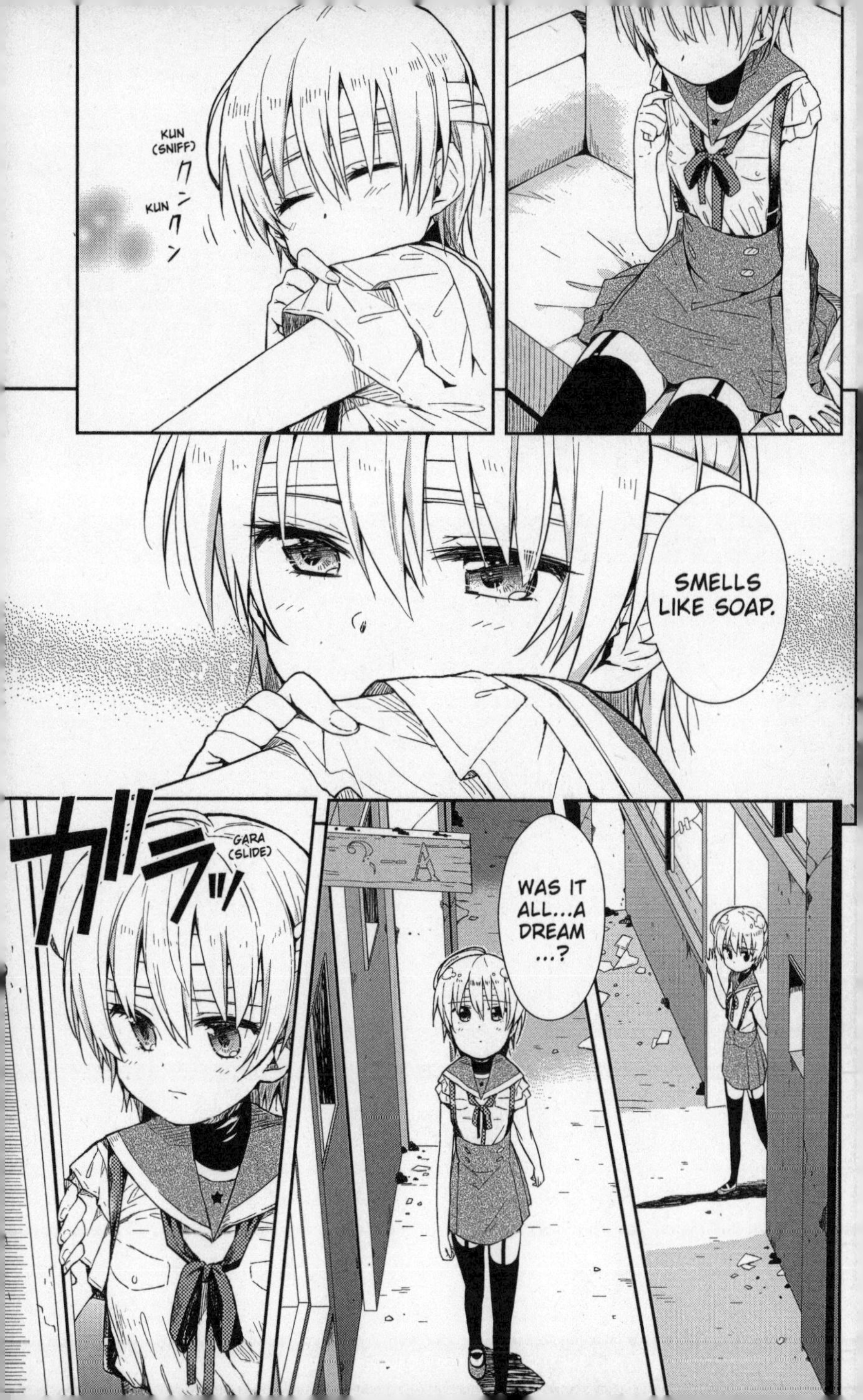

KUN (SNIFF) クン
KUN クン
SMELLS LIKE SOAP.
WAS IT ALL...A DREAM ...?
GARA (SLIDE) ガラッ

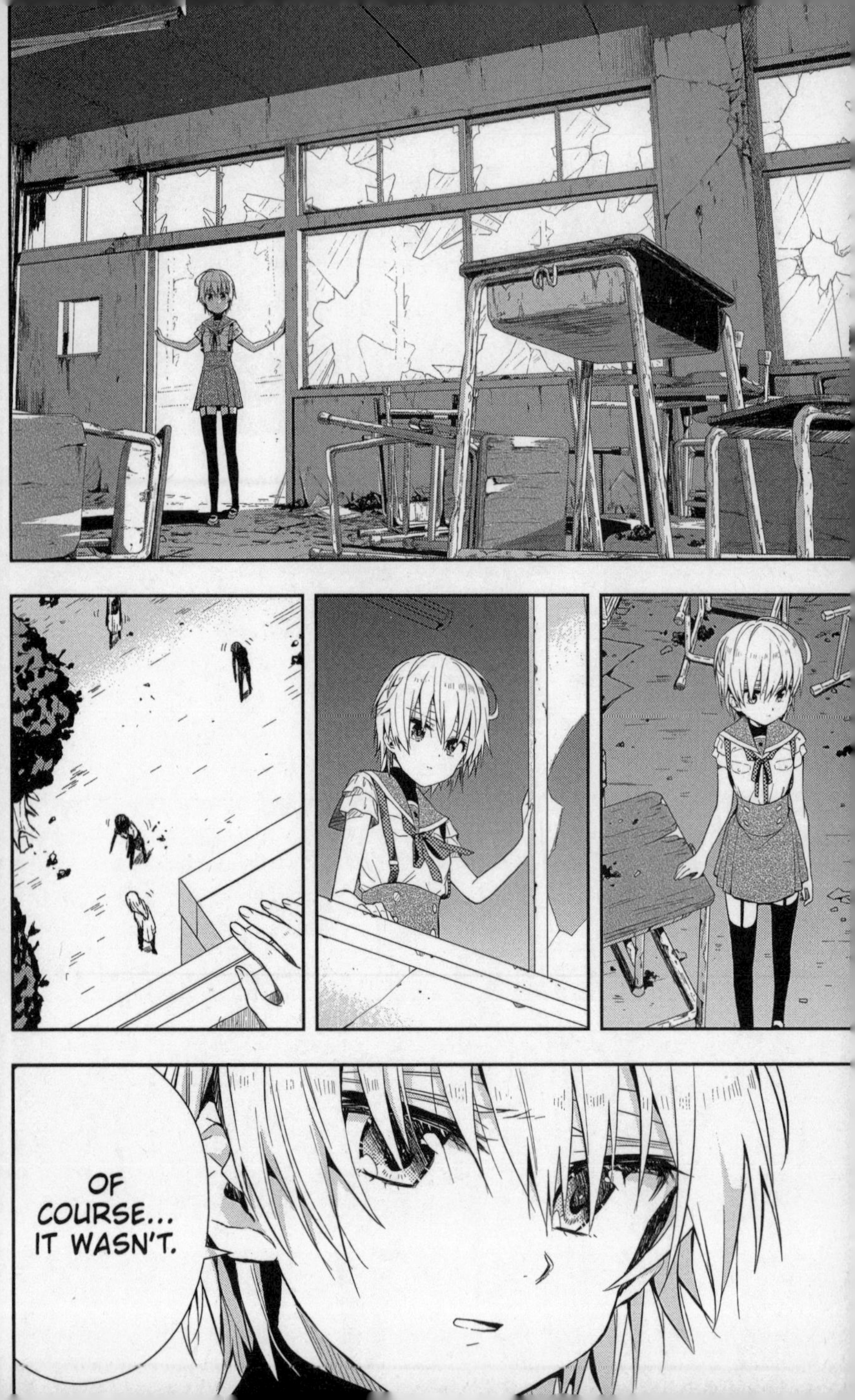
OF COURSE... IT WASN'T.

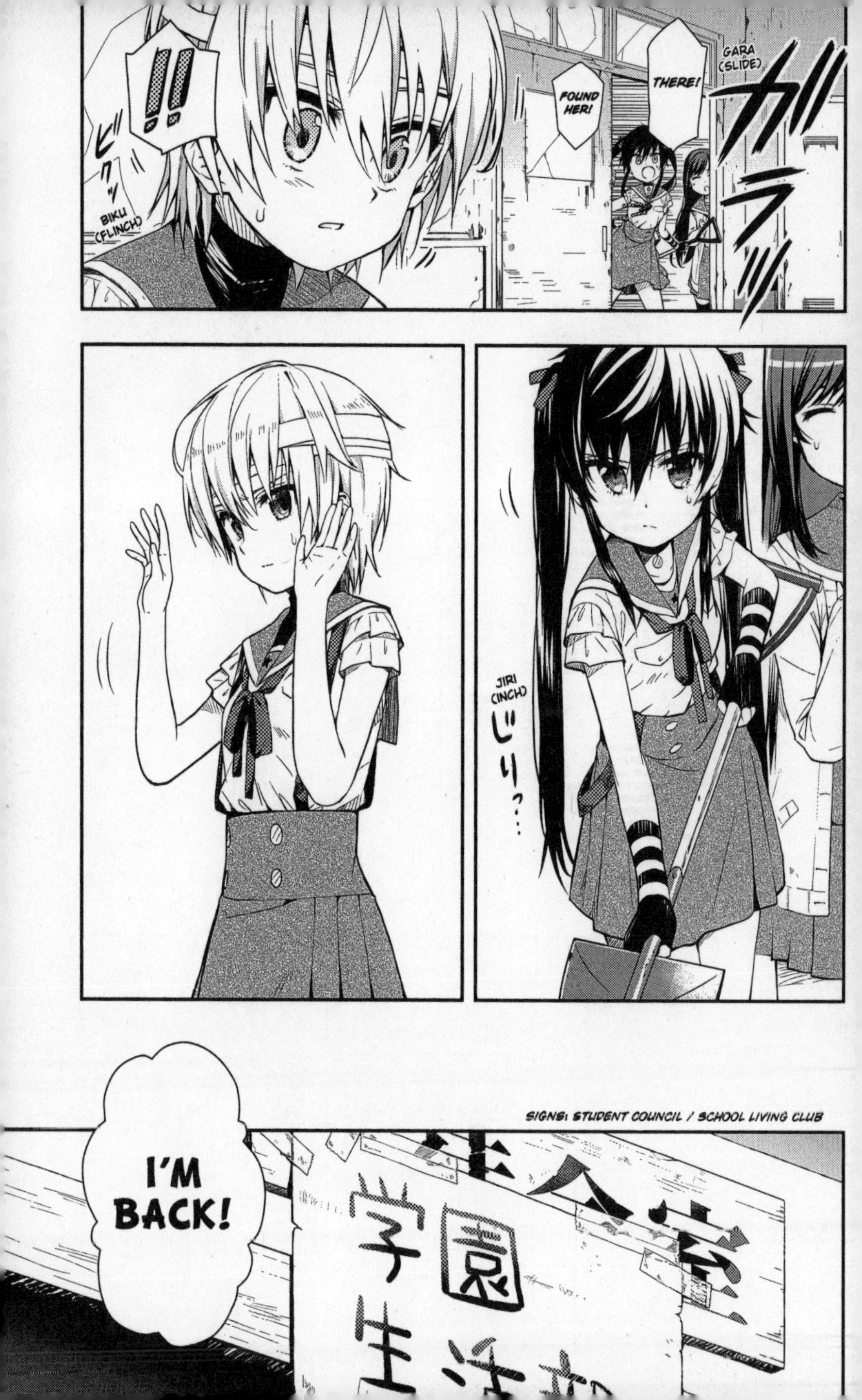
GARA (SLIDE)
ガラッ
THERE!
FOUND HER!
!!
ビクッ
BIKU (FLINCH)
JIRI (INCH)
じりっ…
SIGNS: STUDENT COUNCIL / SCHOOL LIVING CLUB
I'M BACK!

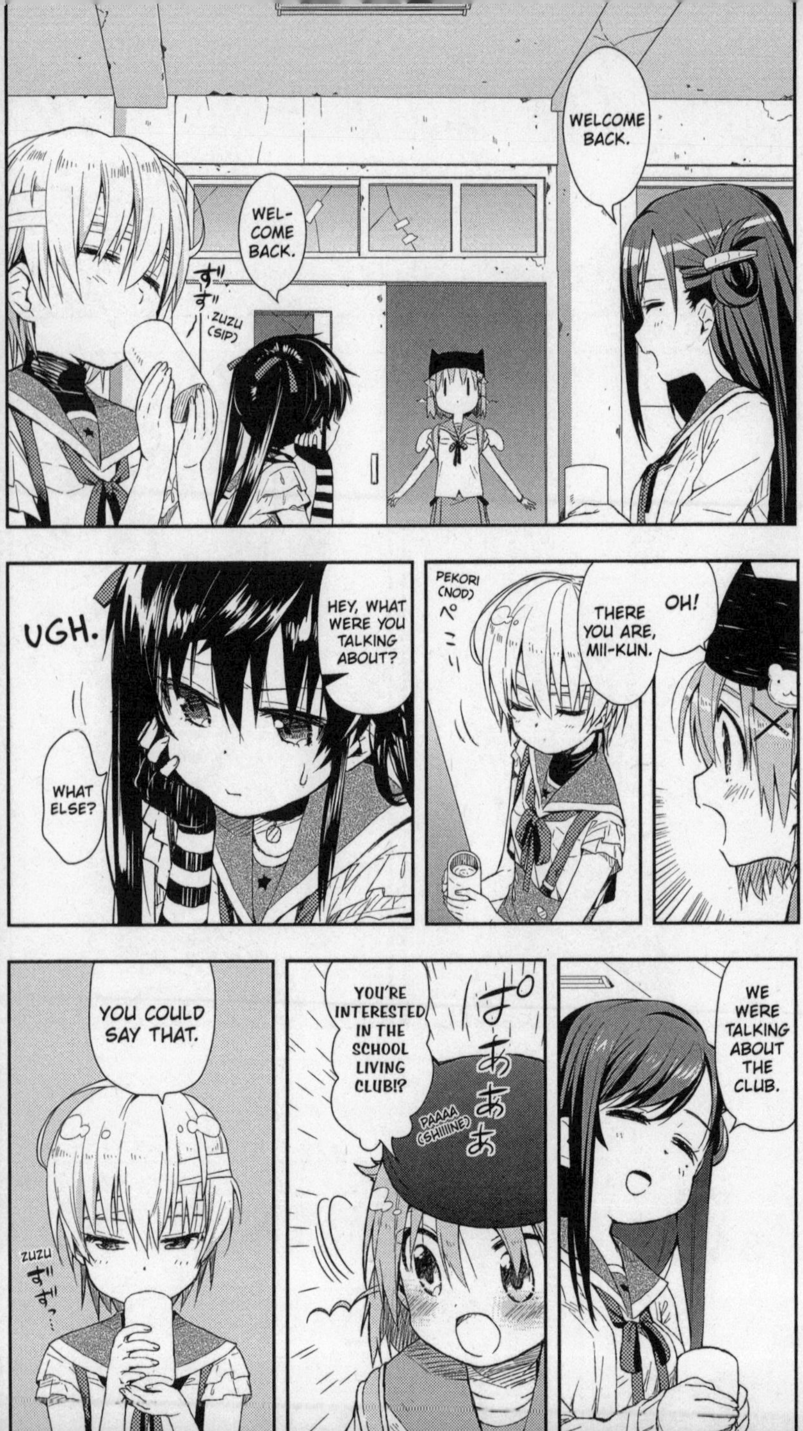
WELCOME BACK.
WEL-COME BACK.
ずずず
ZUZU (SIP)
OH!
THERE YOU ARE, MII-KUN.
ぺこり
PEKORI (NOD)
HEY, WHAT WERE YOU TALKING ABOUT?
UGH.
WHAT ELSE?
WE WERE TALKING ABOUT THE CLUB.
ぱあああ
PAAAA (SHIIINE)
YOU'RE INTERESTED IN THE SCHOOL LIVING CLUB!?
YOU COULD SAY THAT.
ずずっ…
ZUZU

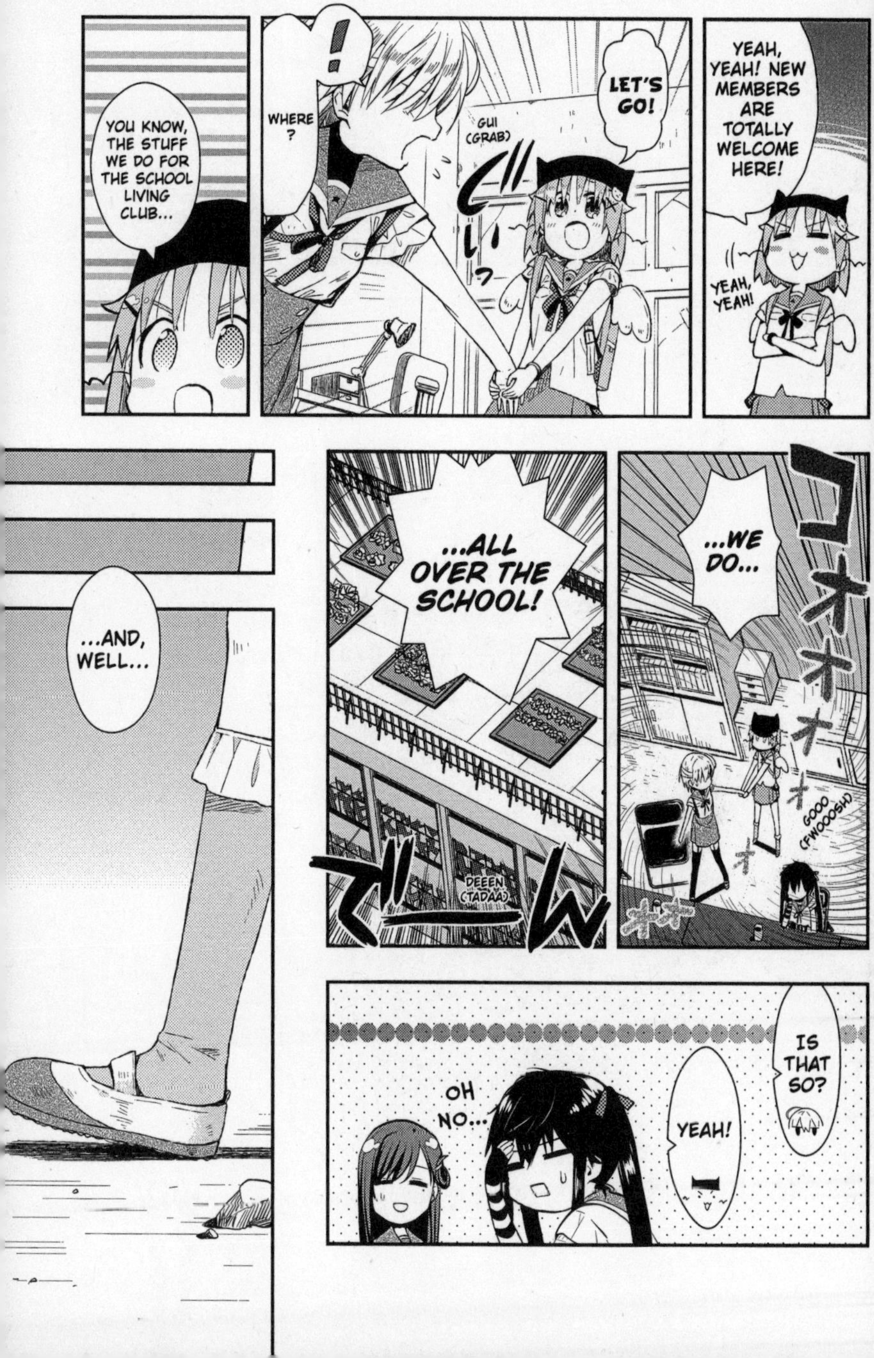
YEAH, YEAH! NEW MEMBERS ARE TOTALLY WELCOME HERE!
YEAH, YEAH!
LET'S GO!
GUI (GRAB)
!
WHERE?
YOU KNOW, THE STUFF WE DO FOR THE SCHOOL LIVING CLUB...
...WE DO...
GOOO (FWOOOSH)
...ALL OVER THE SCHOOL!
DEEEN (TADAA)
IS THAT SO?
YEAH!
OH NO...
...AND, WELL...

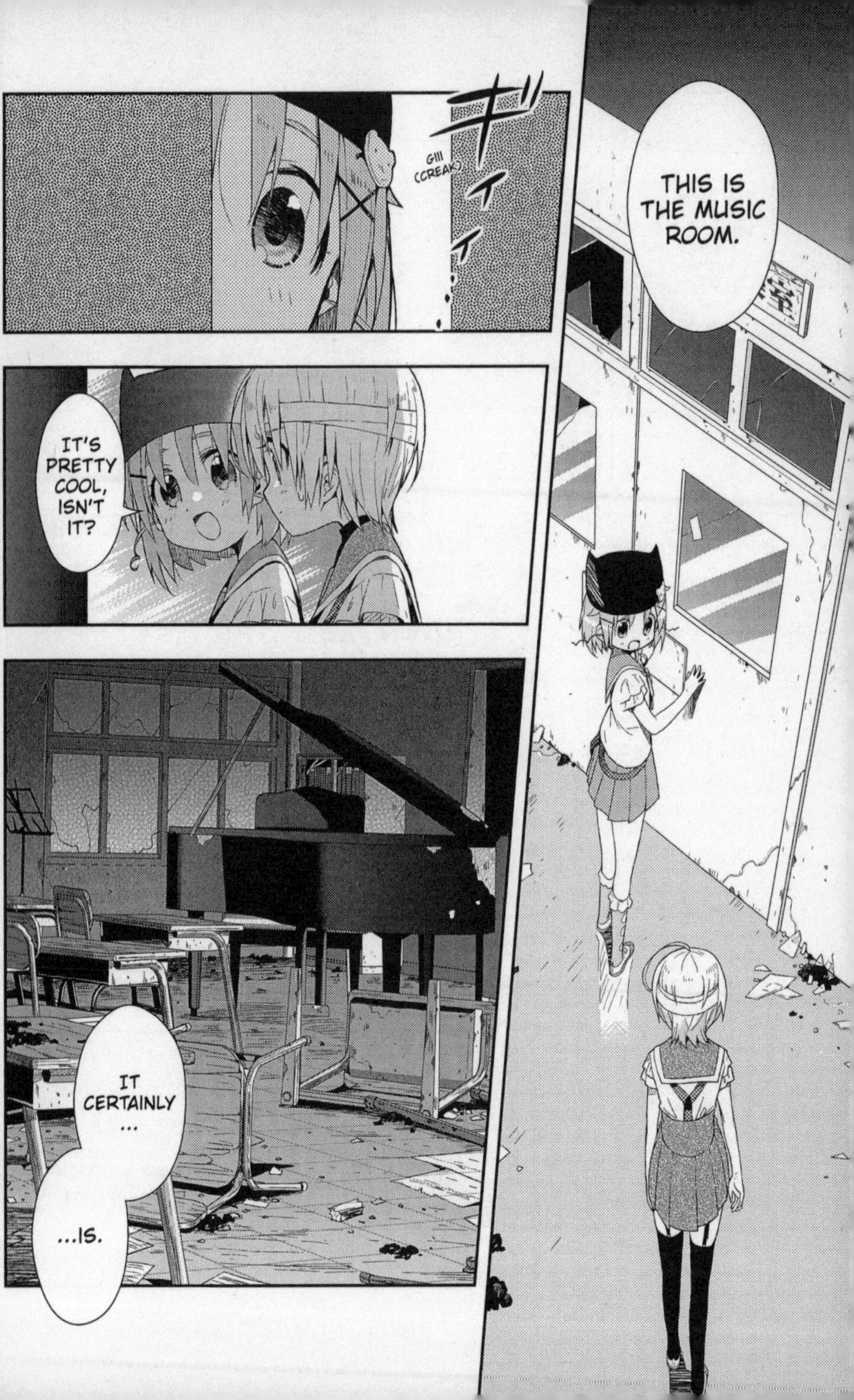
THIS IS THE MUSIC ROOM.
GIII (CREAK)
IT'S PRETTY COOL, ISN'T IT?
IT CERTAINLY ...
...IS.

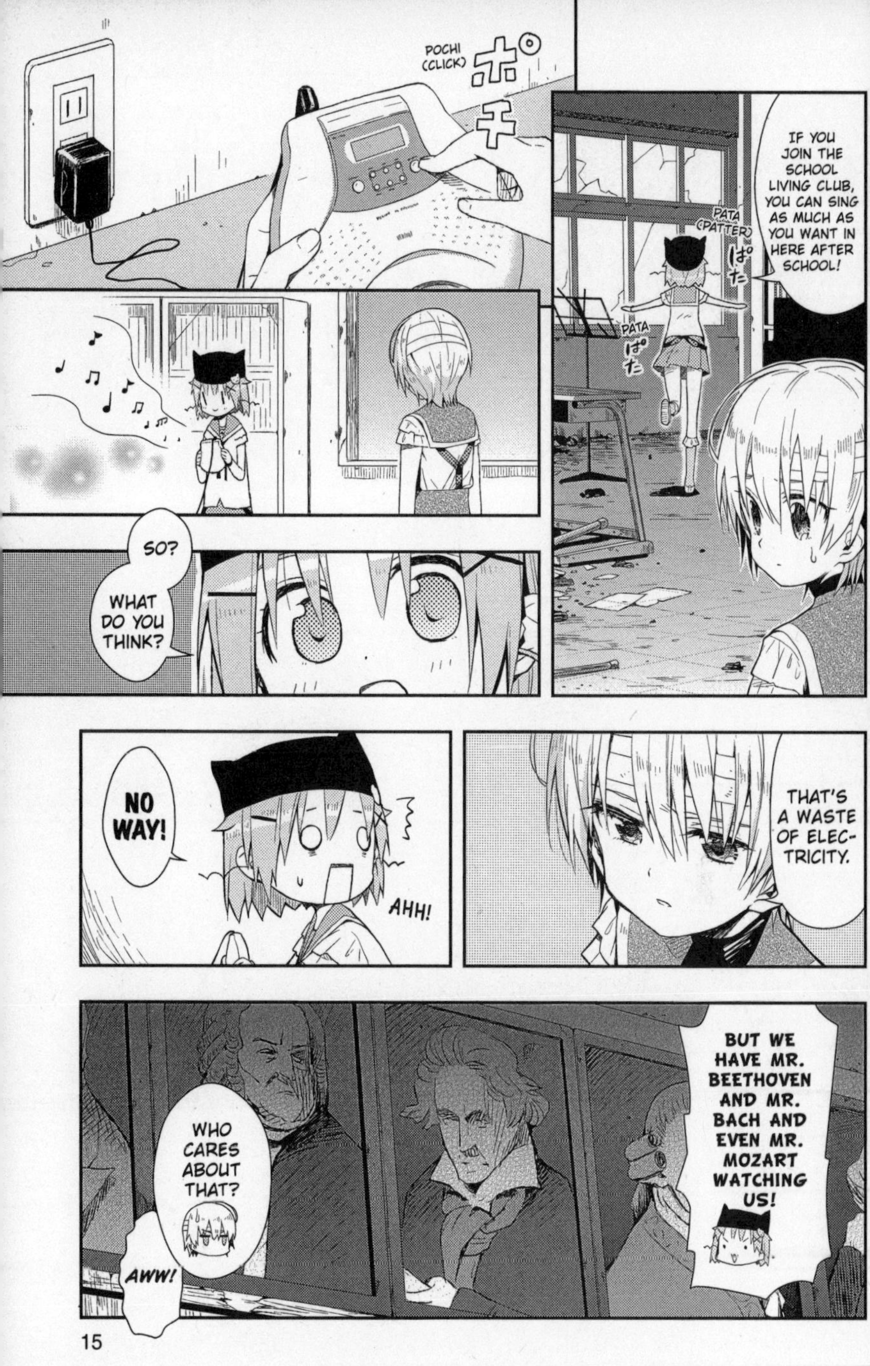
IF YOU JOIN THE SCHOOL LIVING CLUB, YOU CAN SING AS MUCH AS YOU WANT IN HERE AFTER SCHOOL!
PATA (PATTER) ぱた
PATA ぱた
POCHI (CLICK) ポチ
SO?
WHAT DO YOU THINK?
THAT'S A WASTE OF ELECTRICITY.
NO WAY!
AHH!
BUT WE HAVE MR. BEETHOVEN AND MR. BACH AND EVEN MR. MOZART WATCHING US!
WHO CARES ABOUT THAT?
AWW!

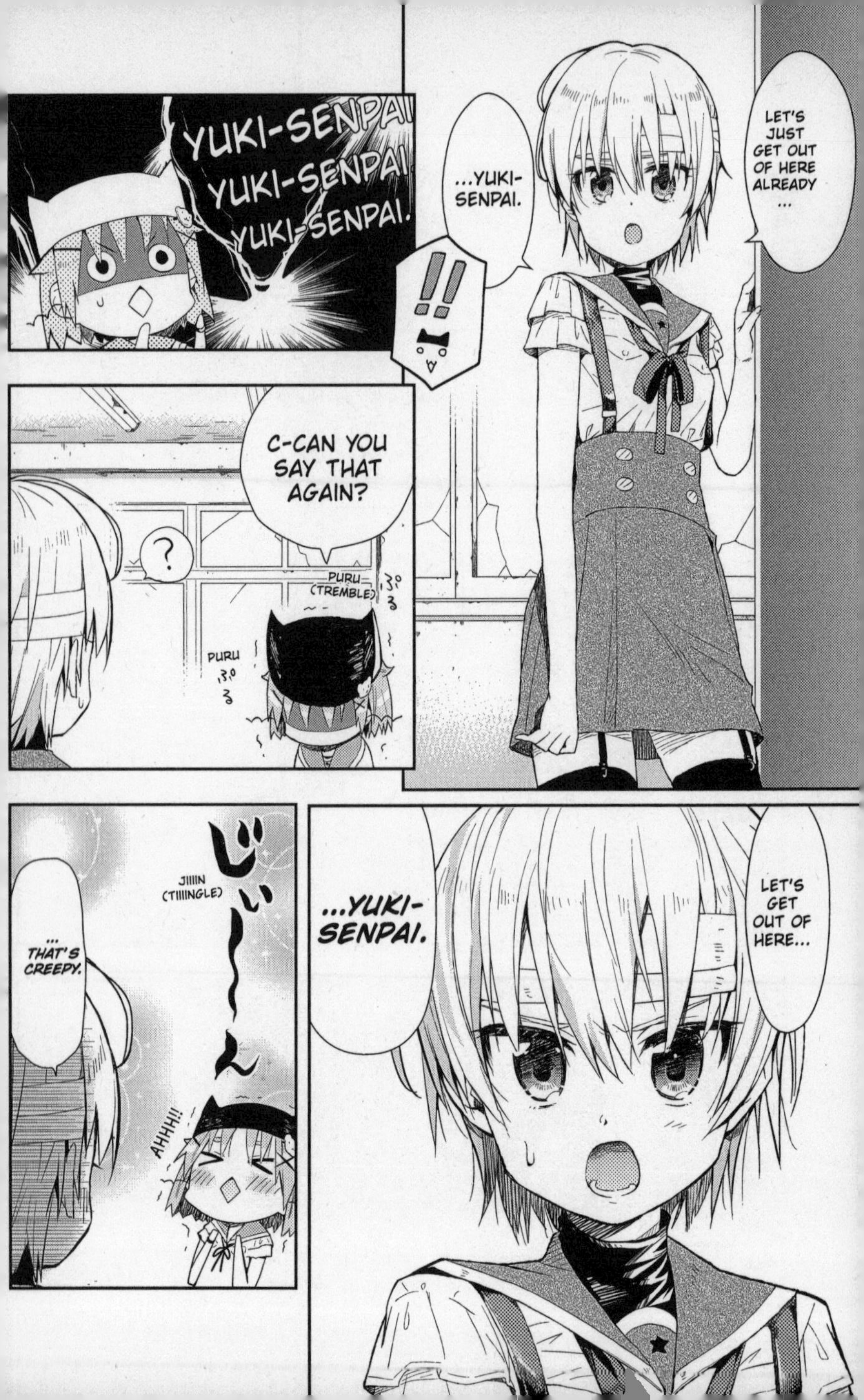
LET'S JUST GET OUT OF HERE ALREADY ...
...YUKI-SENPAI.
!!
YUKI-SENPAI! YUKI-SENPAI! YUKI-SENPAI!
C-CAN YOU SAY THAT AGAIN?
?
PURU (TREMBLE)
PURU
LET'S GET OUT OF HERE...
...YUKI-SENPAI.
じぃーん
JIIIIN (TIIIINGLE)
... THAT'S CREEPY.
AHHH!!

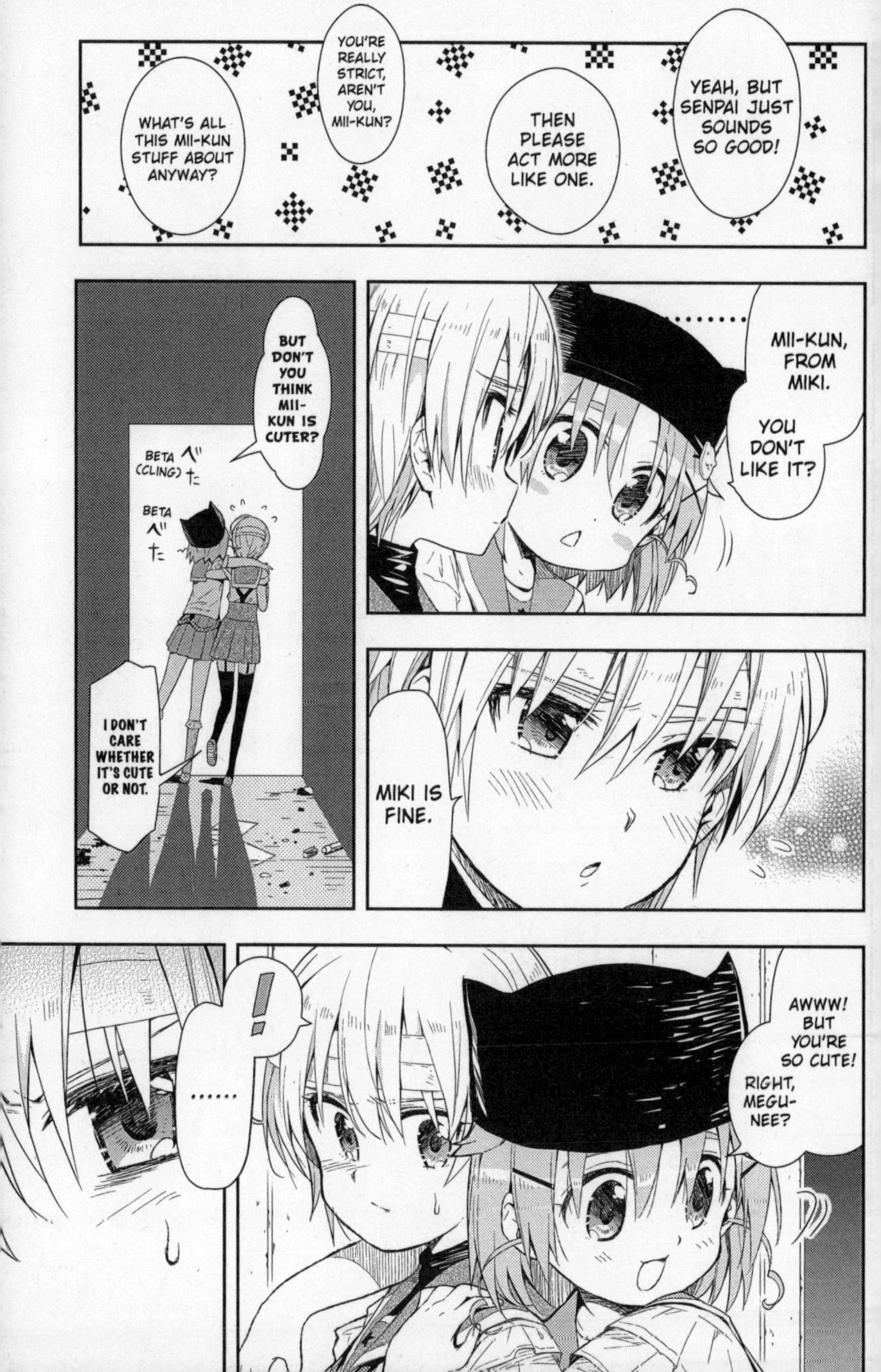
YEAH, BUT SENPAI JUST SOUNDS SO GOOD!
THEN PLEASE ACT MORE LIKE ONE.
YOU'RE REALLY STRICT, AREN'T YOU, MII-KUN?
WHAT'S ALL THIS MII-KUN STUFF ABOUT ANYWAY?
......
MII-KUN, FROM MIKI.
YOU DON'T LIKE IT?
MIKI IS FINE.
BUT DON'T YOU THINK MII-KUN IS CUTER?
BETA べた (CLING)
BETA べた
I DON'T CARE WHETHER IT'S CUTE OR NOT.
AWWW! BUT YOU'RE SO CUTE!
RIGHT, MEGU-NEE?
!
......

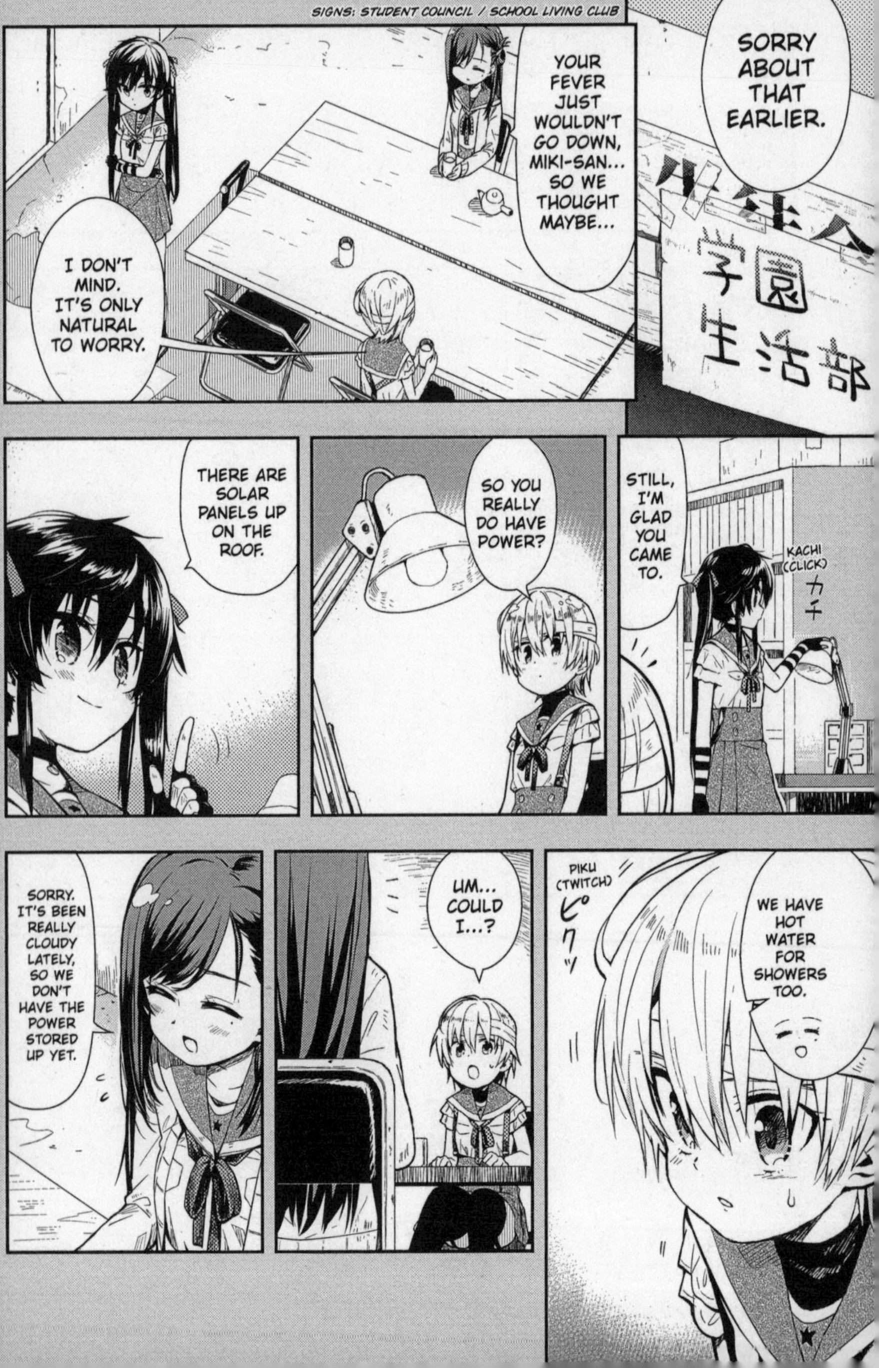
SIGNS: STUDENT COUNCIL / SCHOOL LIVING CLUB
SORRY ABOUT THAT EARLIER.
学園生活部
YOUR FEVER JUST WOULDN'T GO DOWN, MIKI-SAN... SO WE THOUGHT MAYBE...
I DON'T MIND. IT'S ONLY NATURAL TO WORRY.
STILL, I'M GLAD YOU CAME TO.
KACHI (CLICK)
カチ
SO YOU REALLY DO HAVE POWER?
THERE ARE SOLAR PANELS UP ON THE ROOF.
WE HAVE HOT WATER FOR SHOWERS TOO.
PIKU (TWITCH)
ピクッ
UM... COULD I...?
SORRY. IT'S BEEN REALLY CLOUDY LATELY, SO WE DON'T HAVE THE POWER STORED UP YET.

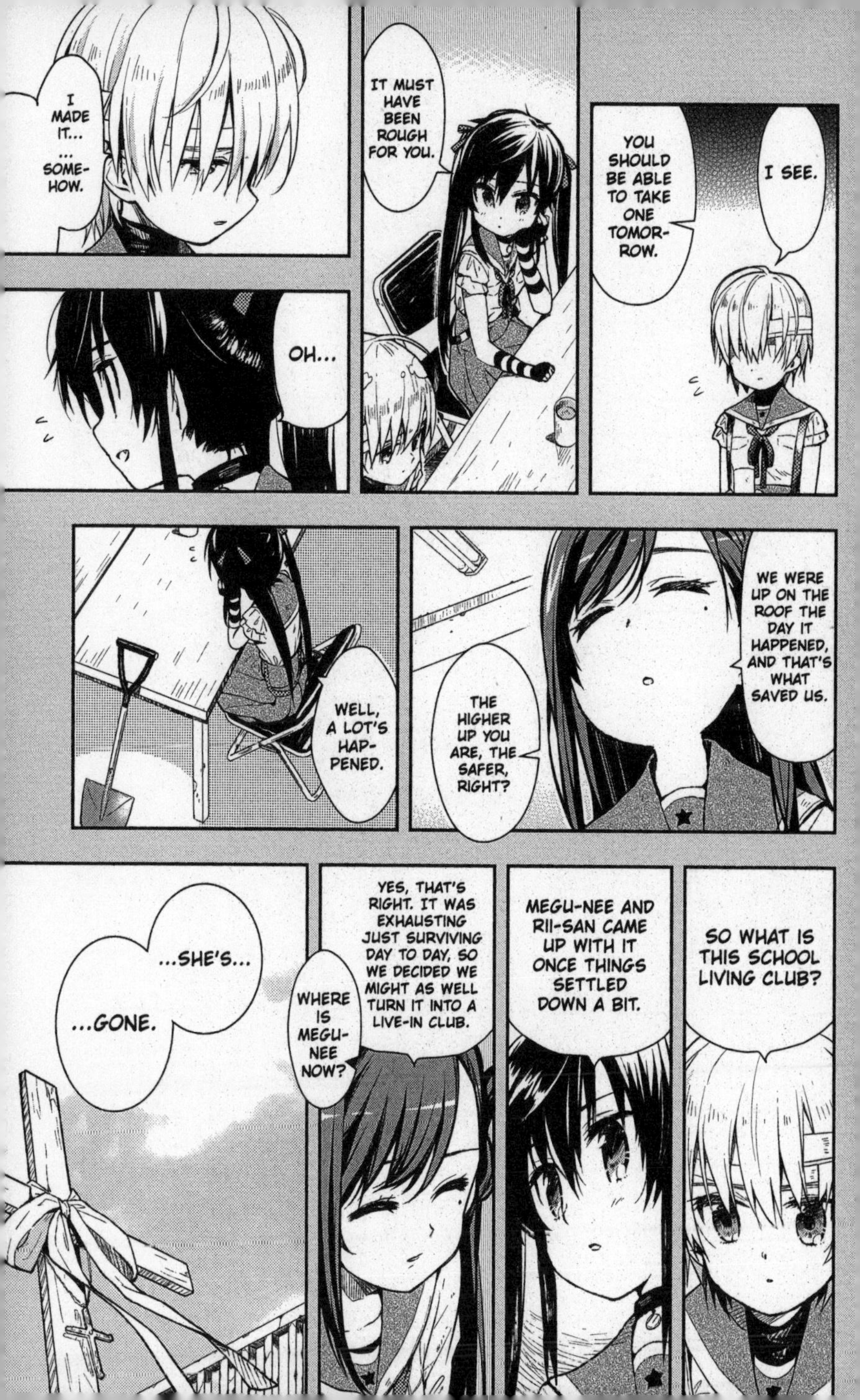
I SEE.
YOU SHOULD BE ABLE TO TAKE ONE TOMORROW.
IT MUST HAVE BEEN ROUGH FOR YOU.
I MADE IT... ... SOMEHOW.
OH...
WE WERE UP ON THE ROOF THE DAY IT HAPPENED, AND THAT'S WHAT SAVED US.
THE HIGHER UP YOU ARE, THE SAFER, RIGHT?
WELL, A LOT'S HAPPENED.
SO WHAT IS THIS SCHOOL LIVING CLUB?
MEGU-NEE AND RII-SAN CAME UP WITH IT ONCE THINGS SETTLED DOWN A BIT.
YES, THAT'S RIGHT. IT WAS EXHAUSTING JUST SURVIVING DAY TO DAY, SO WE DECIDED WE MIGHT AS WELL TURN IT INTO A LIVE-IN CLUB.
WHERE IS MEGU-NEE NOW?
...SHE'S...
...GONE.

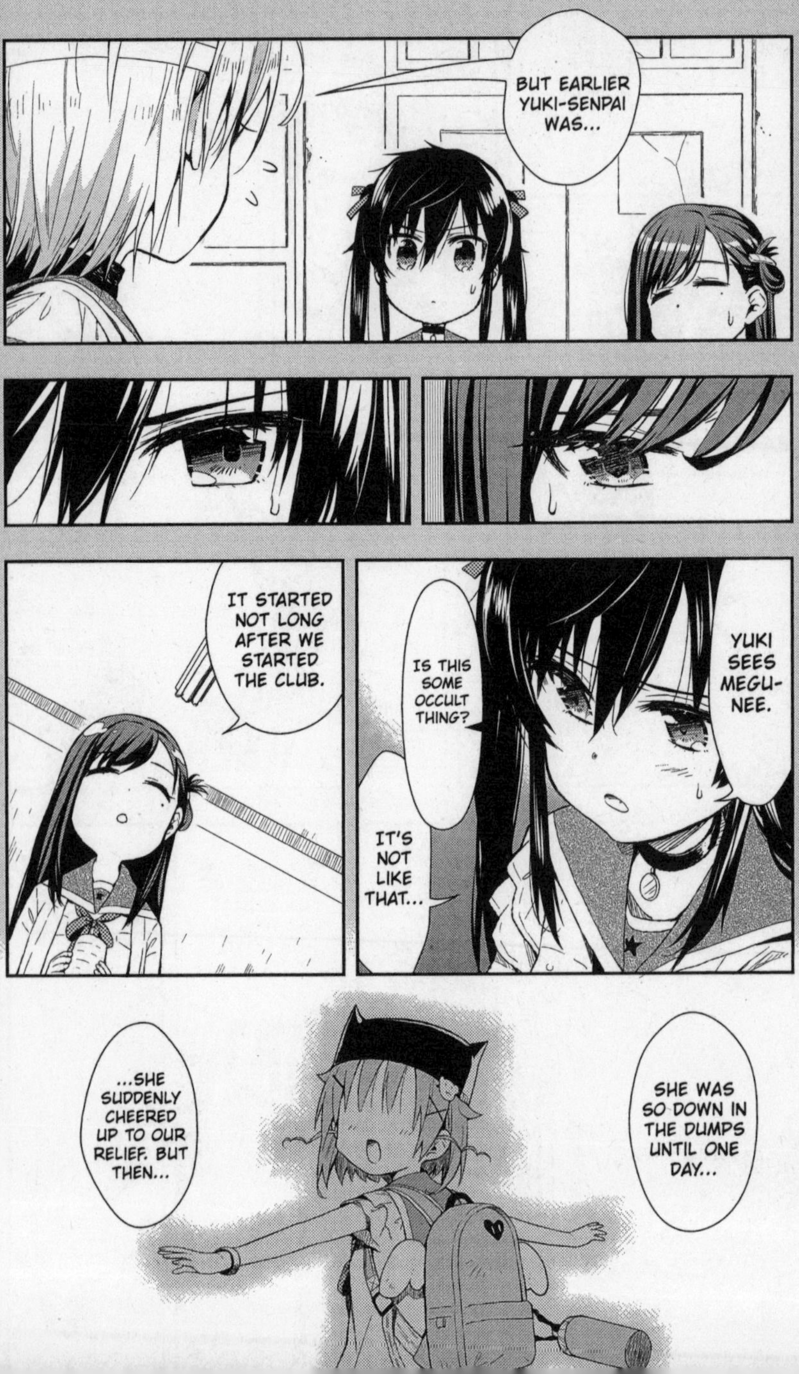
BUT EARLIER YUKI-SENPAI WAS...
YUKI SEES MEGU-NEE.
IS THIS SOME OCCULT THING?
IT'S NOT LIKE THAT...
IT STARTED NOT LONG AFTER WE STARTED THE CLUB.
SHE WAS SO DOWN IN THE DUMPS UNTIL ONE DAY...
...SHE SUDDENLY CHEERED UP TO OUR RELIEF. BUT THEN...

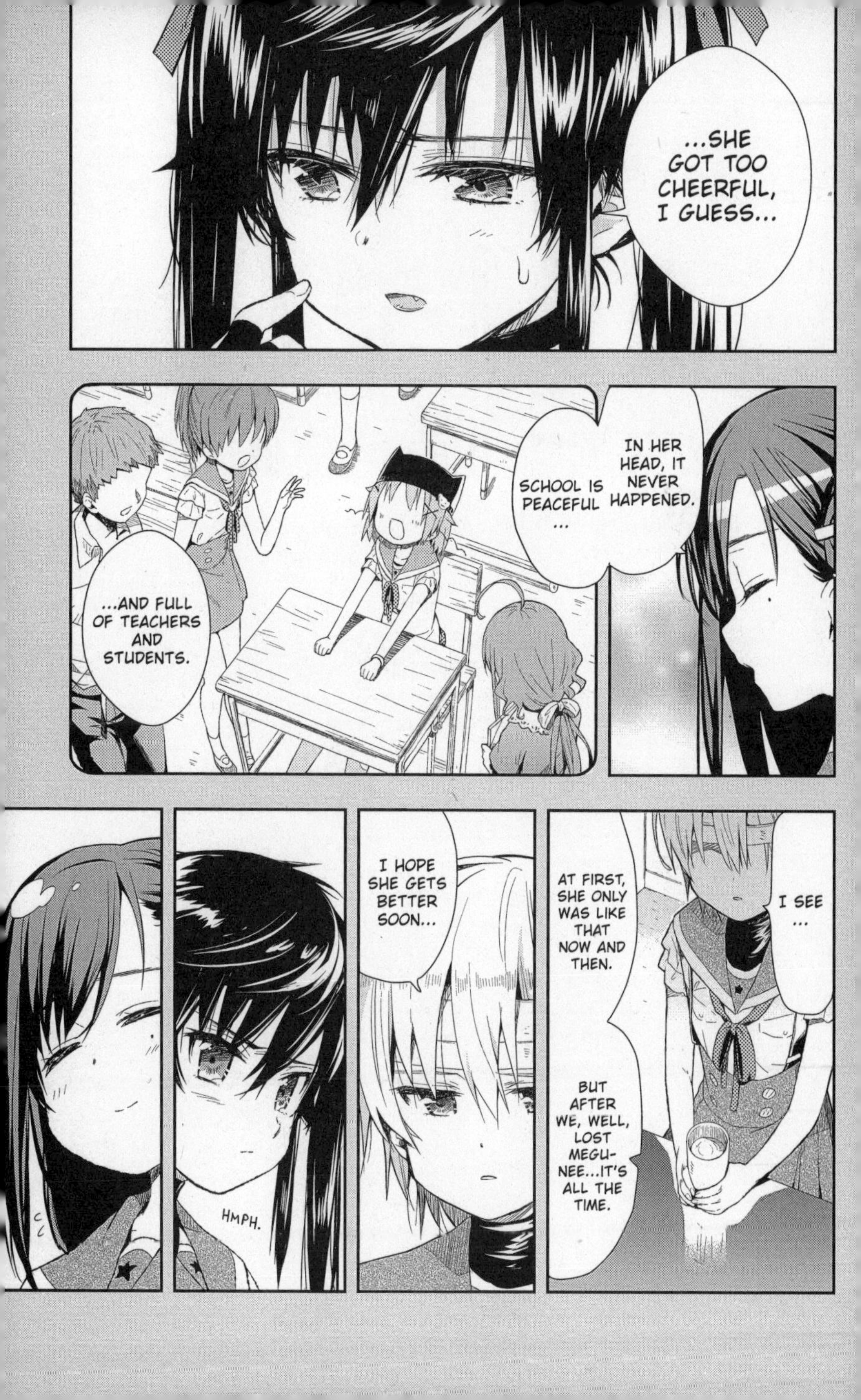
...SHE GOT TOO CHEERFUL, I GUESS...
IN HER HEAD, IT NEVER HAPPENED.
SCHOOL IS PEACEFUL...
...AND FULL OF TEACHERS AND STUDENTS.
I SEE...
AT FIRST, SHE ONLY WAS LIKE THAT NOW AND THEN.
BUT AFTER WE, WELL, LOST MEGU-NEE...IT'S ALL THE TIME.
I HOPE SHE GETS BETTER SOON...
HMPH.

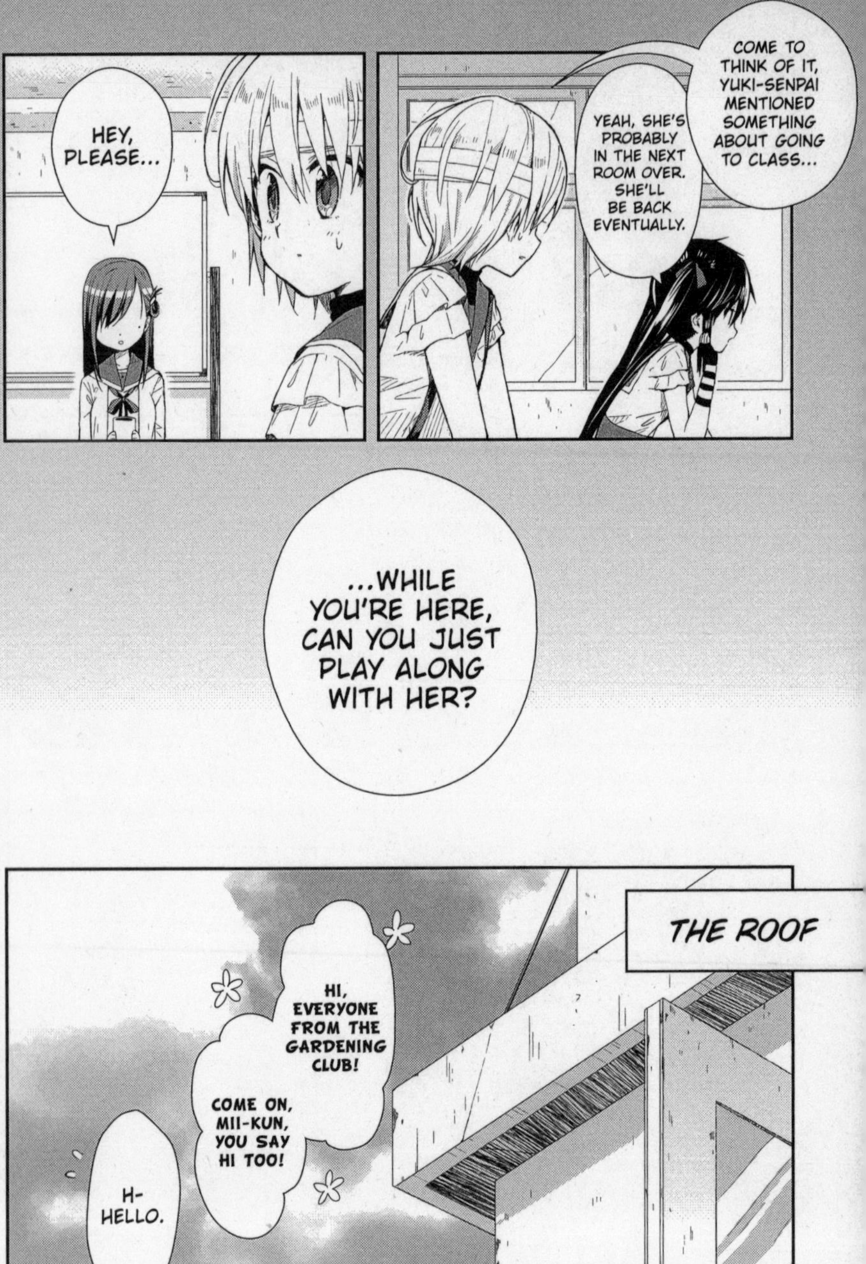
COME TO THINK OF IT, YUKI-SENPAI MENTIONED SOMETHING ABOUT GOING TO CLASS...
YEAH, SHE'S PROBABLY IN THE NEXT ROOM OVER. SHE'LL BE BACK EVENTUALLY.
HEY, PLEASE...
...WHILE YOU'RE HERE, CAN YOU JUST PLAY ALONG WITH HER?
THE ROOF
HI, EVERYONE FROM THE GARDENING CLUB!
COME ON, MII-KUN, YOU SAY HI TOO!
H-HELLO.

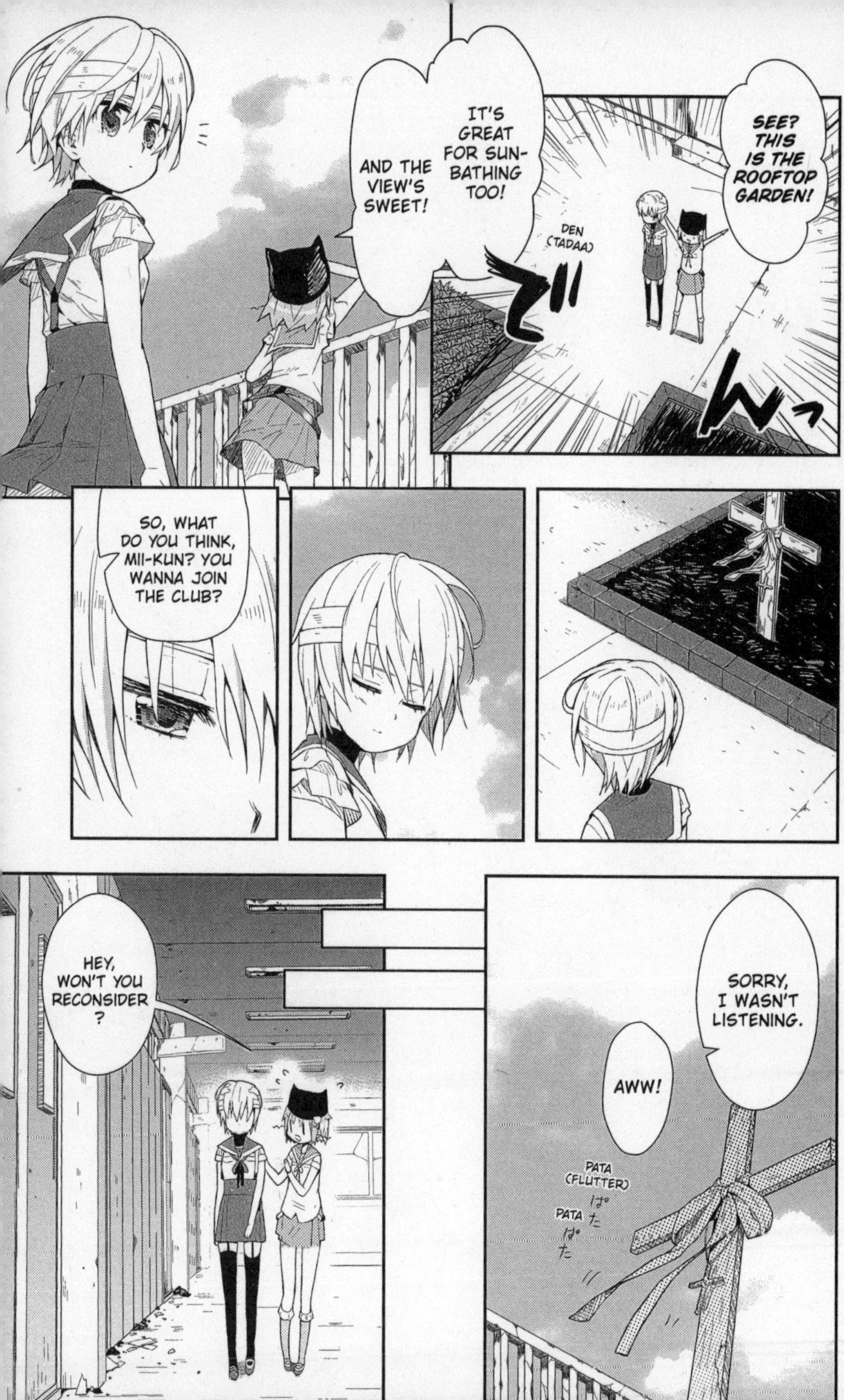
SEE? THIS IS THE ROOFTOP GARDEN!
DEN (TADAA)
IT'S GREAT FOR SUN-BATHING TOO!
AND THE VIEW'S SWEET!
SO, WHAT DO YOU THINK, MII-KUN? YOU WANNA JOIN THE CLUB?
SORRY, I WASN'T LISTENING.
AWW!
PATA (FLUTTER)
ぱた
PATA
ぱた
HEY, WON'T YOU RECONSIDER?

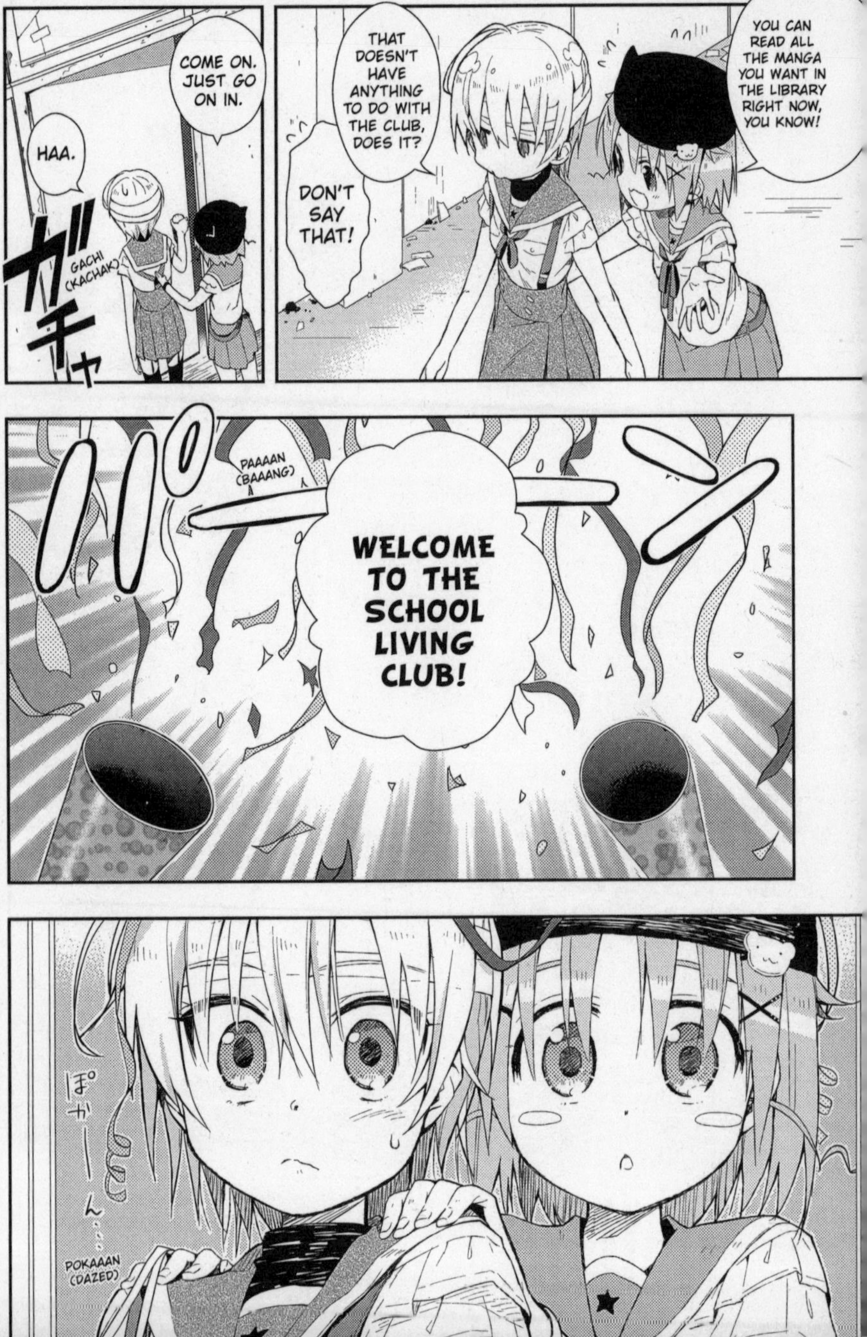

YOU CAN READ ALL THE MANGA YOU WANT IN THE LIBRARY RIGHT NOW, YOU KNOW!
THAT DOESN'T HAVE ANYTHING TO DO WITH THE CLUB, DOES IT?
DON'T SAY THAT!
COME ON. JUST GO ON IN.
HAA.
GACHI (KACHAK)
PAAAAN (BAAANG)
WELCOME TO THE SCHOOL LIVING CLUB!
POKAAAN (DAZED)

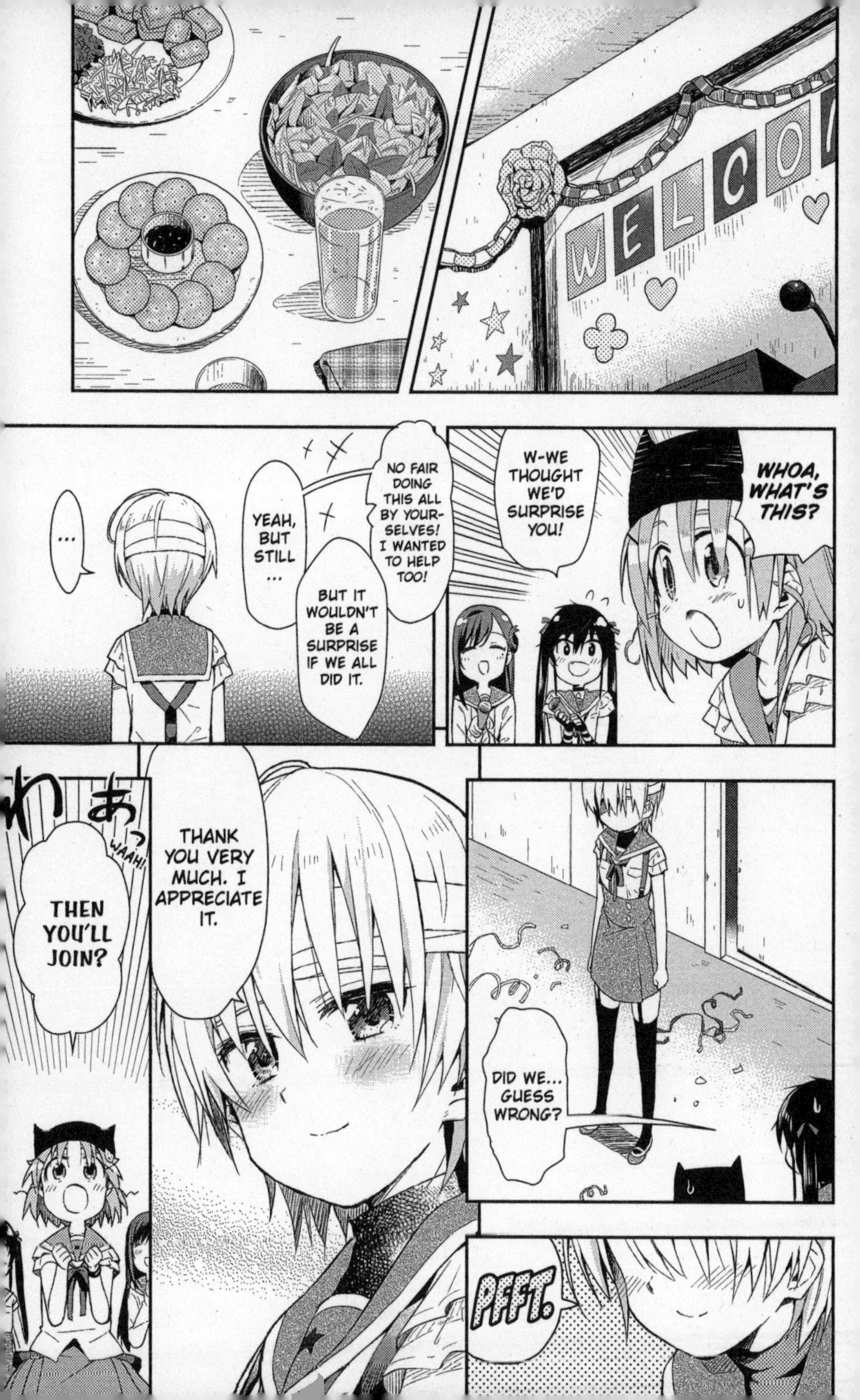
WELCO
WHOA, WHAT'S THIS?
W-WE THOUGHT WE'D SURPRISE YOU!
NO FAIR DOING THIS ALL BY YOUR-SELVES! I WANTED TO HELP TOO!
BUT IT WOULDN'T BE A SURPRISE IF WE ALL DID IT.
YEAH, BUT STILL ...
...
DID WE... GUESS WRONG?
PFFT.
THANK YOU VERY MUCH. I APPRECIATE IT.
わあっ
WAAH!
THEN YOU'LL JOIN?

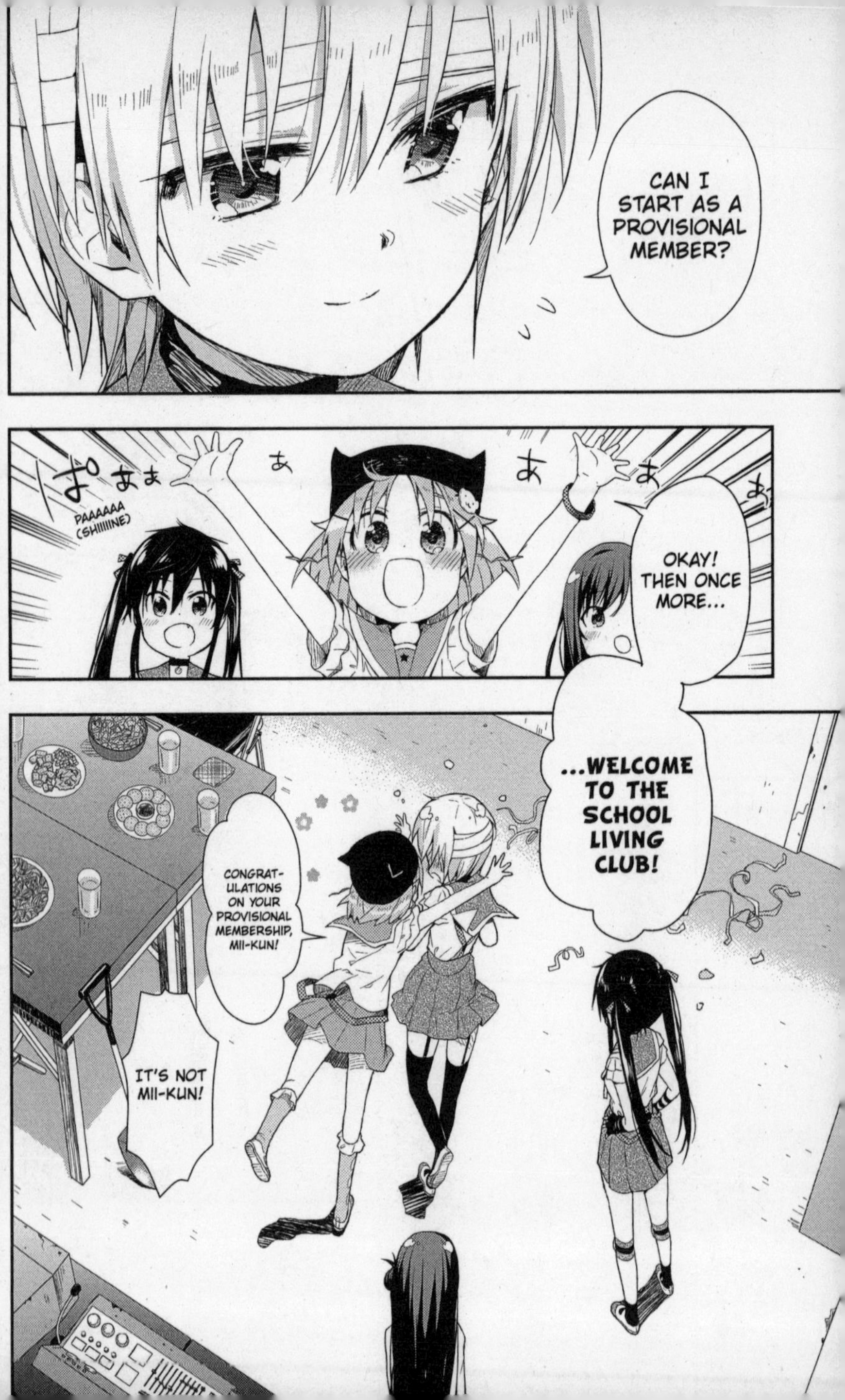
CAN I START AS A PROVISIONAL MEMBER?
PAAAAAA (SHIIIIINE)
OKAY! THEN ONCE MORE...
...WELCOME TO THE SCHOOL LIVING CLUB!
CONGRAT-ULATIONS ON YOUR PROVISIONAL MEMBERSHIP, MII-KUN!
IT'S NOT MII-KUN!

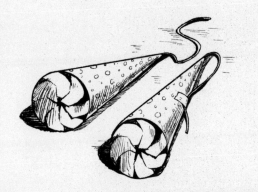

SCHOOL-LIVE!

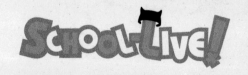

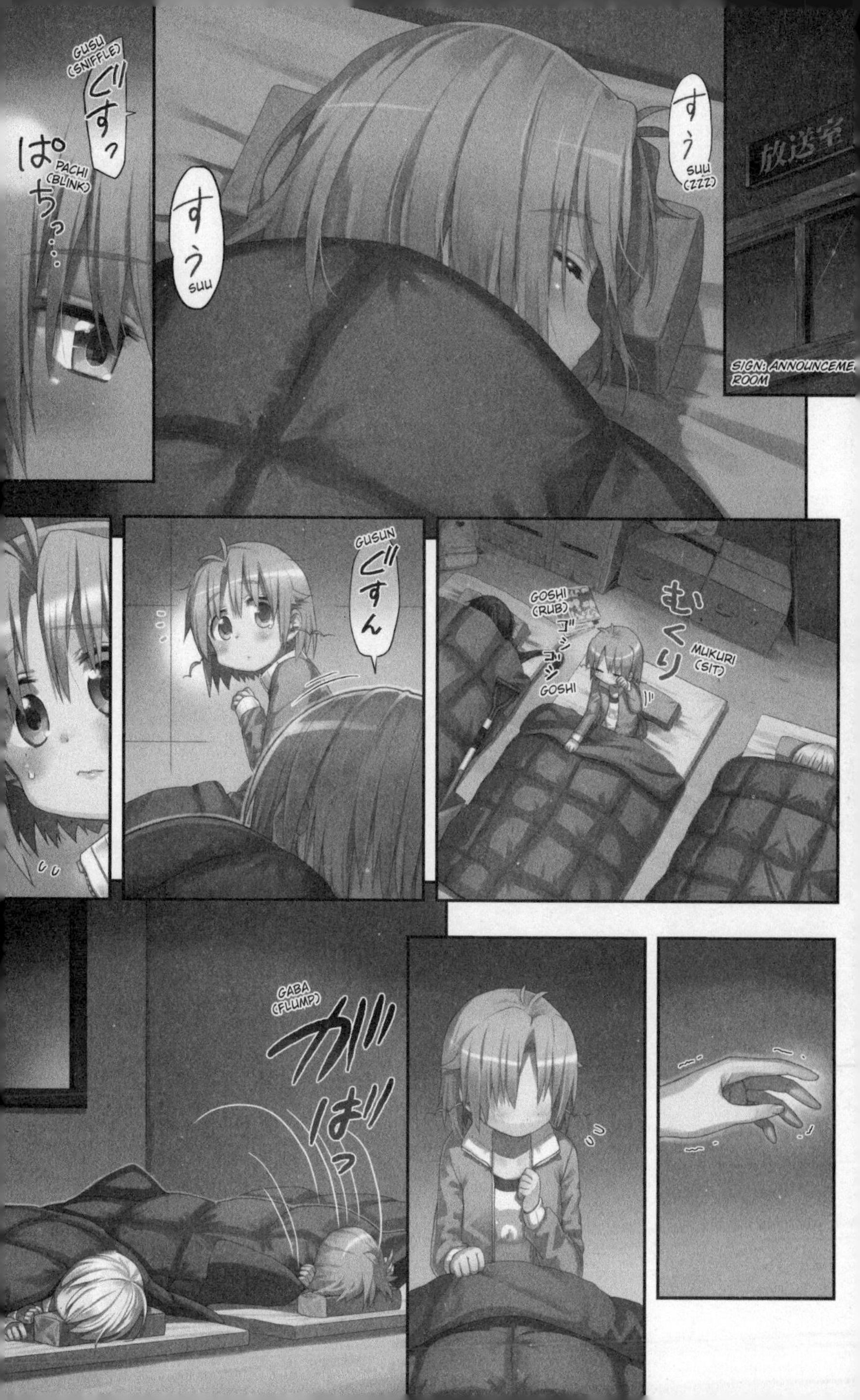
放送室
SIGN: ANNOUNCEME ROOM
すう
SUU (ZZZ)
すう
SUU
ぐすっ
GUSU (SNIFFLE)
ぱちっ…
PACHI (BLINK)
むくり
MUKURI (SIT)
ゴシゴシ
GOSHI (RUB) GOSHI
ぐすん
GUSUN
がばっ
GABA (FLUMP)

Chapter 14 Field Day

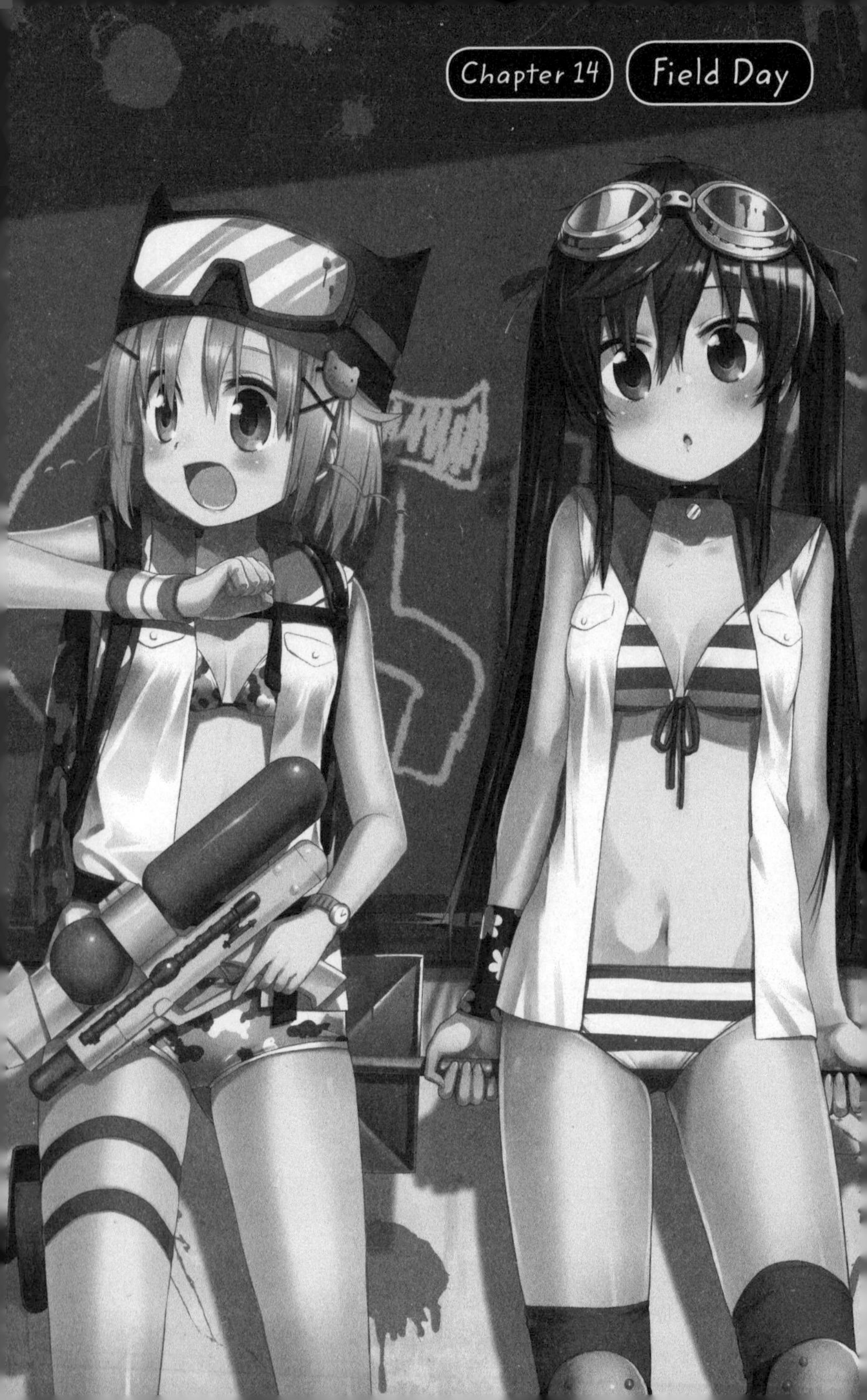

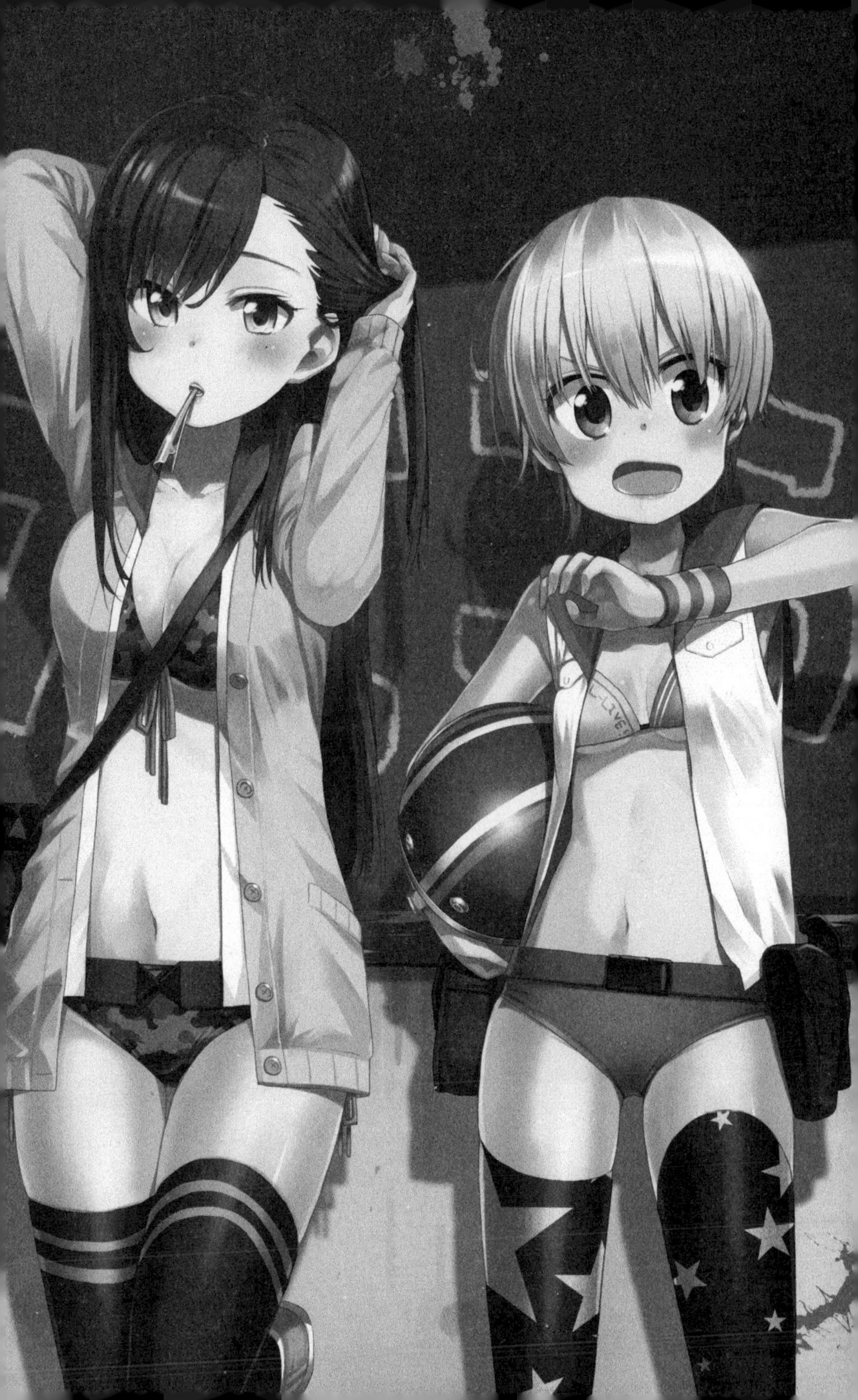

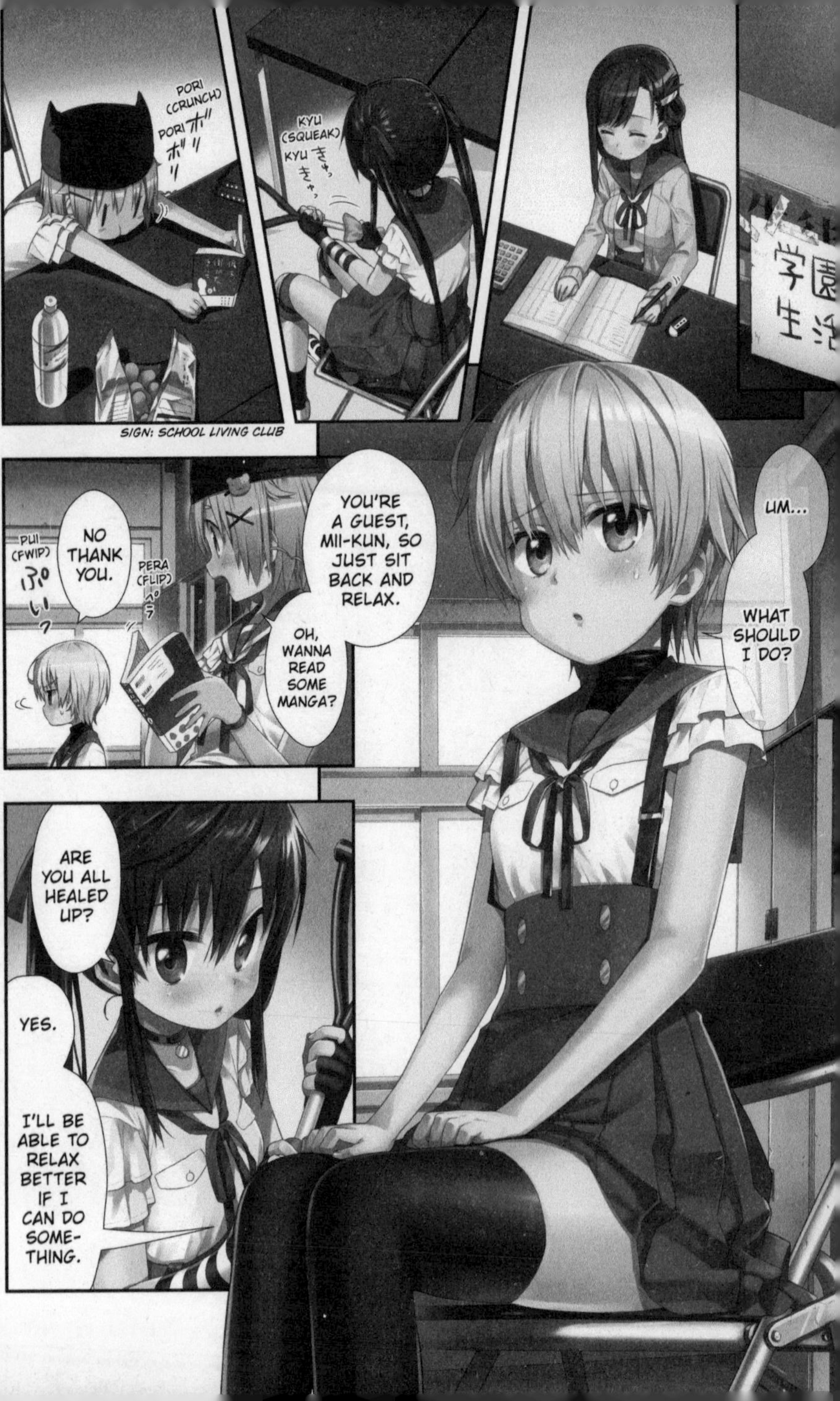
学園生活
KYU (SQUEAK) KYU きゅっ きゅっ
PORI (CRUNCH) PORI ポリ ポリ
SIGN: SCHOOL LIVING CLUB
UM...
WHAT SHOULD I DO?
YOU'RE A GUEST, MII-KUN, SO JUST SIT BACK AND RELAX.
OH, WANNA READ SOME MANGA?
PERA (FLIP) ペラ
NO THANK YOU.
PUI (FWIP) ぷいっ
ARE YOU ALL HEALED UP?
YES.
I'LL BE ABLE TO RELAX BETTER IF I CAN DO SOME-THING.

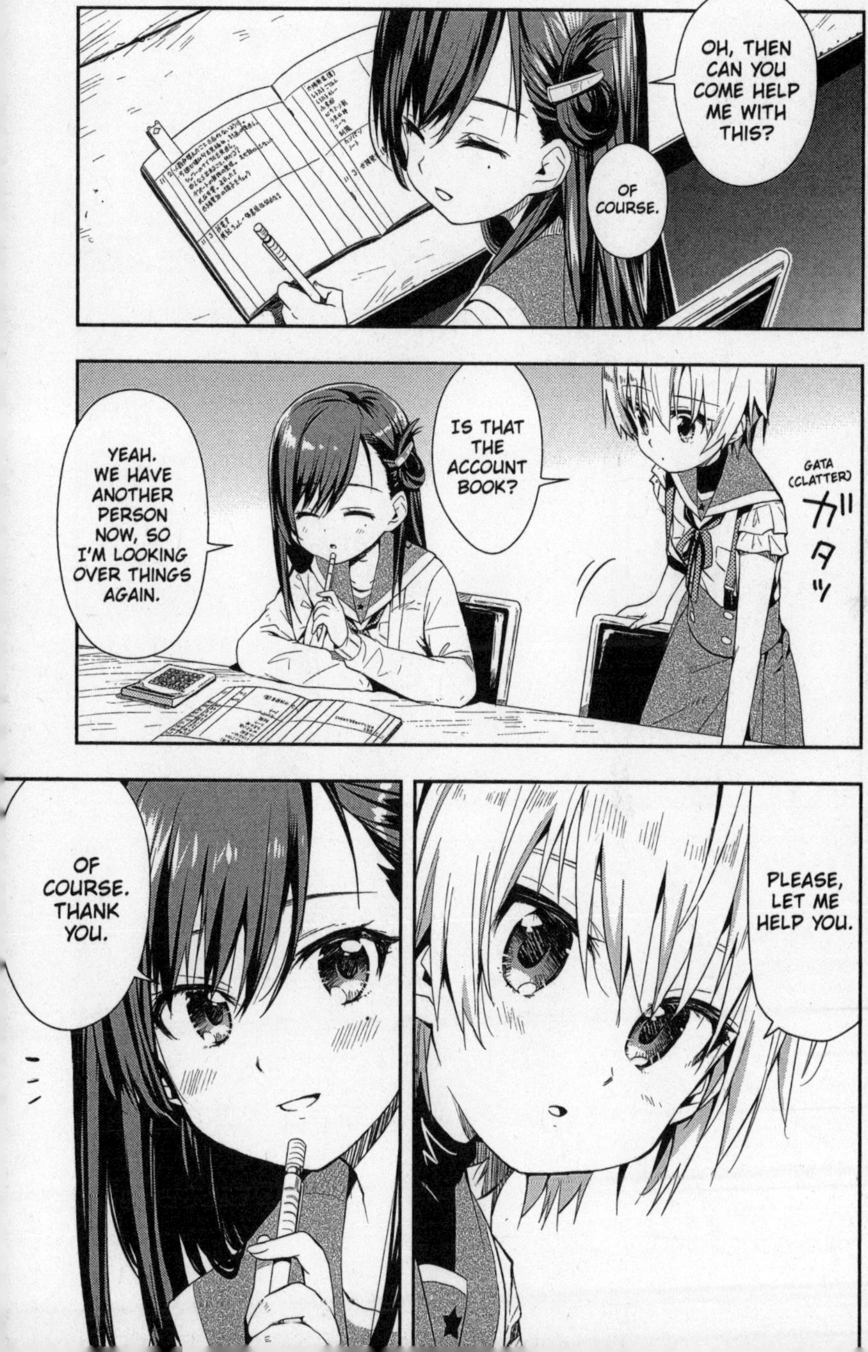
OH, THEN CAN YOU COME HELP ME WITH THIS?
OF COURSE.
GATA (CLATTER)
ガタッ
IS THAT THE ACCOUNT BOOK?
YEAH. WE HAVE ANOTHER PERSON NOW, SO I'M LOOKING OVER THINGS AGAIN.
PLEASE, LET ME HELP YOU.
OF COURSE. THANK YOU.

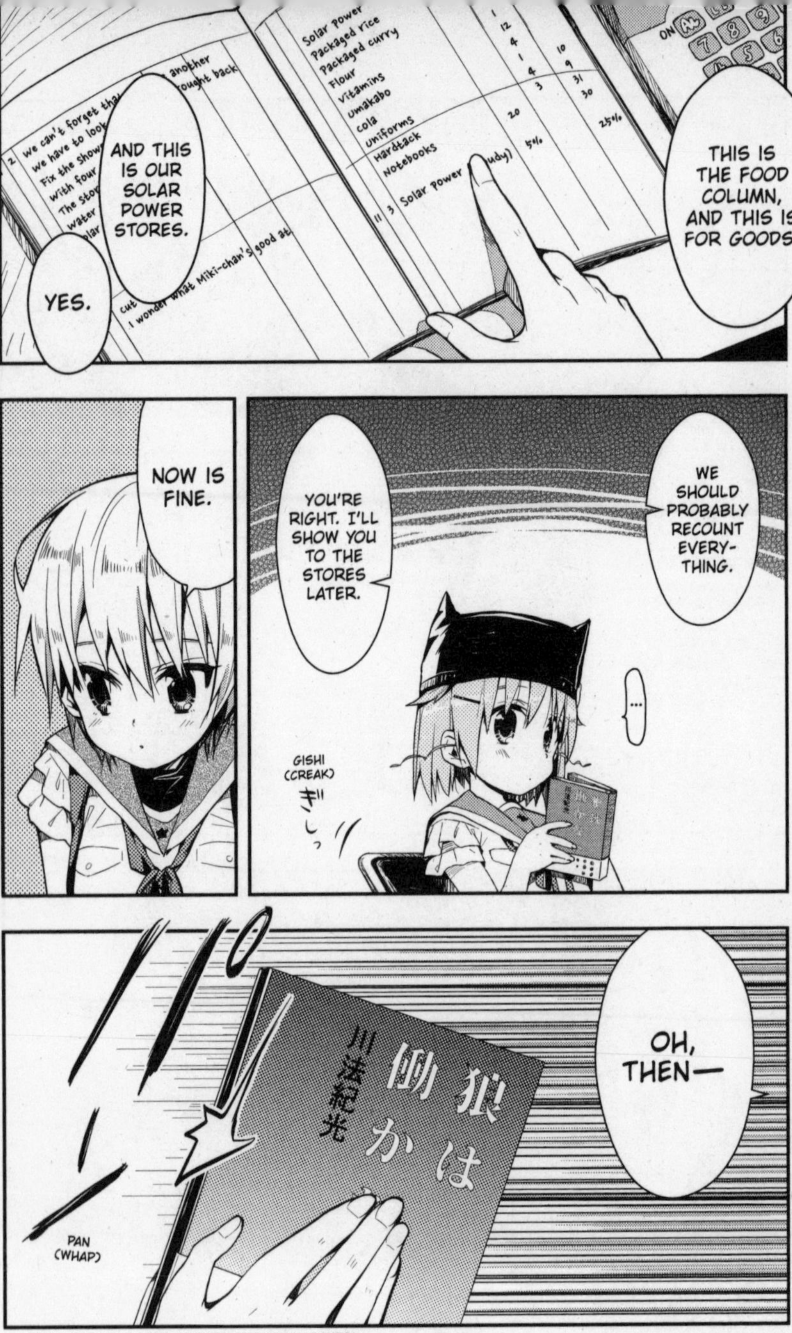

THIS IS THE FOOD COLUMN, AND THIS IS FOR GOODS.
AND THIS IS OUR SOLAR POWER STORES.
YES.
Solar power
Packaged rice
Packaged curry
Flour
Vitamins
Umakabo
cola
uniforms
Hardtack
Notebooks
I wonder what Miki-chan's good at
WE SHOULD PROBABLY RECOUNT EVERY-THING.
YOU'RE RIGHT. I'LL SHOW YOU TO THE STORES LATER.
...
GISHI (CREAK)
ぎしっ
NOW IS FINE.
OH, THEN—
狼は
働か
PAN (WHAP)

BOOK: THE WOLF DOESN'T WORK, NORIMITSU SANPOU

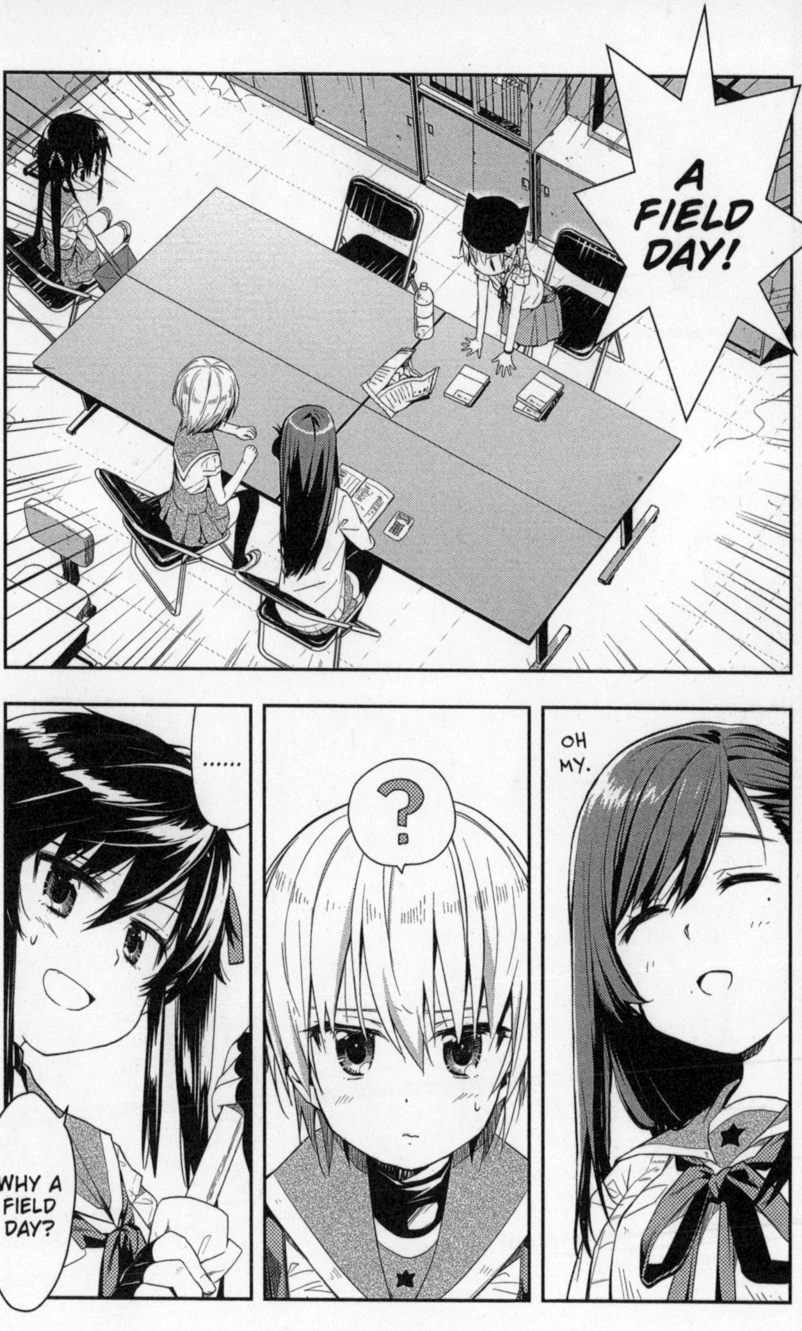
A FIELD DAY!
OH MY.
?
......
WHY A FIELD DAY?

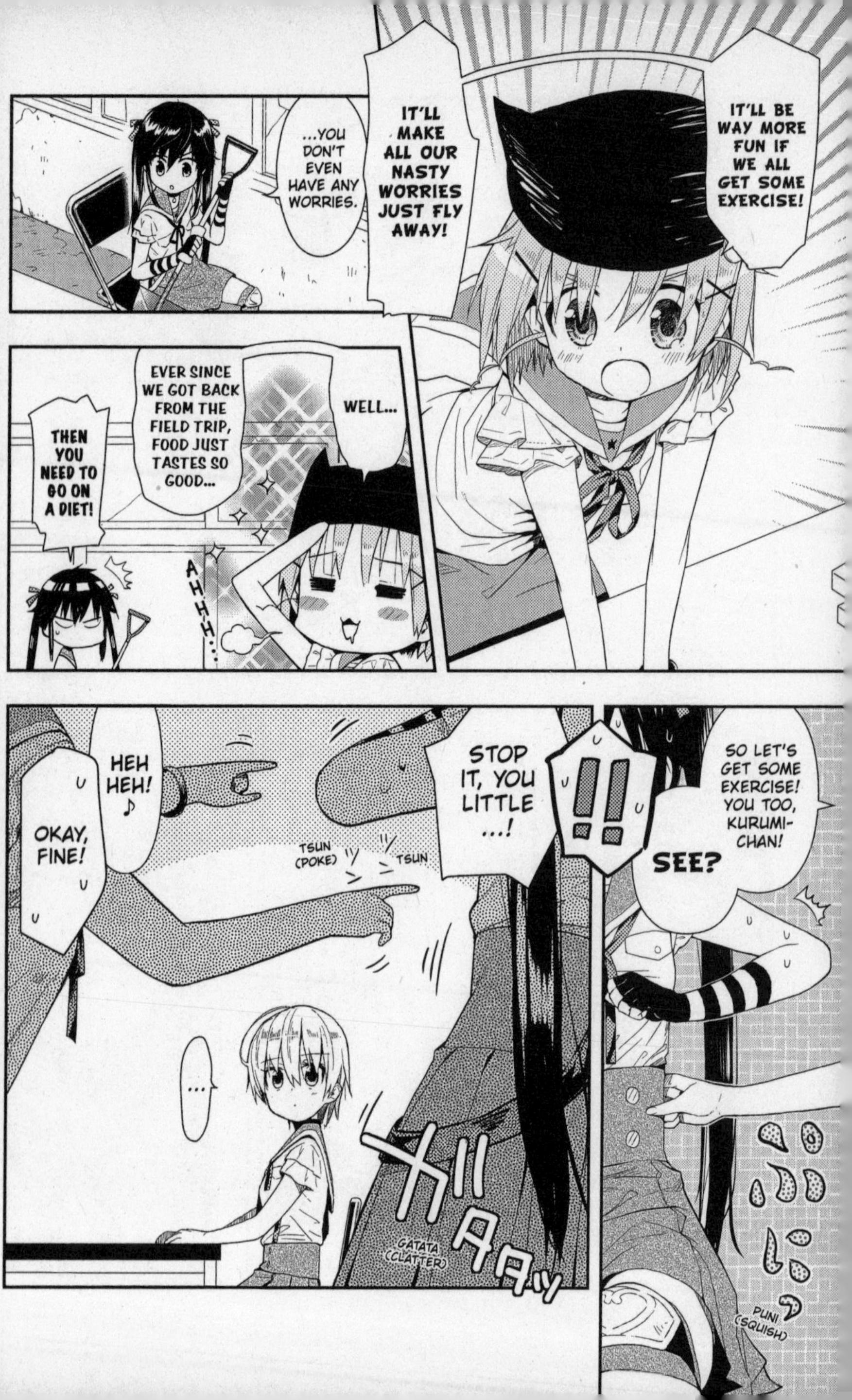
IT'LL BE WAY MORE FUN IF WE ALL GET SOME EXERCISE!
IT'LL MAKE ALL OUR NASTY WORRIES JUST FLY AWAY!
...YOU DON'T EVEN HAVE ANY WORRIES.
WELL...
EVER SINCE WE GOT BACK FROM THE FIELD TRIP, FOOD JUST TASTES SO GOOD...
AHHHH...
THEN YOU NEED TO GO ON A DIET!
SO LET'S GET SOME EXERCISE! YOU TOO, KURUMI-CHAN!
SEE?
PUNI (SQUISH)
!!
STOP IT, YOU LITTLE ...!
HEH HEH! ♪
OKAY, FINE!
TSUN (POKE)
TSUN
...
GATATA (CLATTER)

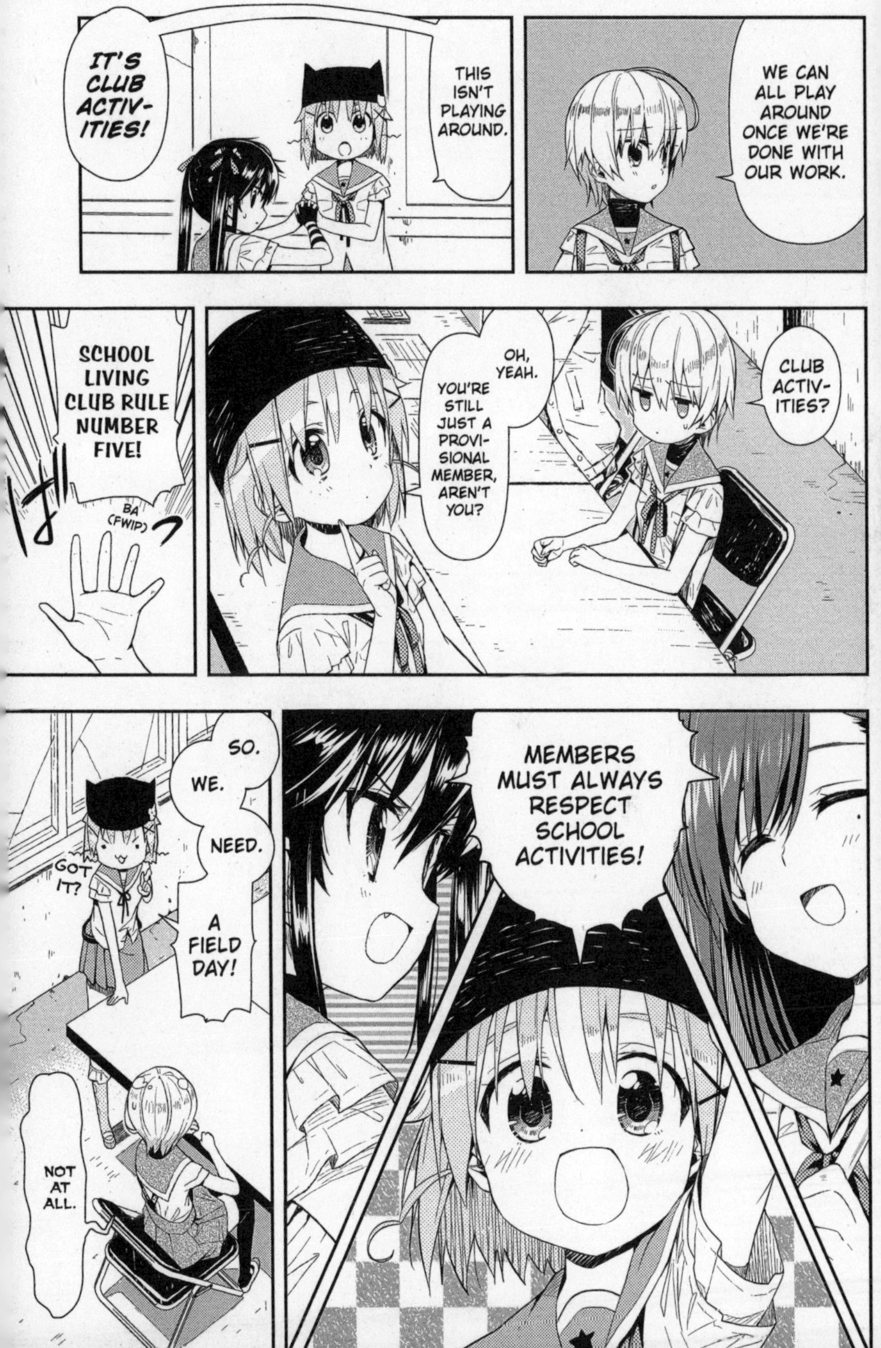
WE CAN ALL PLAY AROUND ONCE WE'RE DONE WITH OUR WORK.
THIS ISN'T PLAYING AROUND.
IT'S CLUB ACTIVITIES!
CLUB ACTIVITIES?
OH, YEAH.
YOU'RE STILL JUST A PROVISIONAL MEMBER, AREN'T YOU?
SCHOOL LIVING CLUB RULE NUMBER FIVE!
BA (FWIP)
MEMBERS MUST ALWAYS RESPECT SCHOOL ACTIVITIES!
SO.
WE.
NEED.
A FIELD DAY!
GOT IT?
NOT AT ALL.

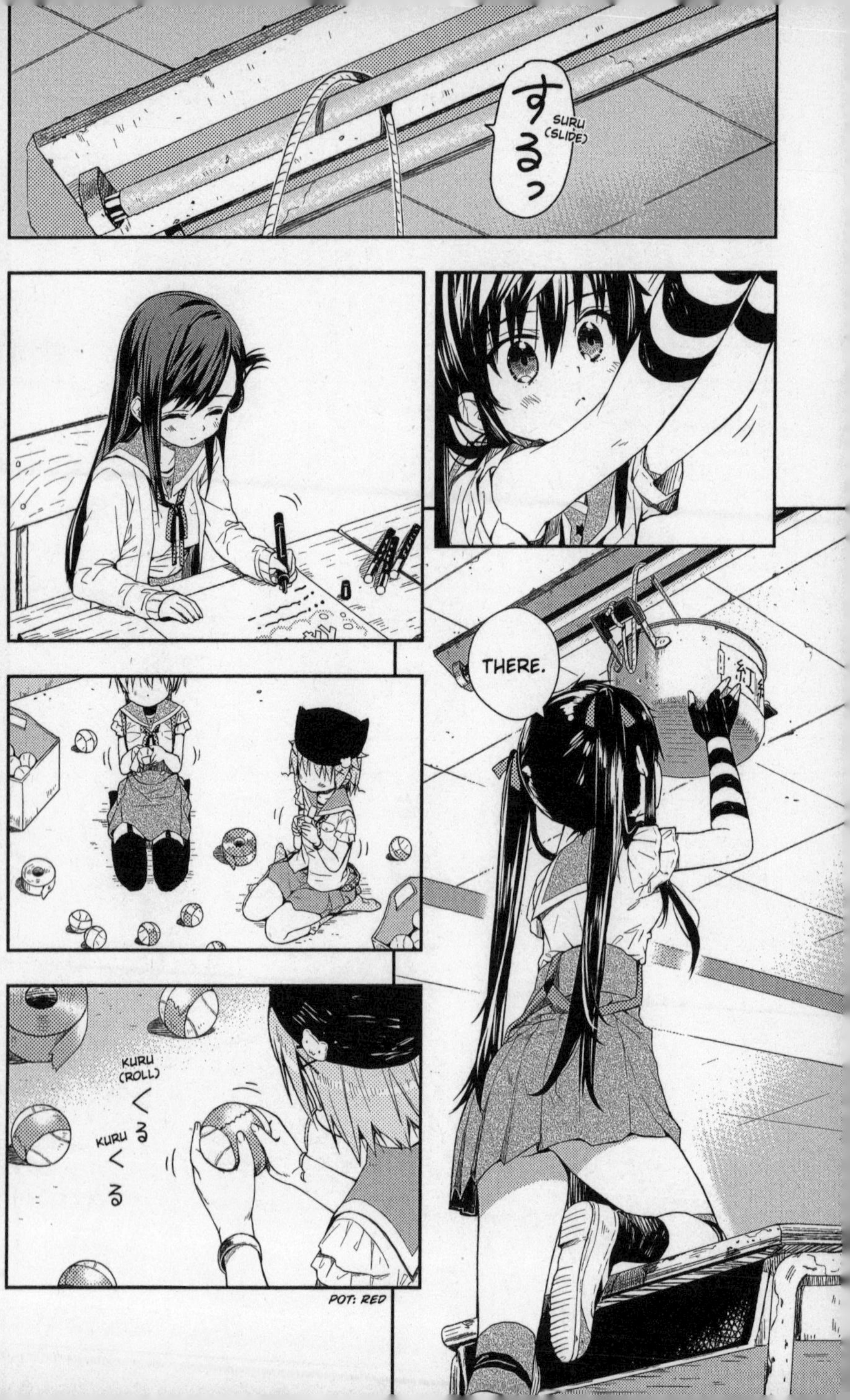
するっ
SURU (SLIDE)
THERE.
POT: RED
くる
KURU (ROLL)
くる
KURU

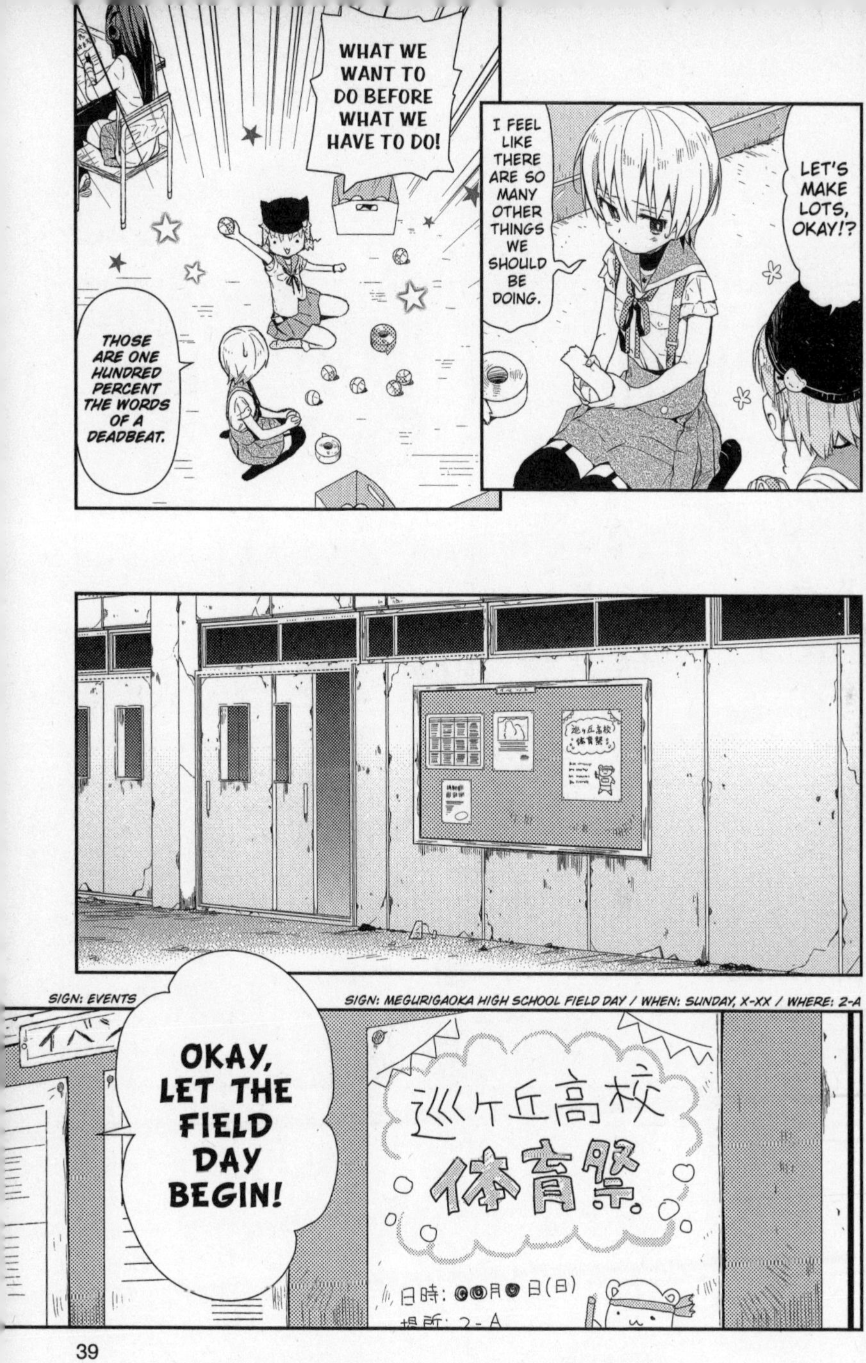
LET'S MAKE LOTS, OKAY!?
I FEEL LIKE THERE ARE SO MANY OTHER THINGS WE SHOULD BE DOING.
WHAT WE WANT TO DO BEFORE WHAT WE HAVE TO DO!
THOSE ARE ONE HUNDRED PERCENT THE WORDS OF A DEADBEAT.
SIGN: MEGURIGAOKA HIGH SCHOOL FIELD DAY / WHEN: SUNDAY, X-XX / WHERE: 2-A
SIGN: EVENTS
巡ヶ丘高校
体育祭
日時：◎◎月◎日(日)
OKAY, LET THE FIELD DAY BEGIN!

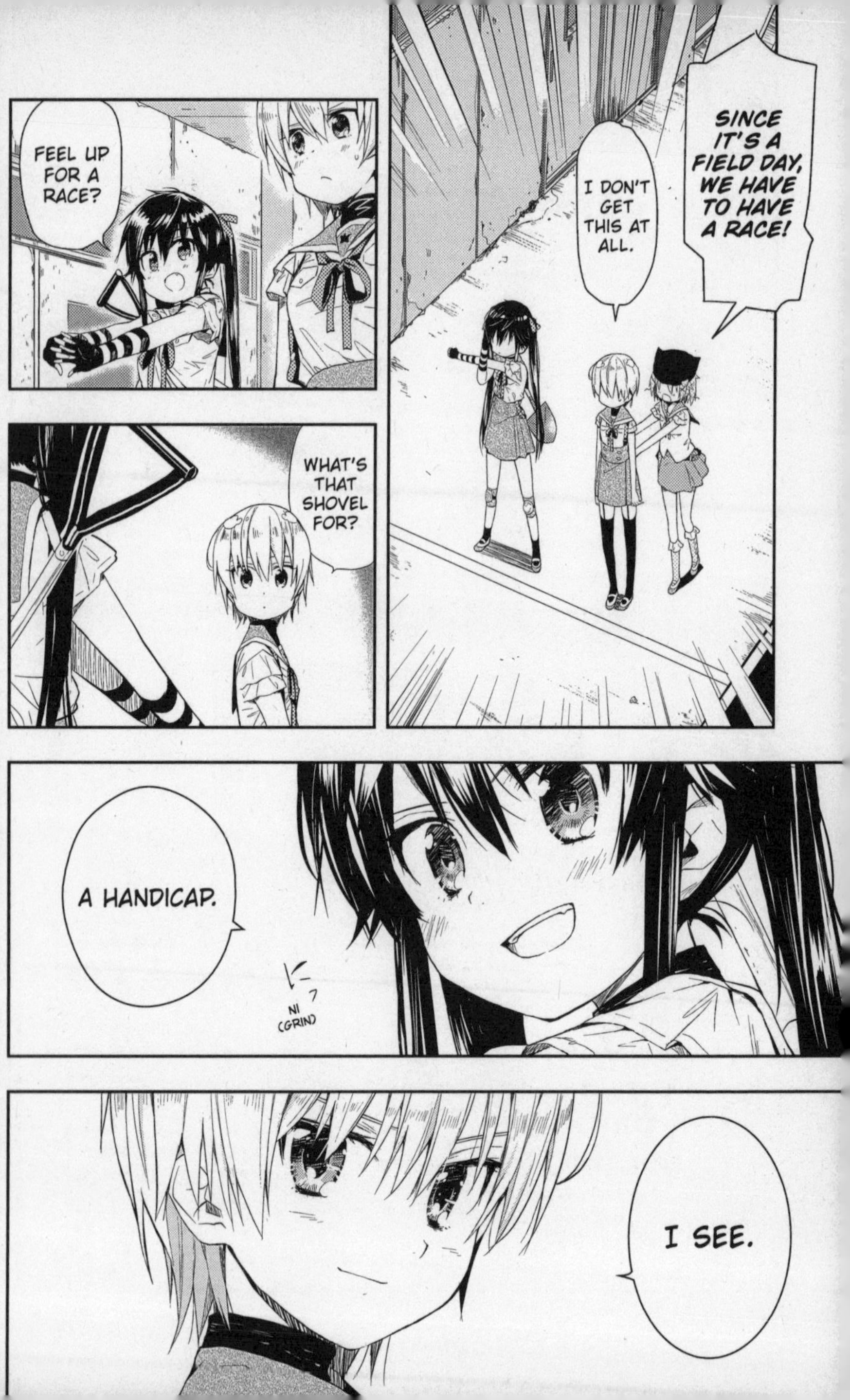
SINCE IT'S A FIELD DAY, WE HAVE TO HAVE A RACE!
I DON'T GET THIS AT ALL.
FEEL UP FOR A RACE?
WHAT'S THAT SHOVEL FOR?
A HANDICAP.
NI (GRIN)
I SEE.

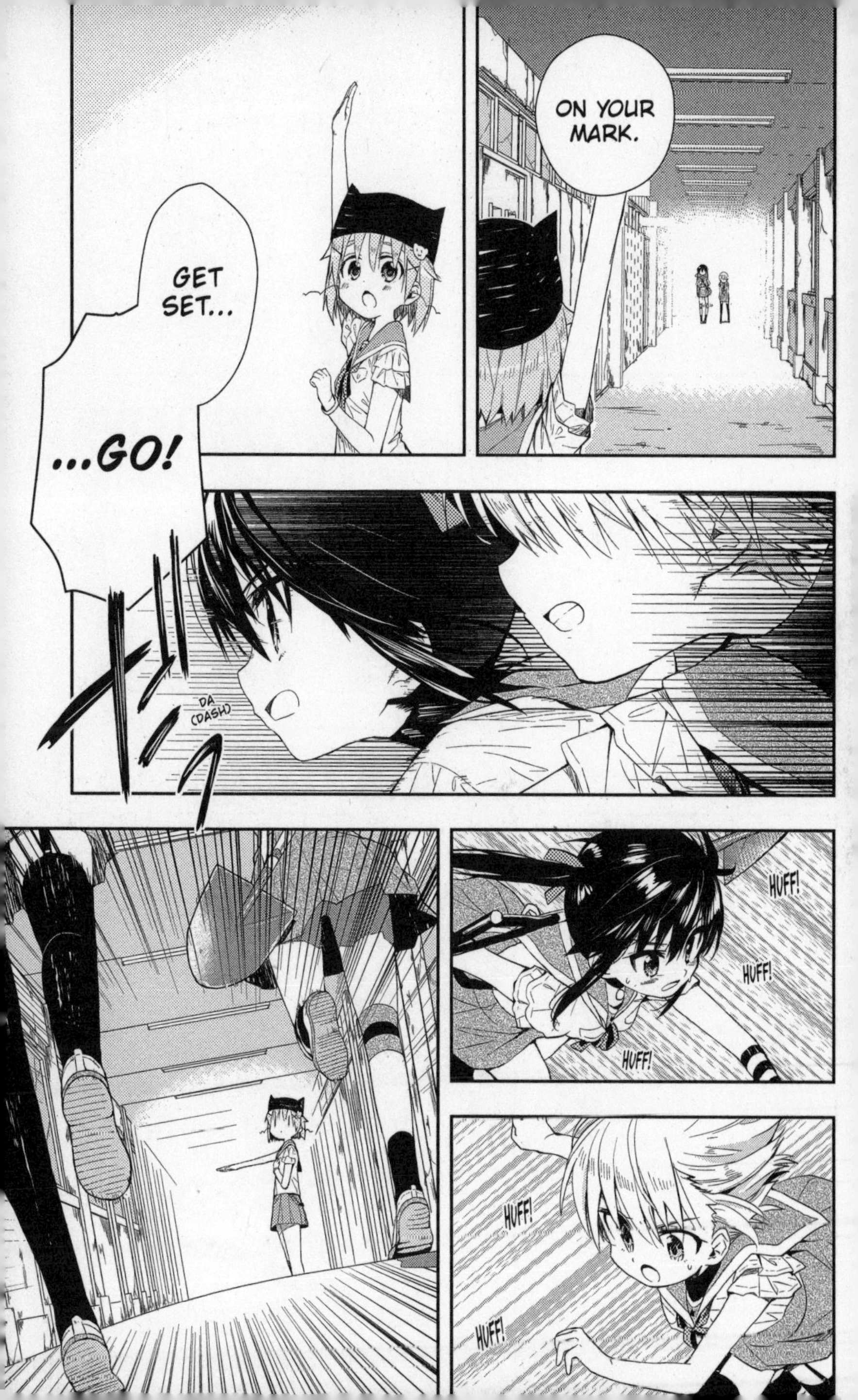
ON YOUR MARK.
GET SET...
...GO!
DA (DASH)
HUFF!
HUFF!
HUFF!
HUFF!
HUFF!

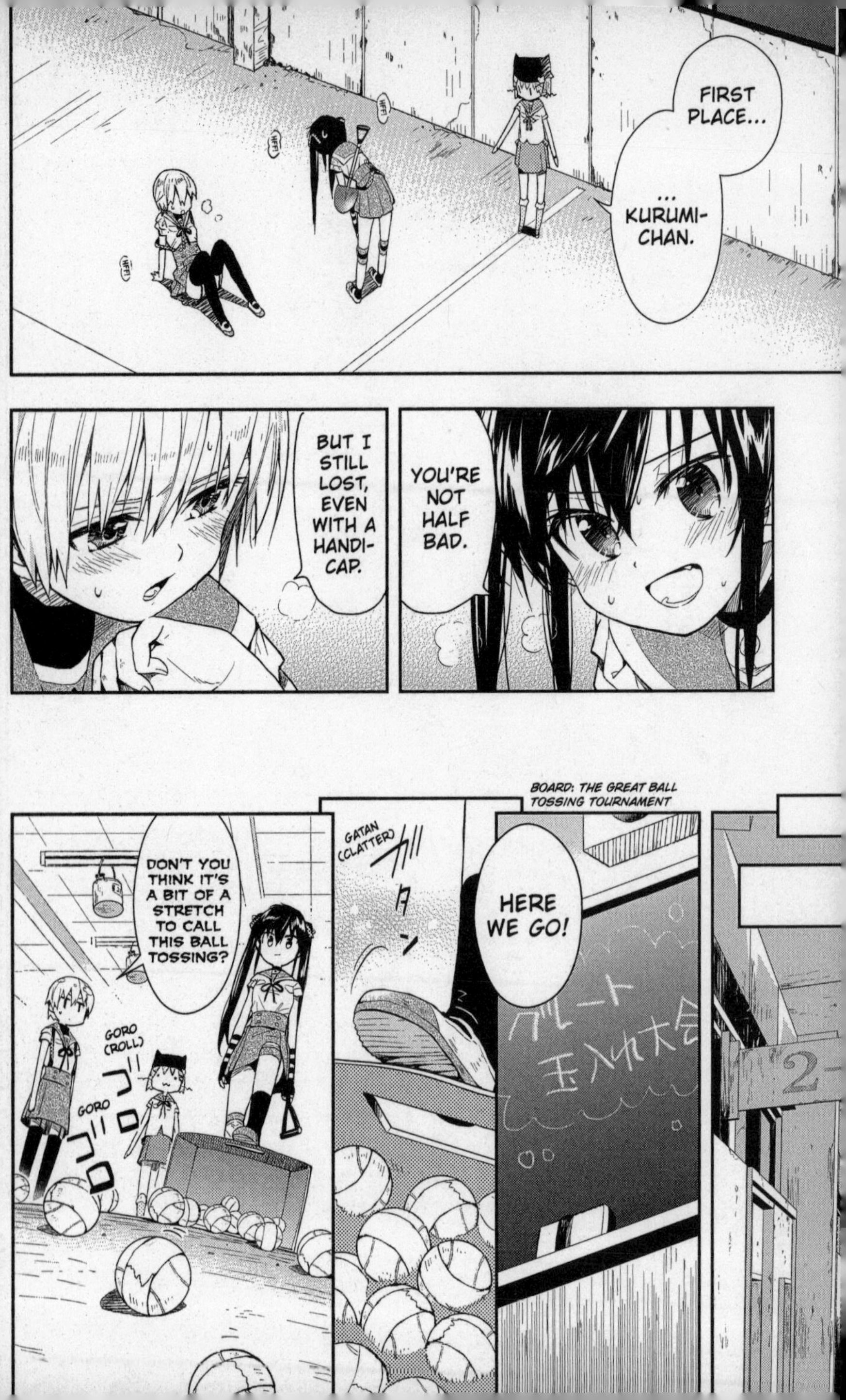
HFF!
HFF!
HFF!
FIRST PLACE...
...KURUMI-CHAN.
YOU'RE NOT HALF BAD.
BUT I STILL LOST, EVEN WITH A HANDICAP.
BOARD: THE GREAT BALL TOSSING TOURNAMENT
グレート
玉入れ大会
HERE WE GO!
GATAN (CLATTER)
DON'T YOU THINK IT'S A BIT OF A STRETCH TO CALL THIS BALL TOSSING?
GORO (ROLL)
GORO

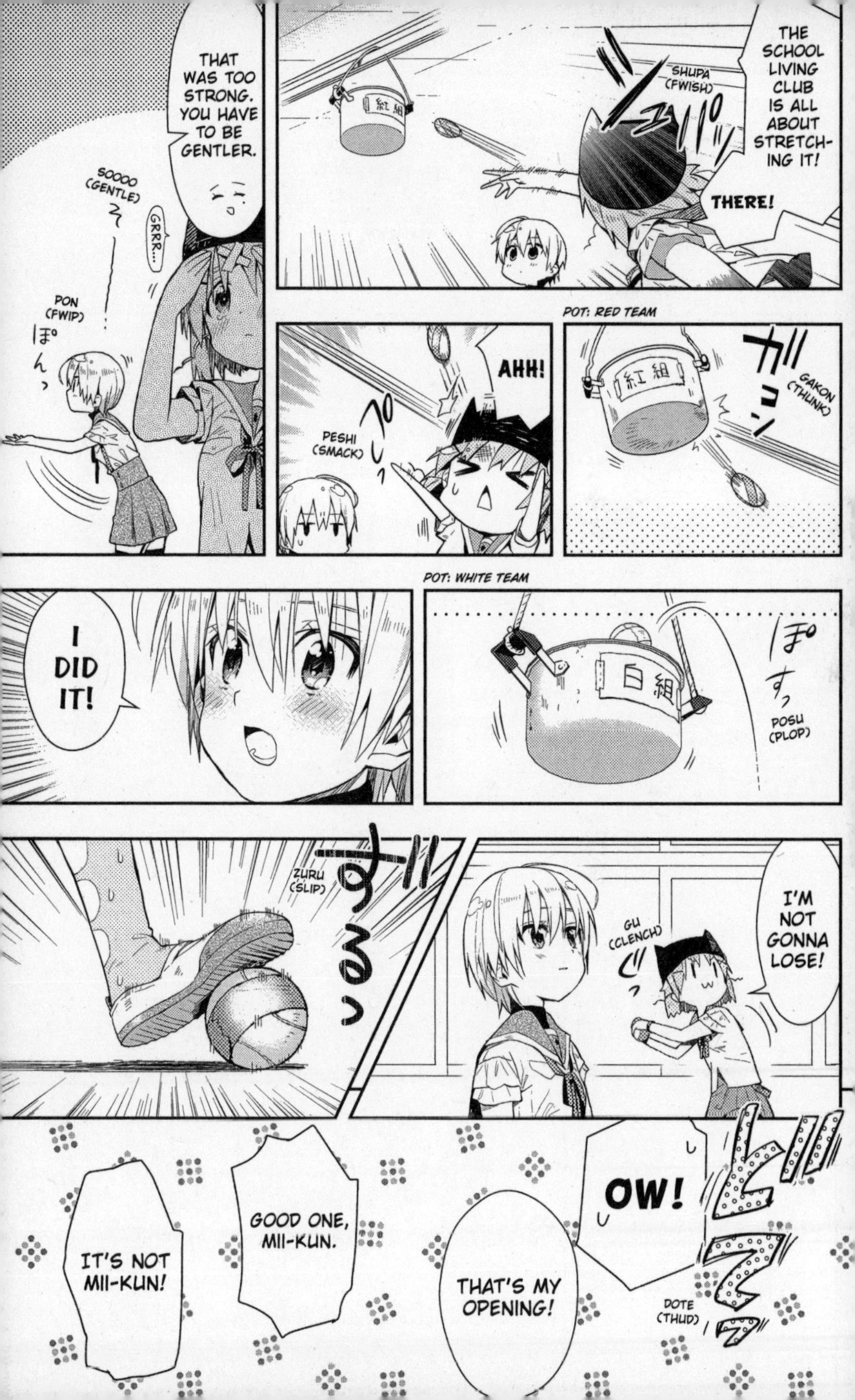
THE SCHOOL LIVING CLUB IS ALL ABOUT STRETCHING IT!
SHUPA (FWISH)
THERE!
POT: RED TEAM
GAKON (THUNK)
AHH!
PESHI (SMACK)
THAT WAS TOO STRONG. YOU HAVE TO BE GENTLER.
SOOOO (GENTLE)
GRRR...
PON (FWIP)
ぽんっ
POT: WHITE TEAM
ぽすっ
POSU (PLOP)
I DID IT!
I'M NOT GONNA LOSE!
GU (CLENCH)
ZURU (SLIP)
OW!
DOTE (THUD)
THAT'S MY OPENING!
GOOD ONE, MII-KUN.
IT'S NOT MII-KUN!

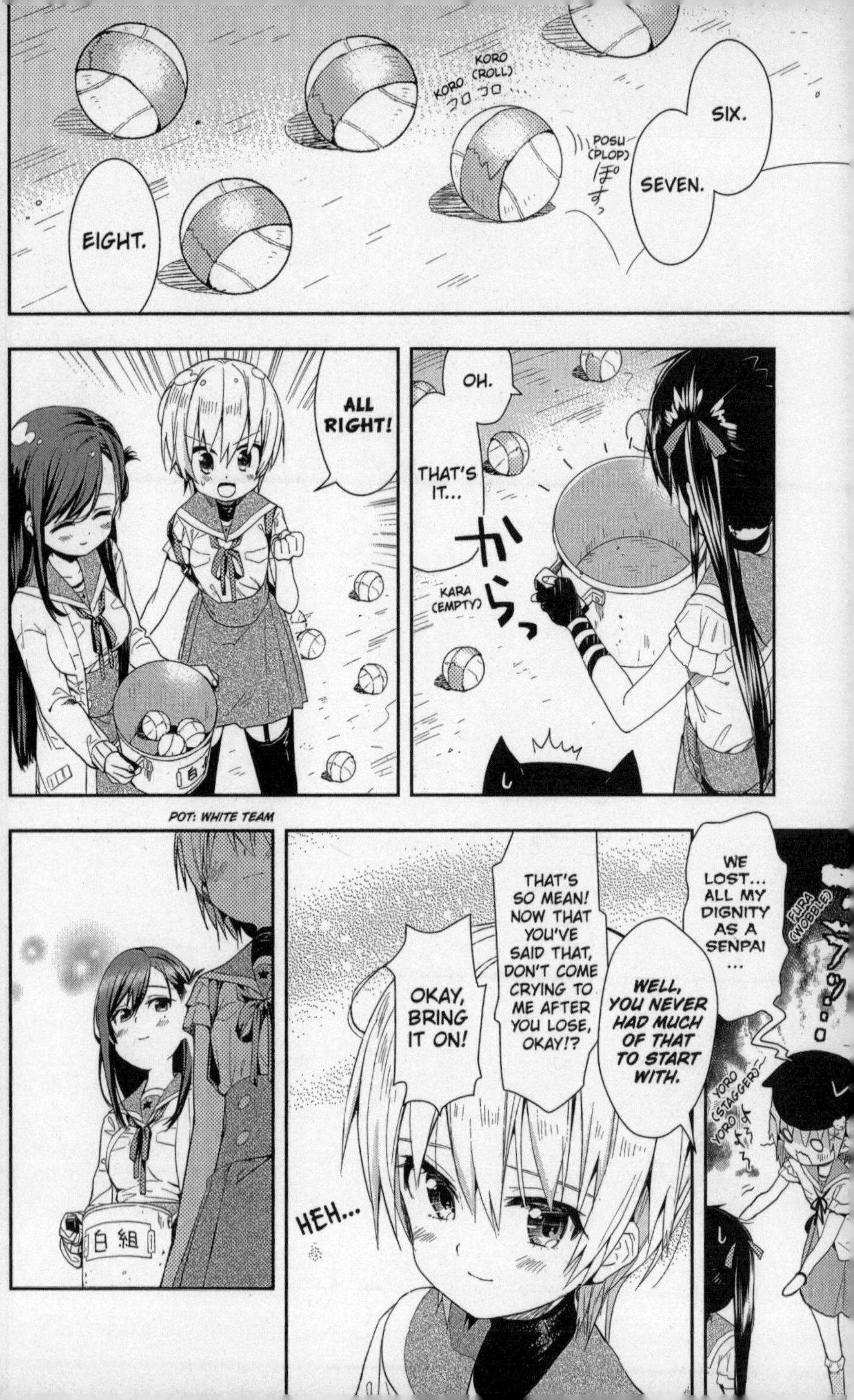

SIX.
SEVEN.
POSU (PLOP)
ぽすっ
KORO KORO (ROLL)
コロコロ...
EIGHT.
OH.
THAT'S IT...
KARA (EMPTY)
からっ
ALL RIGHT!
白
POT: WHITE TEAM
WE LOST... ALL MY DIGNITY AS A SENPAI ...
FURA (WOBBLE)
YORO YORO (STAGGER)
WELL, YOU NEVER HAD MUCH OF THAT TO START WITH.
THAT'S SO MEAN! NOW THAT YOU'VE SAID THAT, DON'T COME CRYING TO ME AFTER YOU LOSE, OKAY!?
OKAY, BRING IT ON!
HEH...
白組

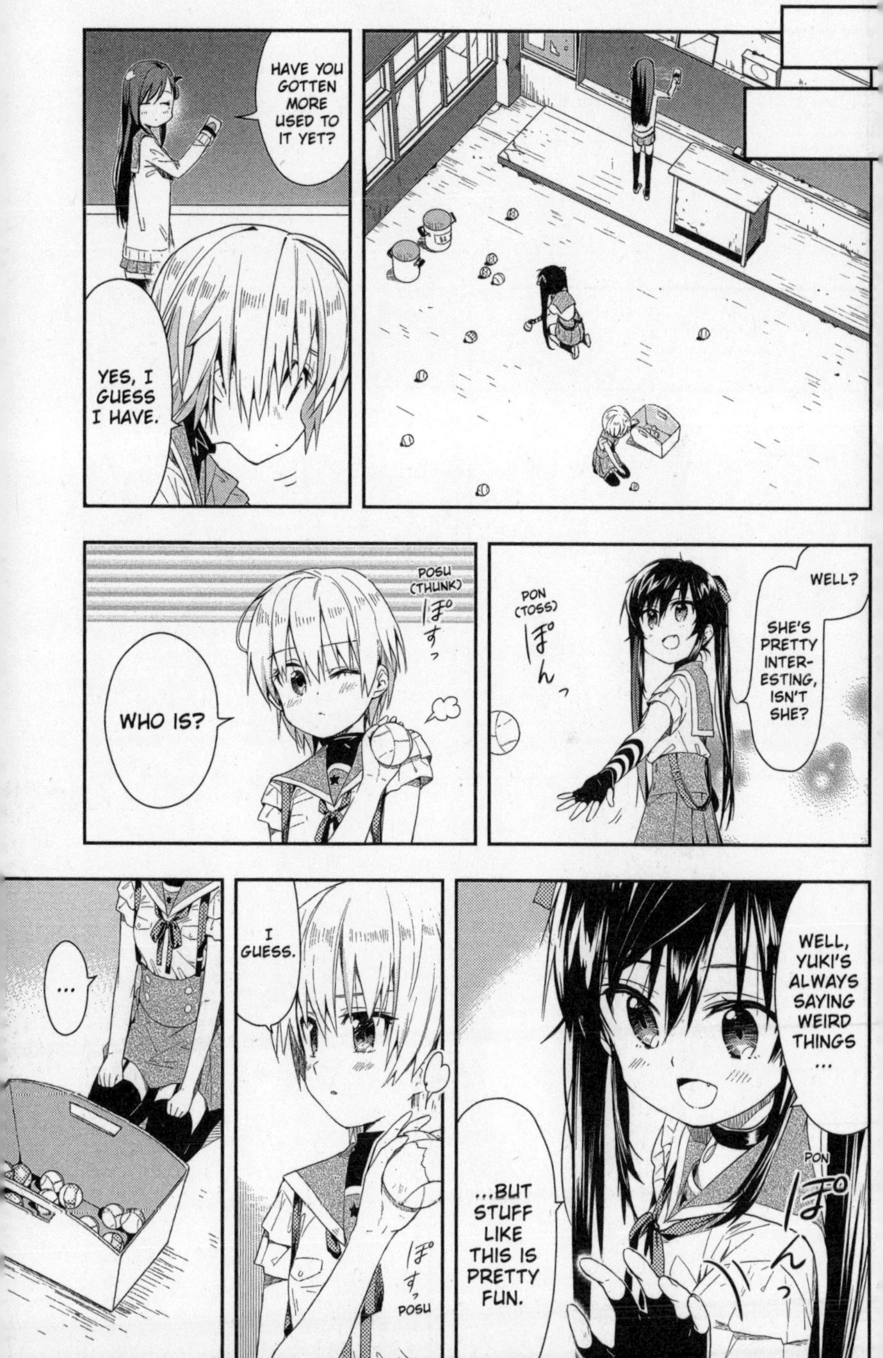
HAVE YOU GOTTEN MORE USED TO IT YET?
YES, I GUESS I HAVE.
WELL?
SHE'S PRETTY INTERESTING, ISN'T SHE?
PON (TOSS)
ぽんっ
POSU (THUNK)
ぽすっ
WHO IS?
WELL, YUKI'S ALWAYS SAYING WEIRD THINGS...
PON
ぽんっ
...BUT STUFF LIKE THIS IS PRETTY FUN.
I GUESS.
ぽすっ
POSU
...

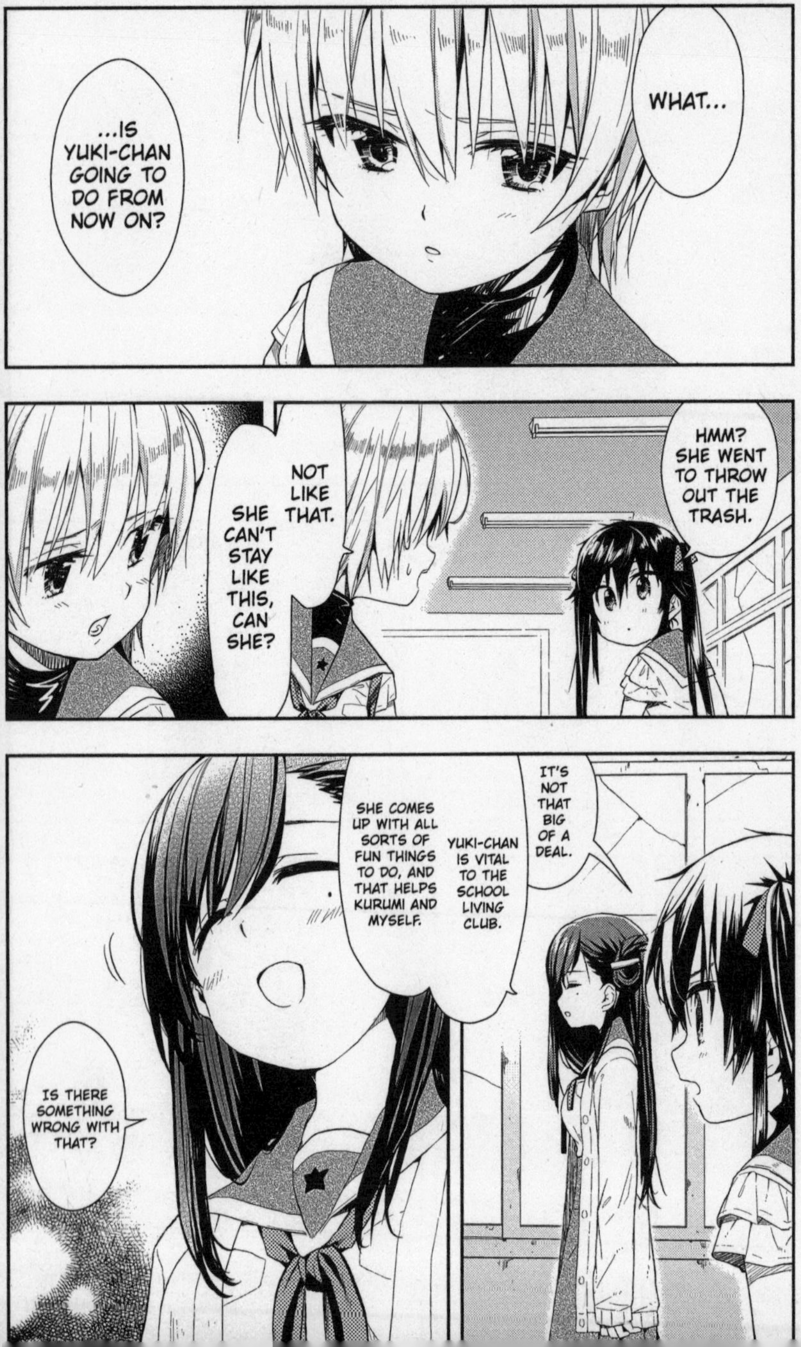
WHAT...
...IS YUKI-CHAN GOING TO DO FROM NOW ON?
HMM? SHE WENT TO THROW OUT THE TRASH.
NOT LIKE THAT.
SHE CAN'T STAY LIKE THIS, CAN SHE?
IT'S NOT THAT BIG OF A DEAL.
YUKI-CHAN IS VITAL TO THE SCHOOL LIVING CLUB.
SHE COMES UP WITH ALL SORTS OF FUN THINGS TO DO, AND THAT HELPS KURUMI AND MYSELF.
IS THERE SOMETHING WRONG WITH THAT?

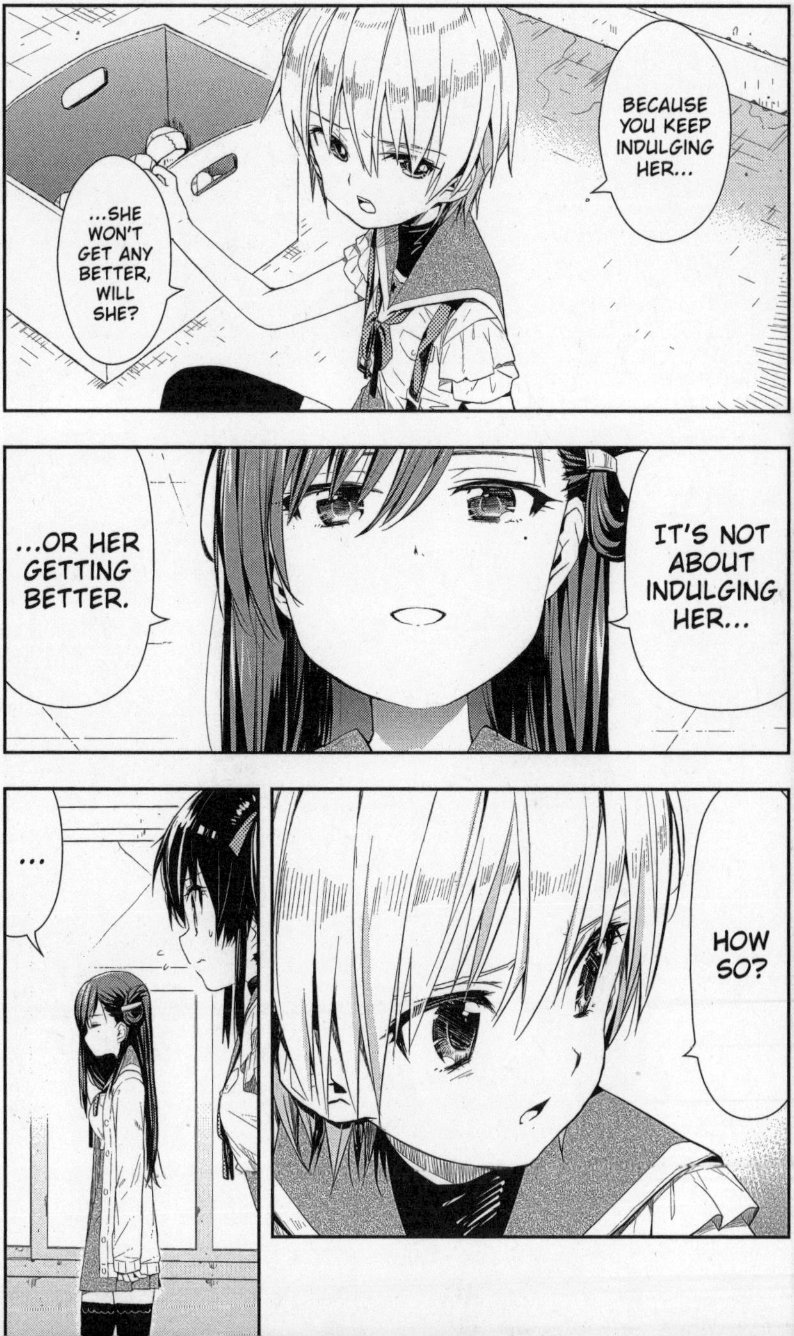
BECAUSE YOU KEEP INDULGING HER...
...SHE WON'T GET ANY BETTER, WILL SHE?
IT'S NOT ABOUT INDULGING HER...
...OR HER GETTING BETTER.
HOW SO?
...

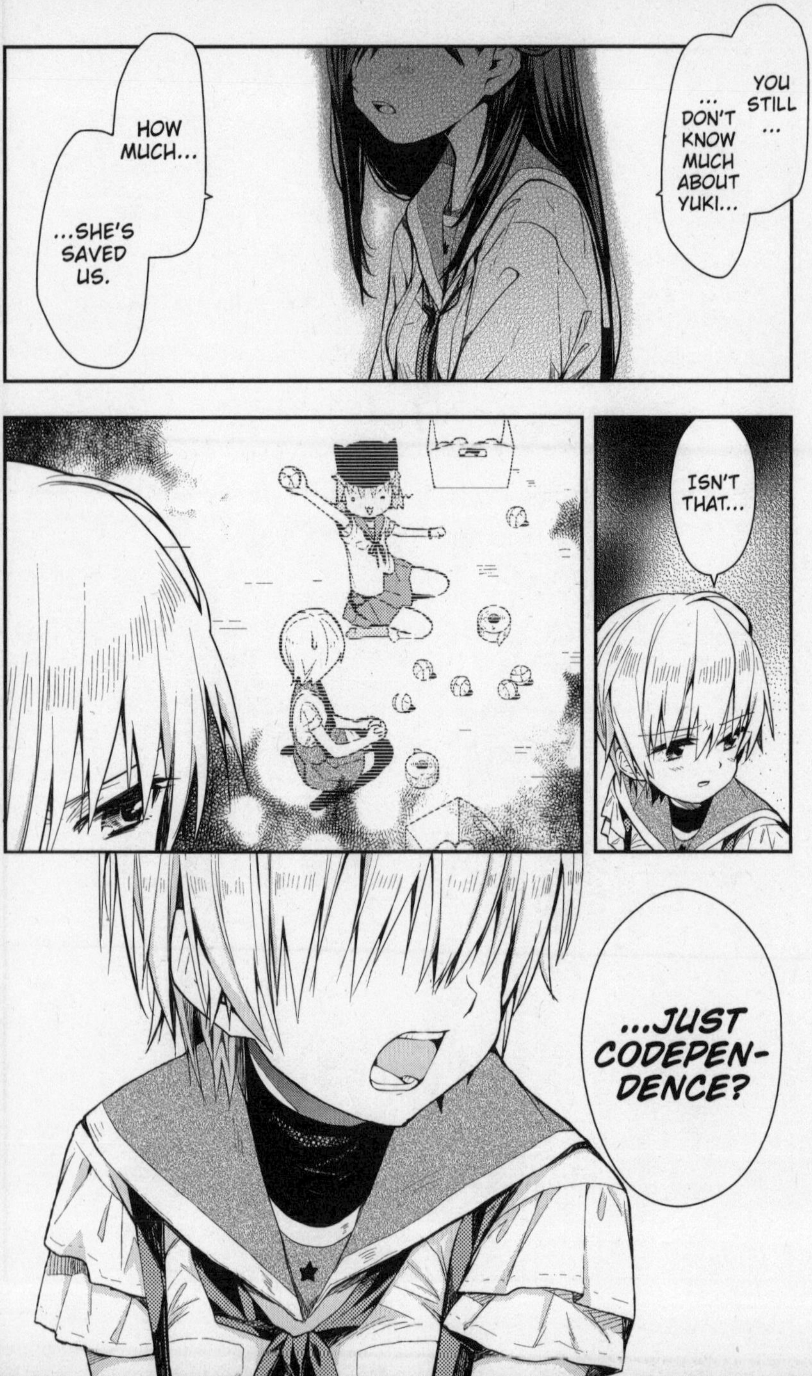
YOU STILL ...
... DON'T KNOW MUCH ABOUT YUKI...
HOW MUCH...
...SHE'S SAVED US.
ISN'T THAT...
...JUST CODEPEN-DENCE?

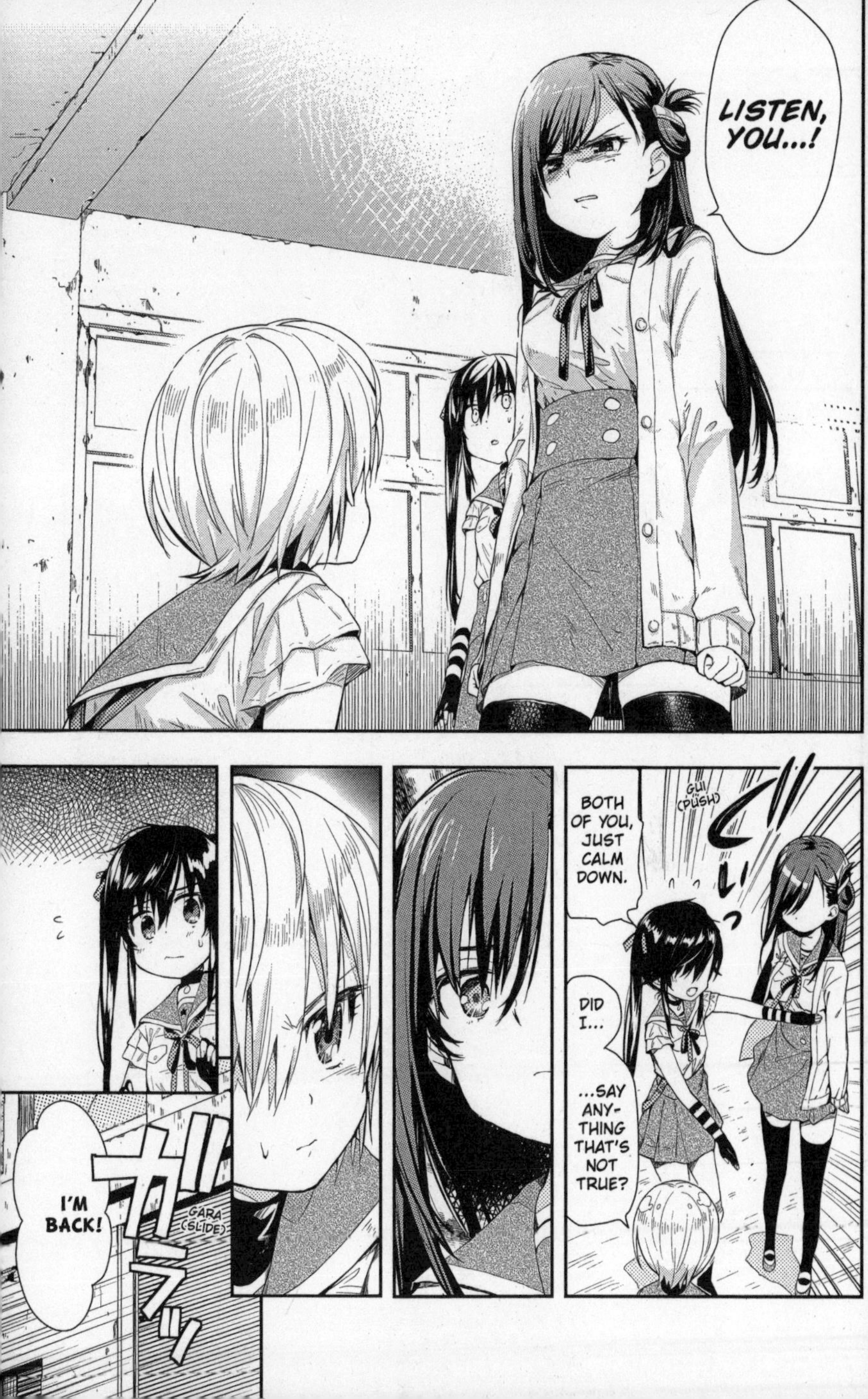
LISTEN, YOU...!
GUI (PUSH)
BOTH OF YOU, JUST CALM DOWN.
DID I...
...SAY ANY-THING THAT'S NOT TRUE?
GARA (SLIDE)
I'M BACK!

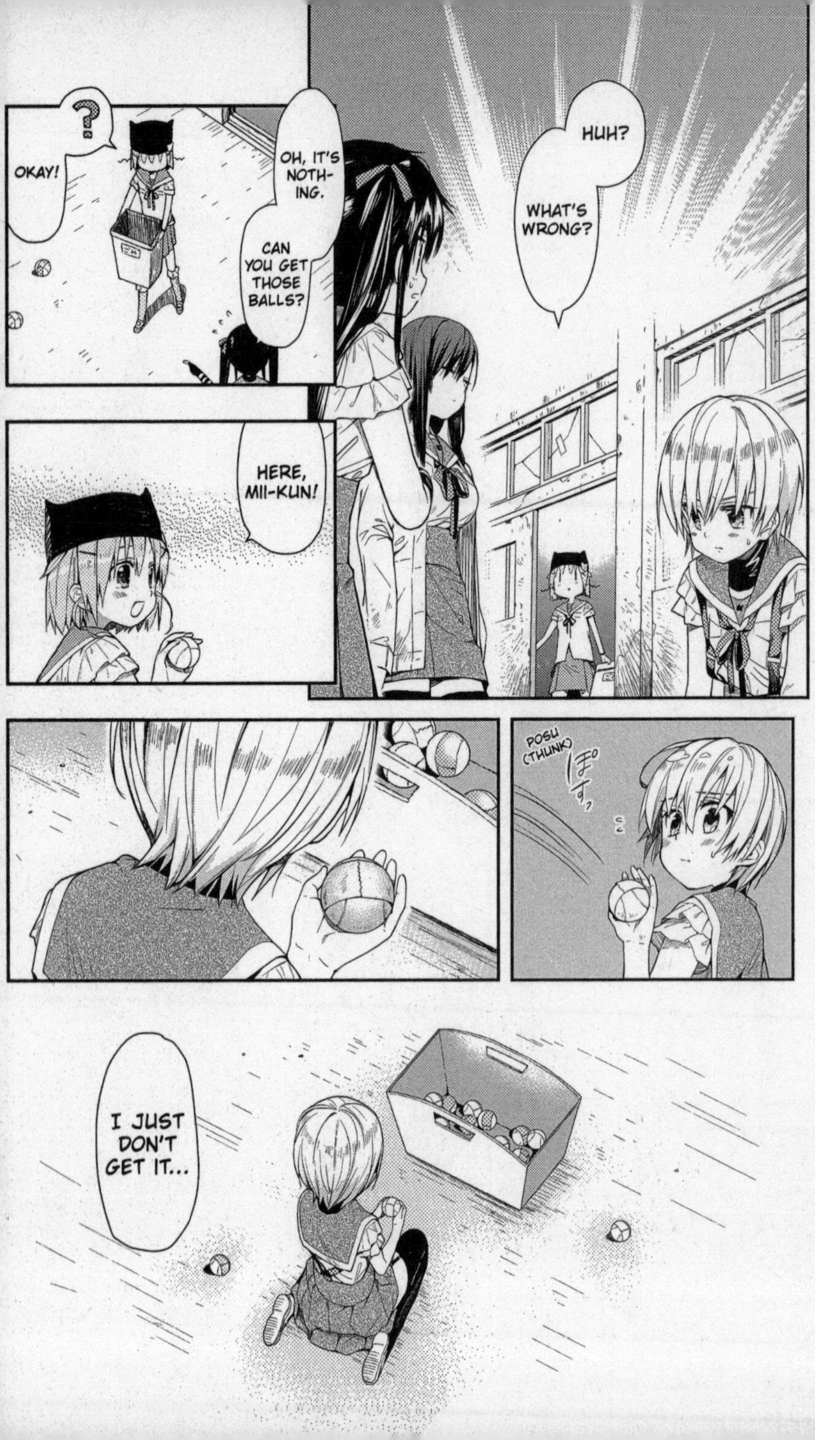
HUH?
WHAT'S WRONG?
OH, IT'S NOTHING.
CAN YOU GET THOSE BALLS?
?
OKAY!
HERE, MII-KUN!
POSU (THUNK)
ぽすっ
I JUST DON'T GET IT...

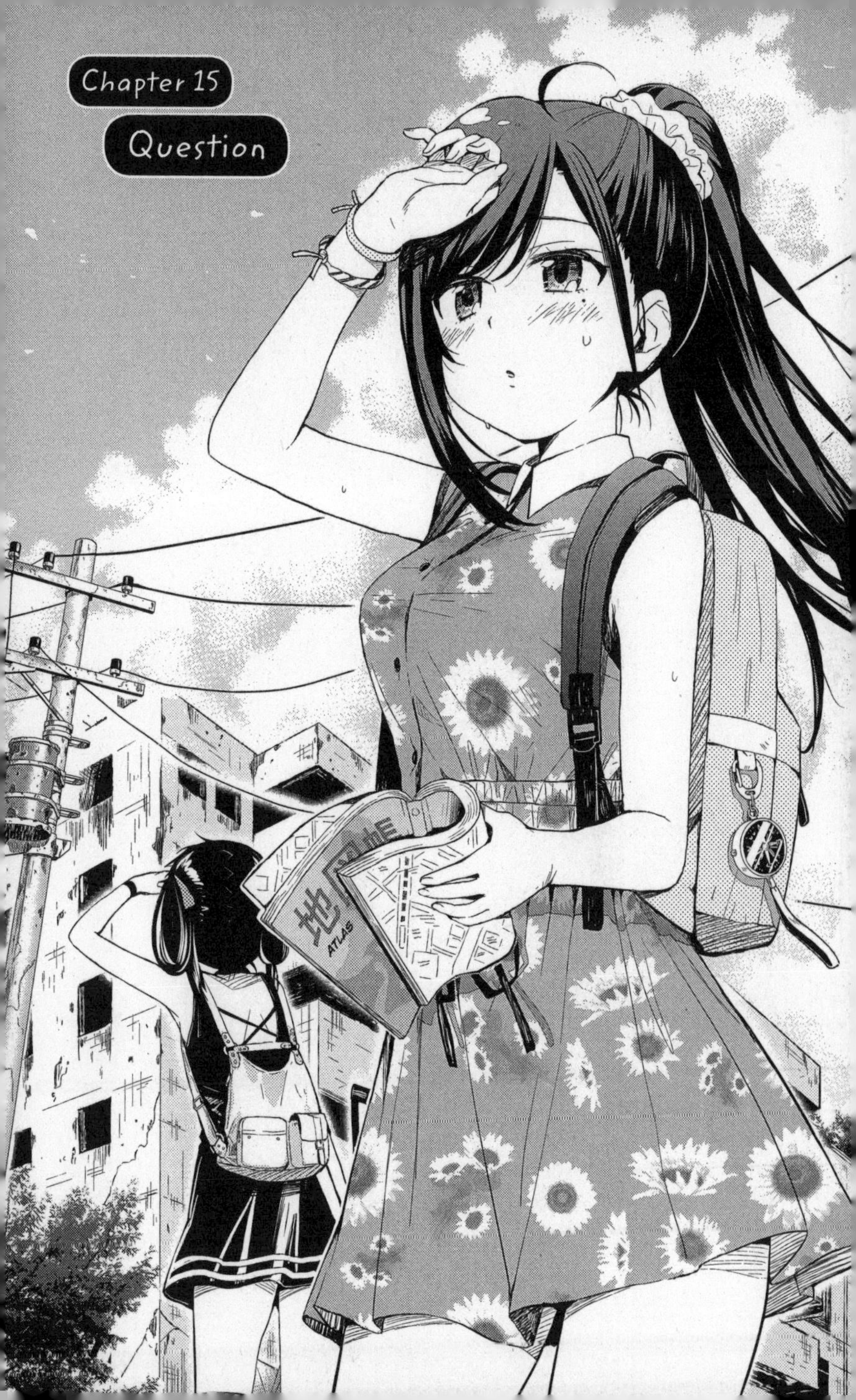
Chapter 15
Question
ATLAS

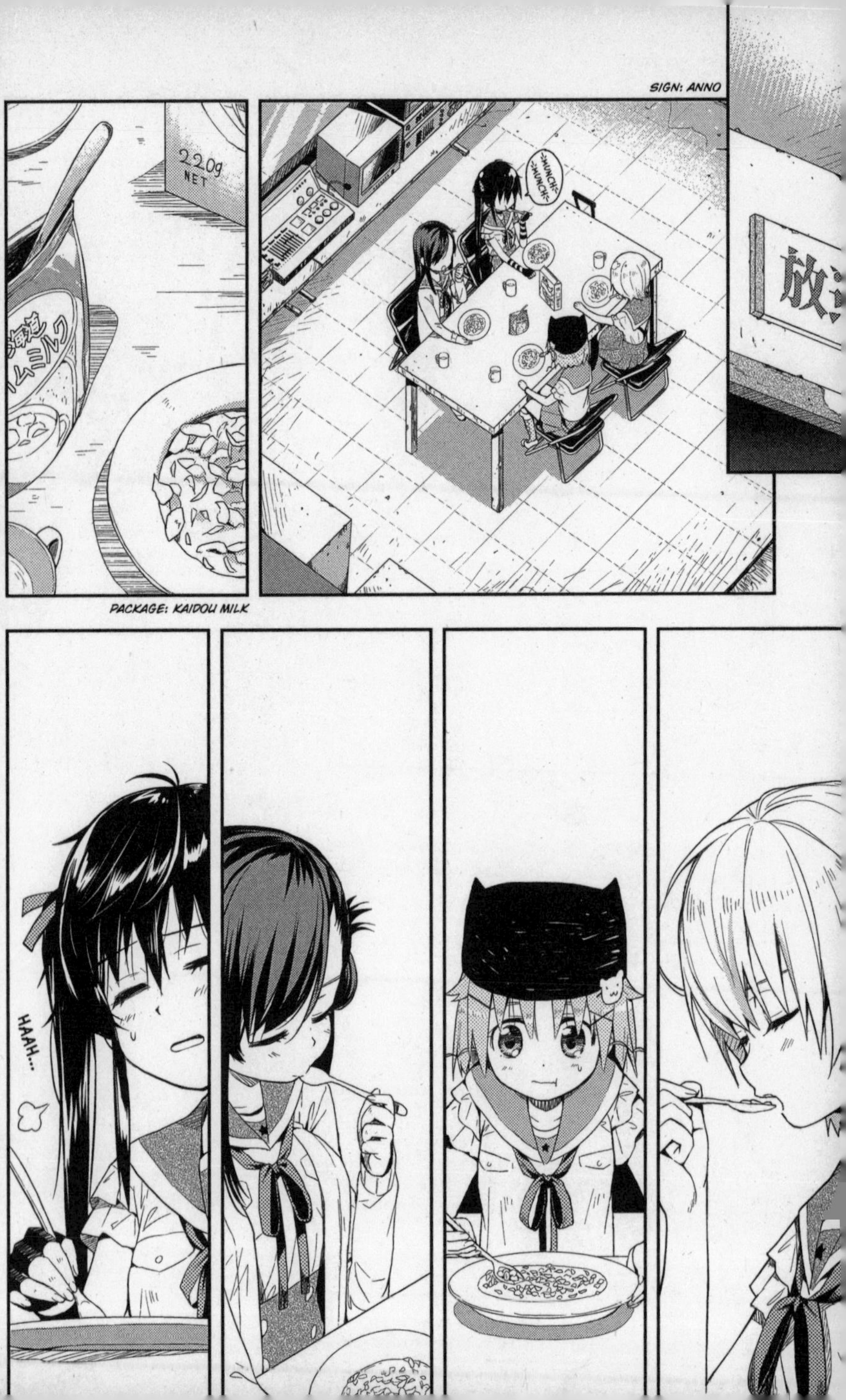
放
SIGN: ANNO
MUNCH
MUNCH
220g
NET
PACKAGE: KAIDOU MILK
HAAH...

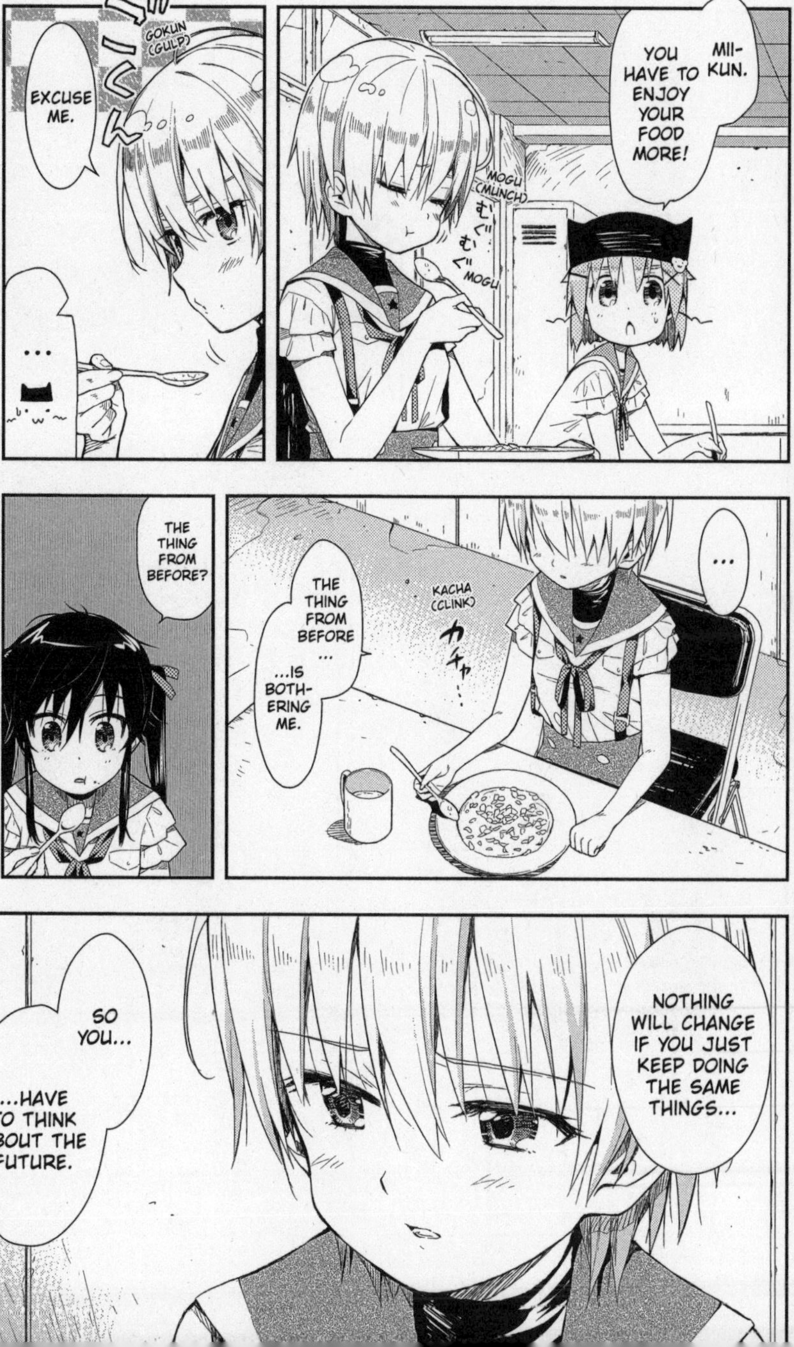
MII-KUN.
YOU HAVE TO ENJOY YOUR FOOD MORE!
MOGU (MUNCH)
むぐ むぐ
MOGU
GOKUN (GULP)
EXCUSE ME.
...
...
KACHA (CLINK)
カチャ
THE THING FROM BEFORE... ...IS BOTHERING ME.
THE THING FROM BEFORE?
NOTHING WILL CHANGE IF YOU JUST KEEP DOING THE SAME THINGS...
SO YOU... ...HAVE TO THINK ABOUT THE FUTURE.

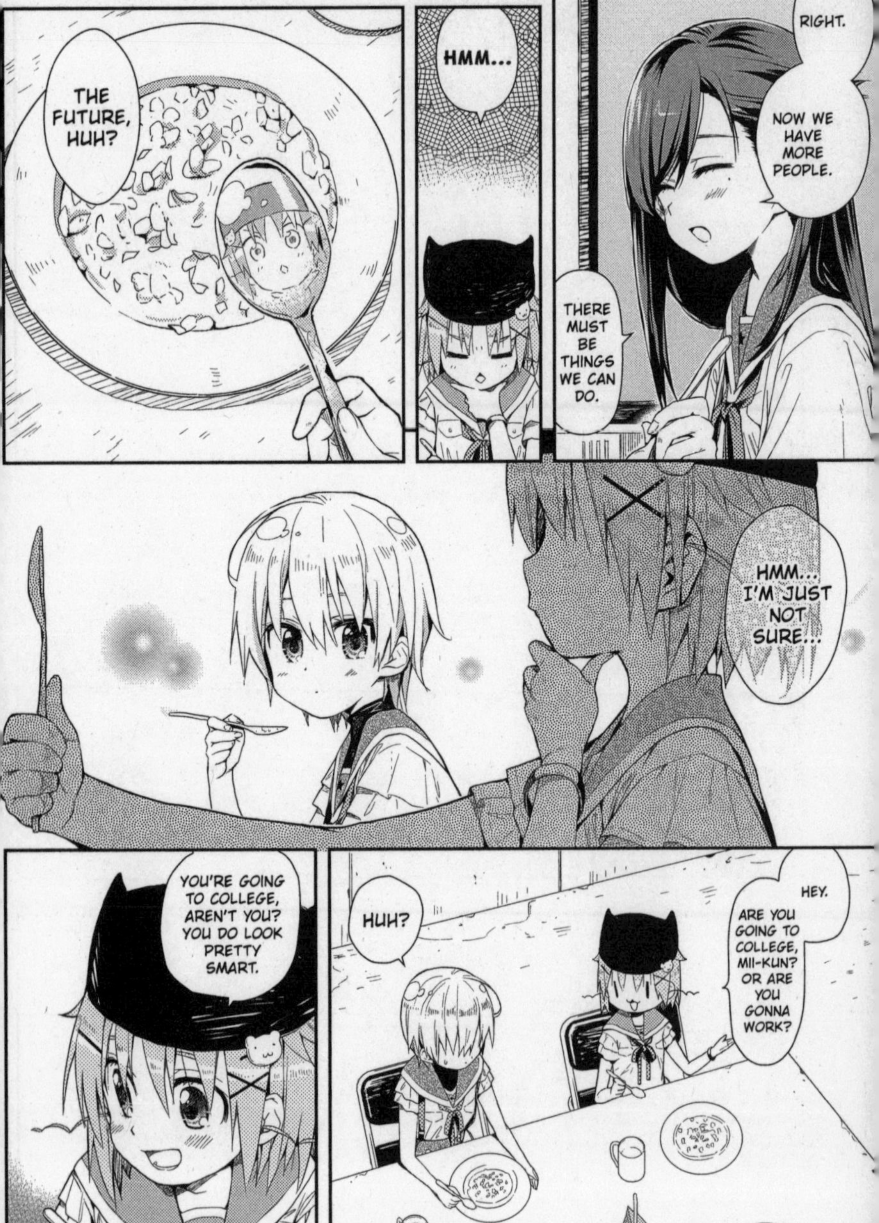
RIGHT.
NOW WE HAVE MORE PEOPLE.
THERE MUST BE THINGS WE CAN DO.
HMM...
THE FUTURE, HUH?
HMM... I'M JUST NOT SURE...
HEY.
ARE YOU GOING TO COLLEGE, MII-KUN? OR ARE YOU GONNA WORK?
HUH?
YOU'RE GOING TO COLLEGE, AREN'T YOU? YOU DO LOOK PRETTY SMART.

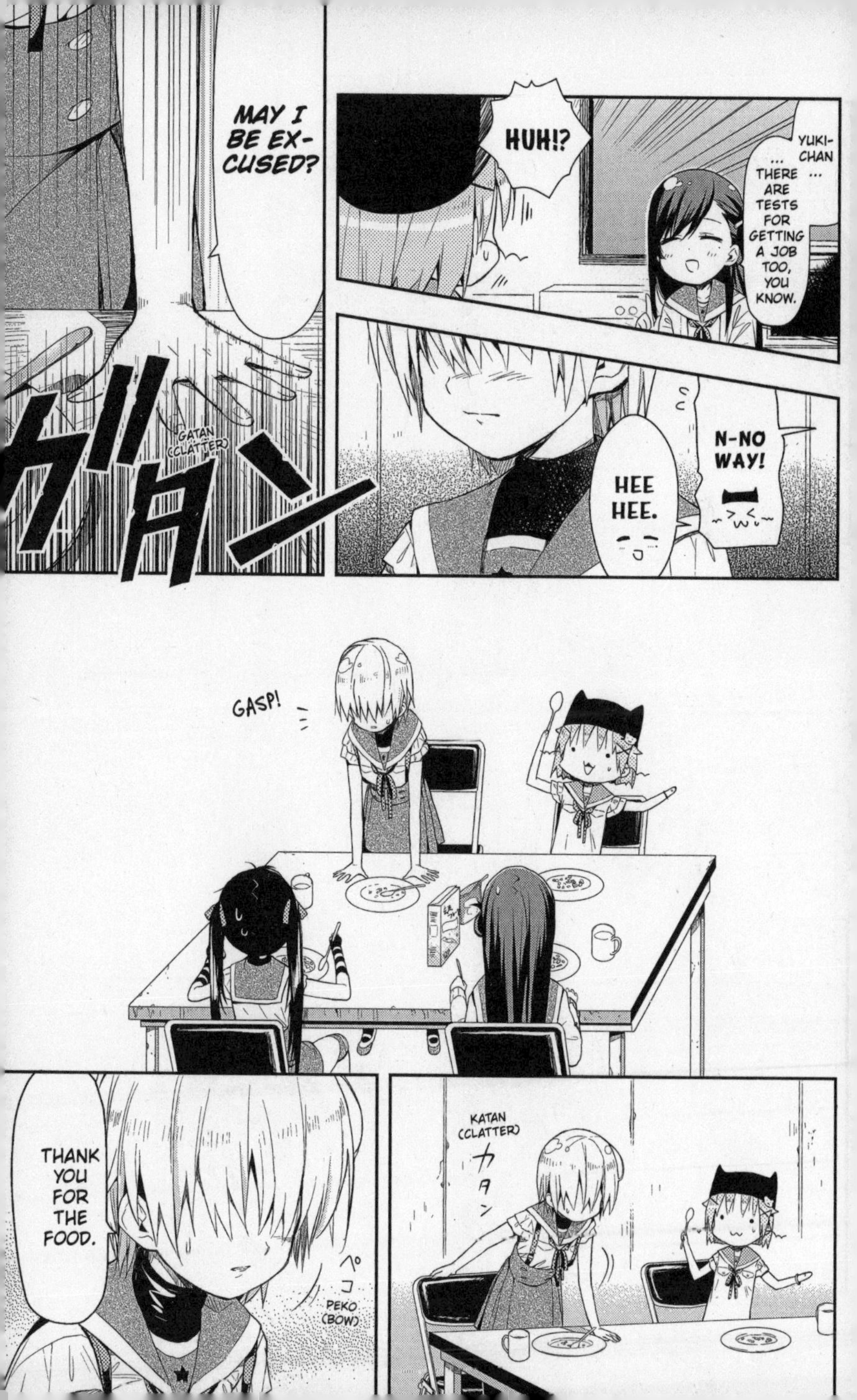

YUKI-CHAN ... THERE ARE TESTS FOR GETTING A JOB TOO, YOU KNOW.
HUH!?
N-NO WAY!
HEE HEE.
MAY I BE EXCUSED?
GATAN (CLATTER)
GASP!
KATAN (CLATTER)
THANK YOU FOR THE FOOD.
PEKO (BOW)

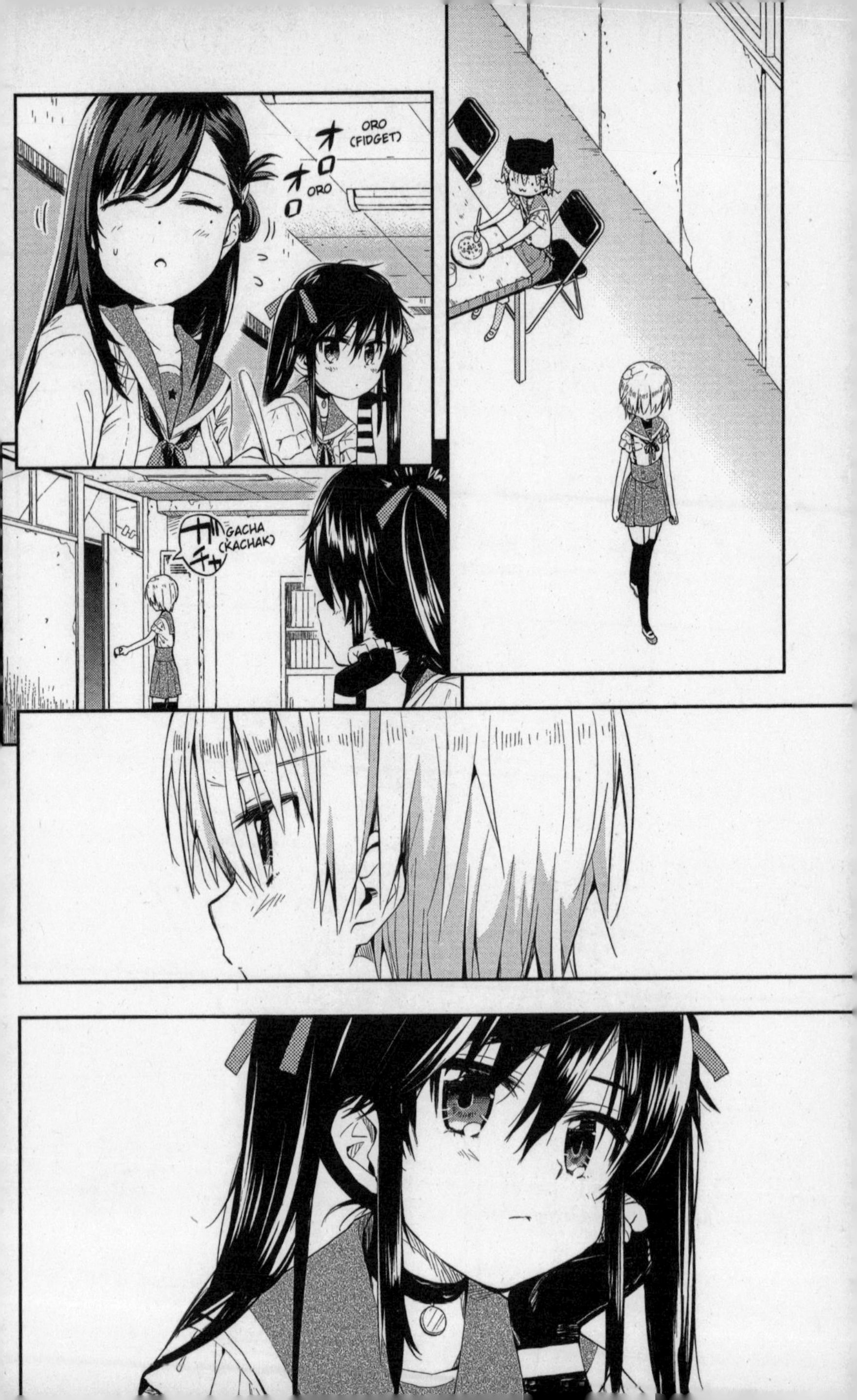
オロオロ
ORO (FIDGET)
ORO
ガチャ
GACHA (KACHAK)

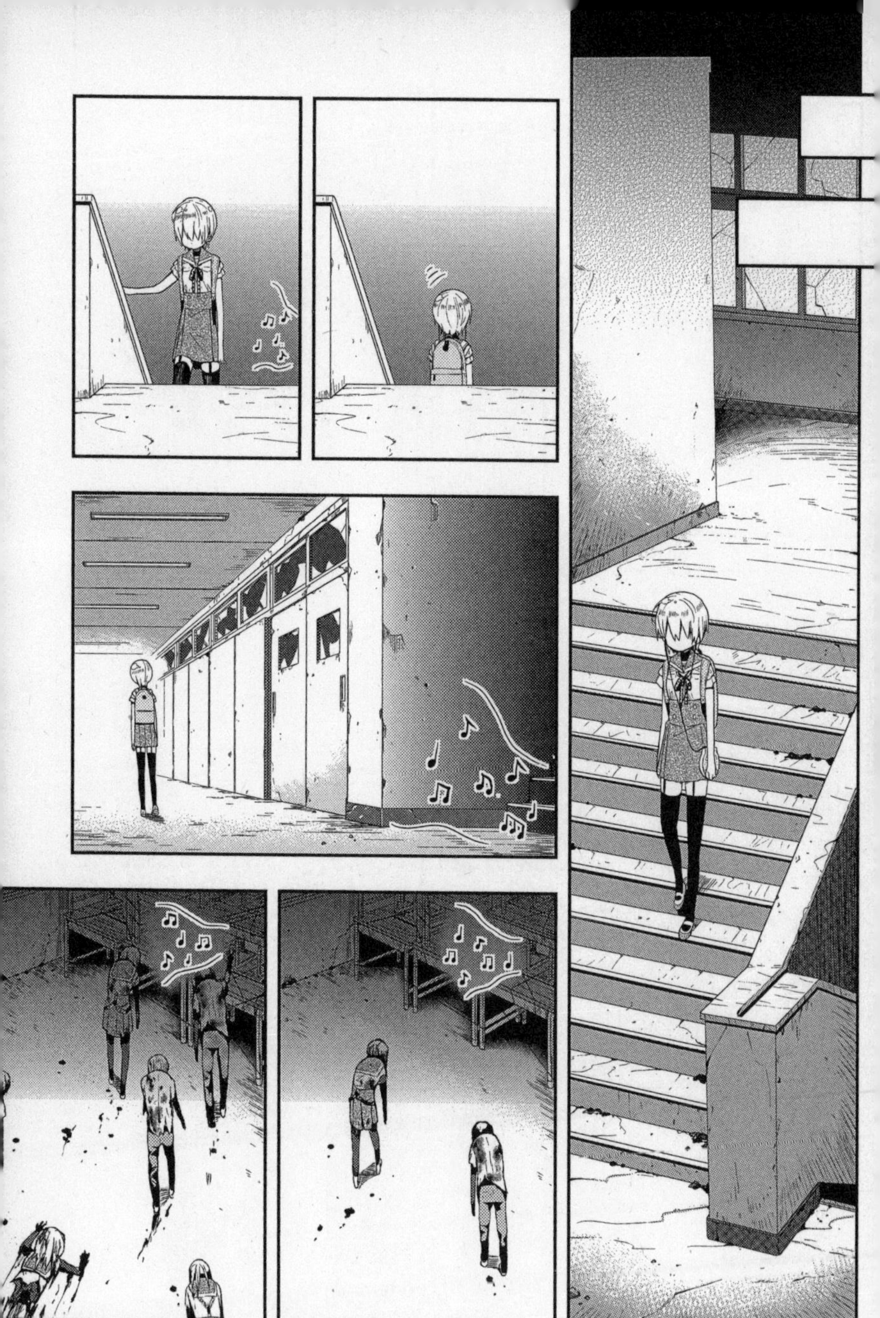

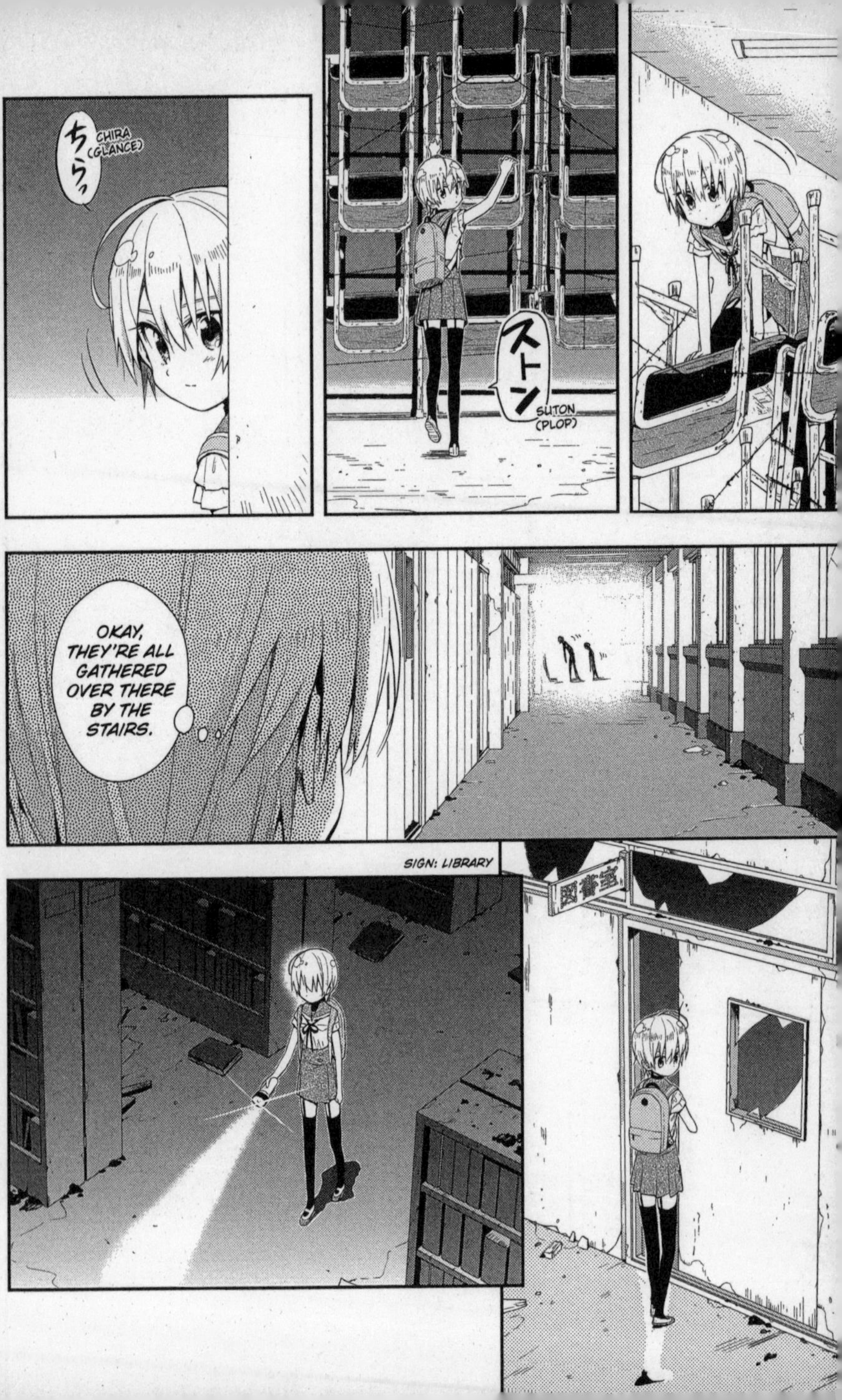
ストン
SUTON (PLOP)
ちらっ
CHIRA (GLANCE)
OKAY, THEY'RE ALL GATHERED OVER THERE BY THE STAIRS.
図書室
SIGN: LIBRARY

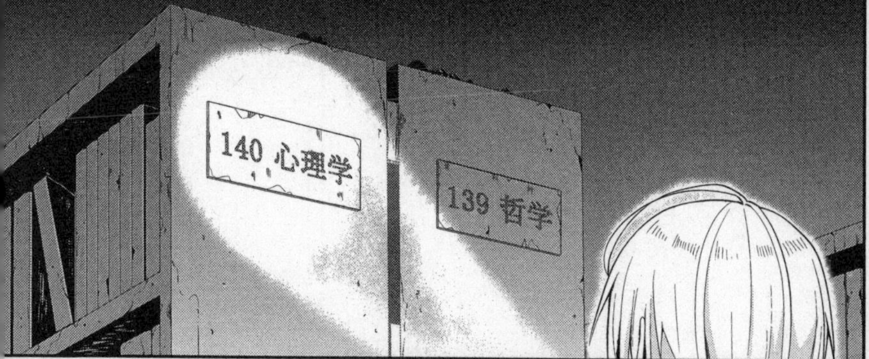
140 心理学
139 哲学

SIGNS: 140 PSYCHOLOGY, 139 PHILOSOPHY

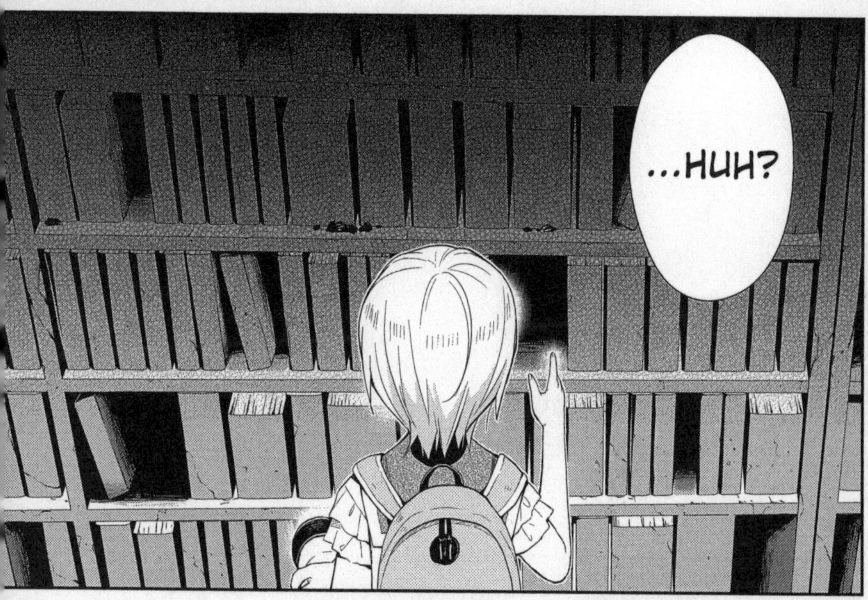
...HUH?

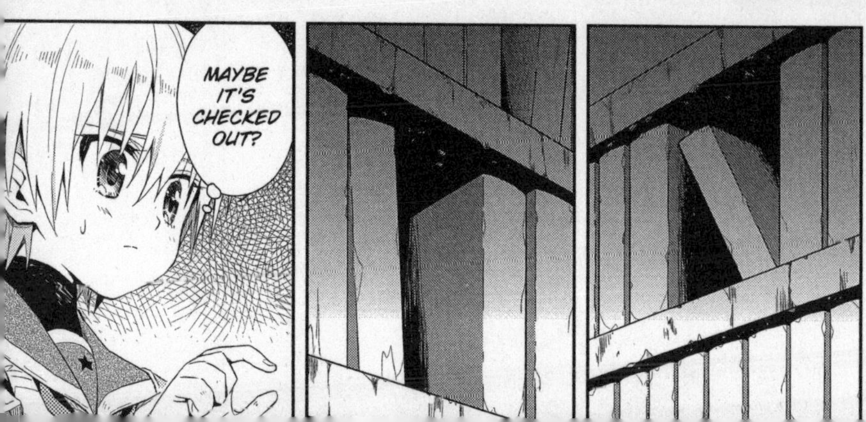
MAYBE IT'S CHECKED OUT?

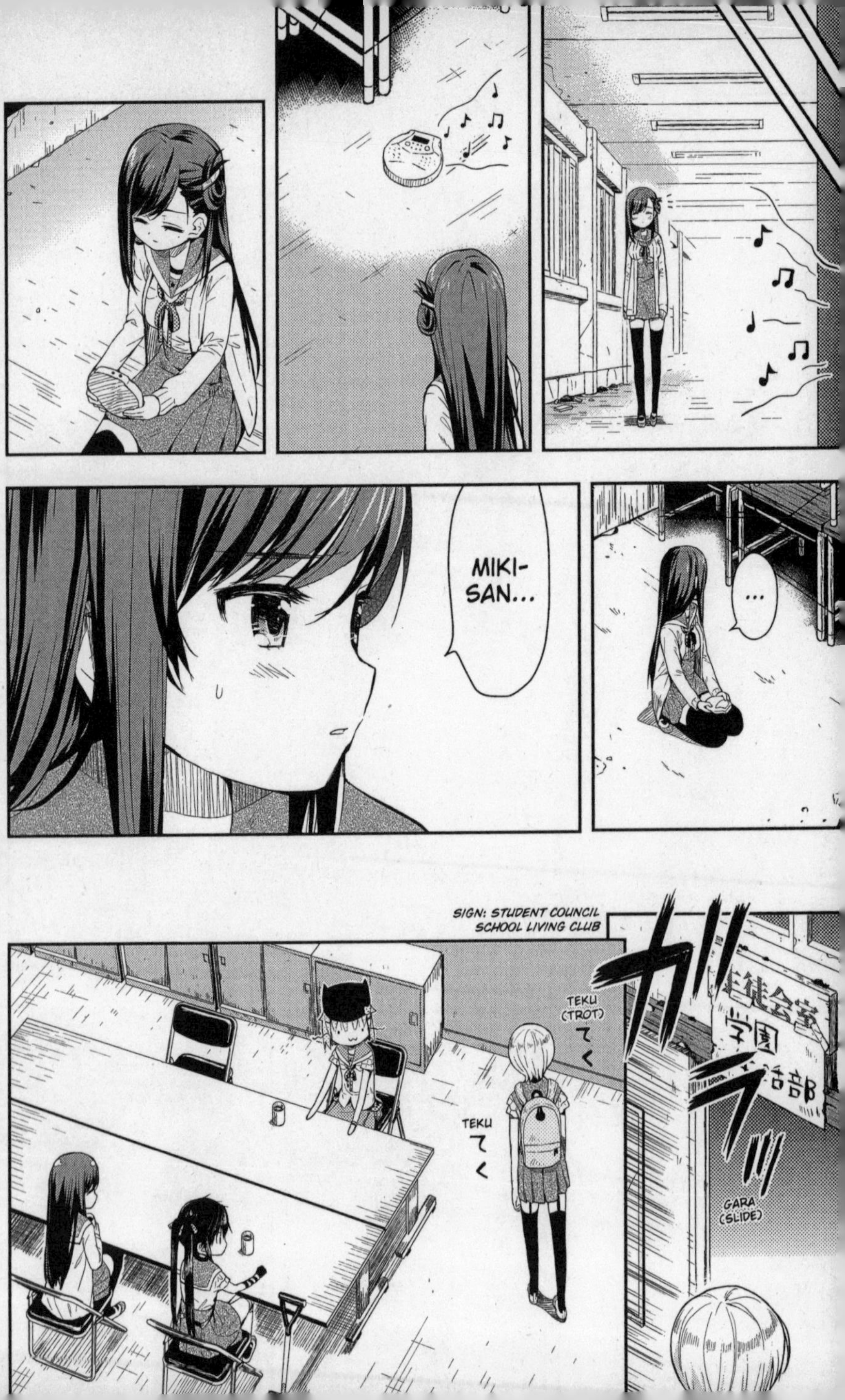
...
MIKI-SAN...
SIGN: STUDENT COUNCIL SCHOOL LIVING CLUB
GARA (SLIDE)
TEKU (TROT) てく
TEKU てく

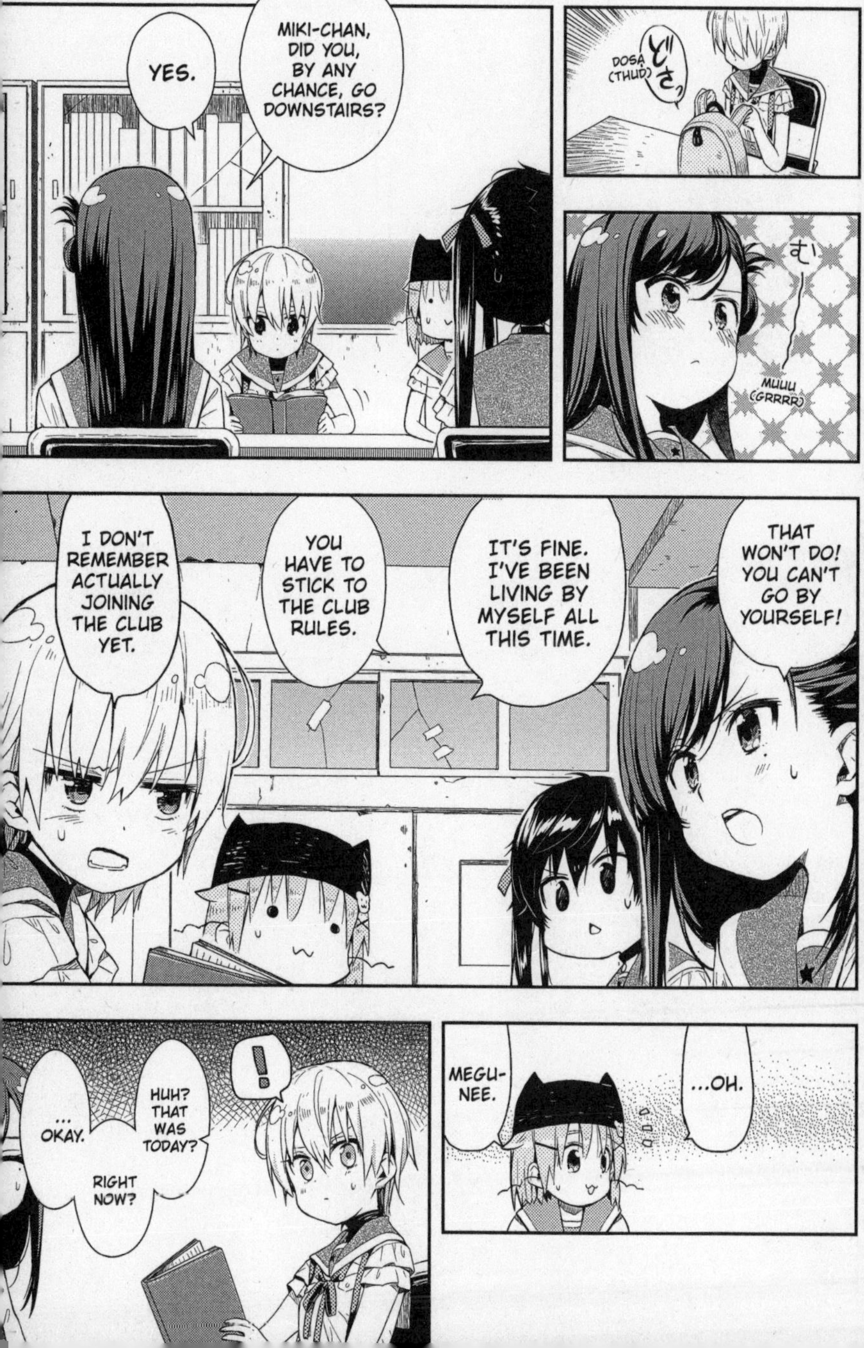
どさっ
DOSA (THUD)
む~
MUUU (GRRRR)
MIKI-CHAN, DID YOU, BY ANY CHANCE, GO DOWNSTAIRS?
YES.
THAT WON'T DO! YOU CAN'T GO BY YOURSELF!
IT'S FINE. I'VE BEEN LIVING BY MYSELF ALL THIS TIME.
YOU HAVE TO STICK TO THE CLUB RULES.
I DON'T REMEMBER ACTUALLY JOINING THE CLUB YET.
...OH.
MEGU-NEE.
!
HUH? THAT WAS TODAY?
RIGHT NOW?
... OKAY.

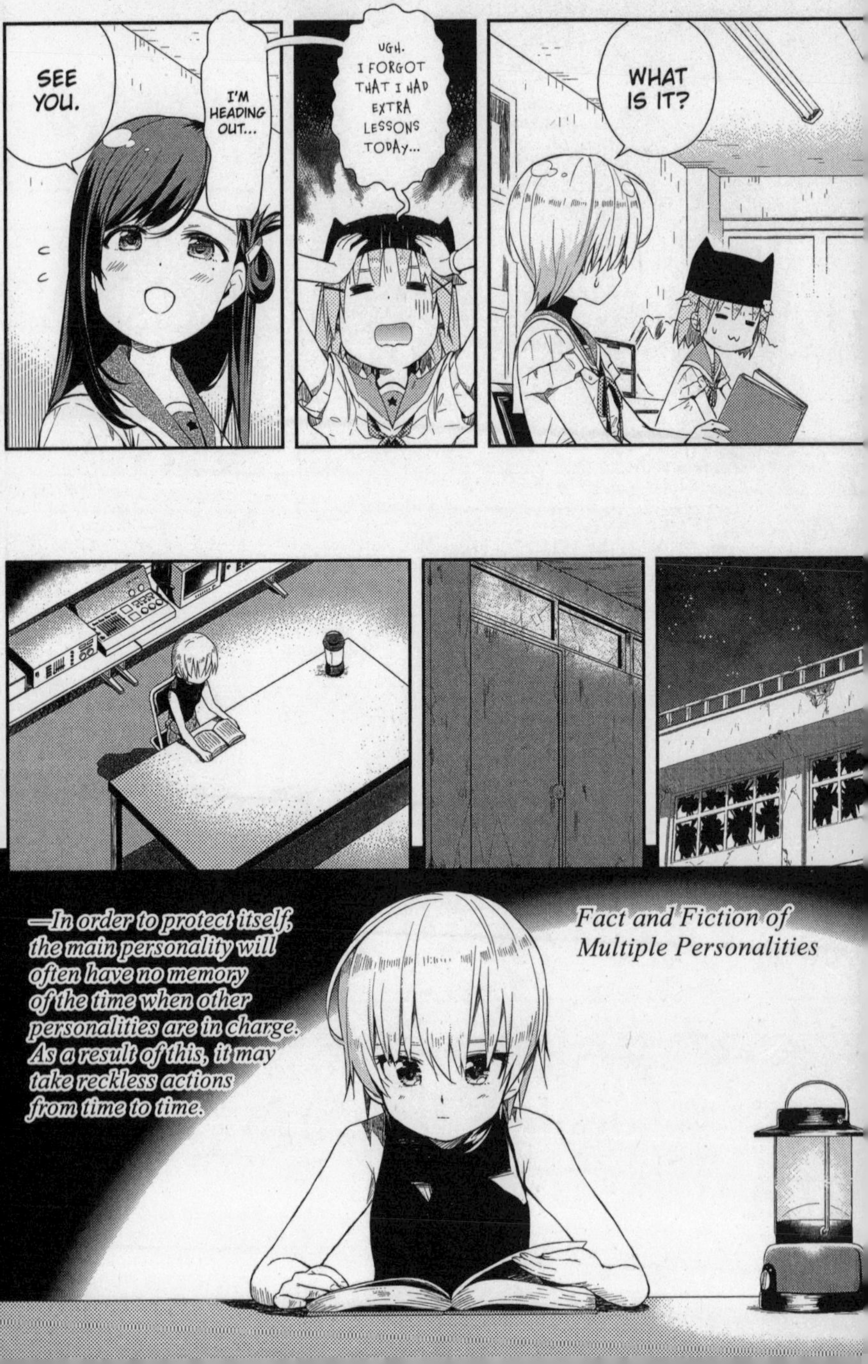
WHAT IS IT?
UGH. I FORGOT THAT I HAD EXTRA LESSONS TODAY...
I'M HEADING OUT...
SEE YOU.
Fact and Fiction of Multiple Personalities
—In order to protect itself, the main personality will often have no memory of the time when other personalities are in charge. As a result of this, it may take reckless actions from time to time.

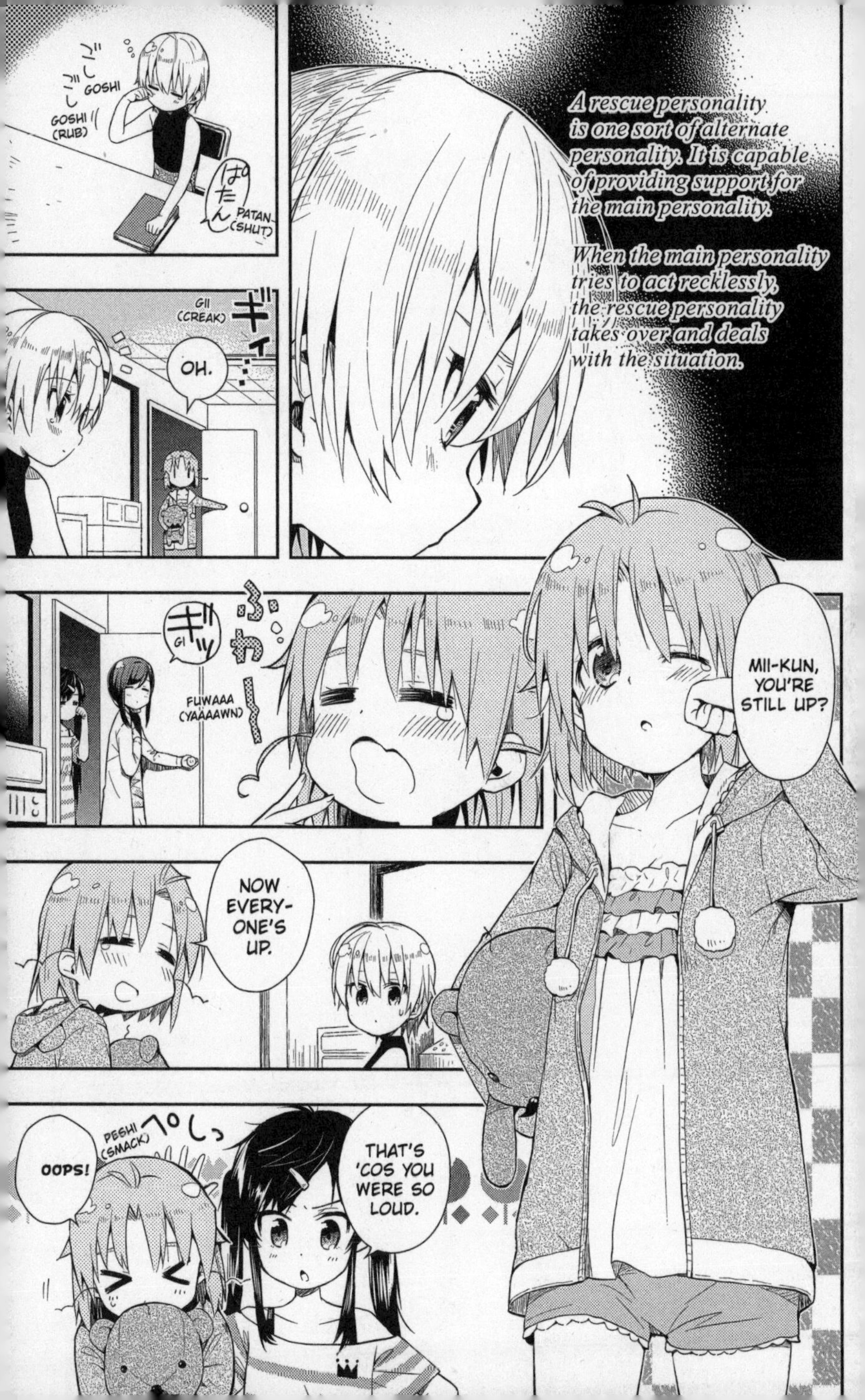

A rescue personality is one sort of alternate personality. It is capable of providing support for the main personality.
When the main personality tries to act recklessly, the rescue personality takes over and deals with the situation.
ごしごし
GOSHI GOSHI (RUB)
ぱたん
PATAN (SHUT)
ギィ…
GII (CREAK)
OH.
MII-KUN, YOU'RE STILL UP?
ギッ
GI
ふわ～
FUWAAA (YAAAAWN)
NOW EVERY-ONE'S UP.
THAT'S 'COS YOU WERE SO LOUD.
ペしっ
PESHI (SMACK)
OOPS!

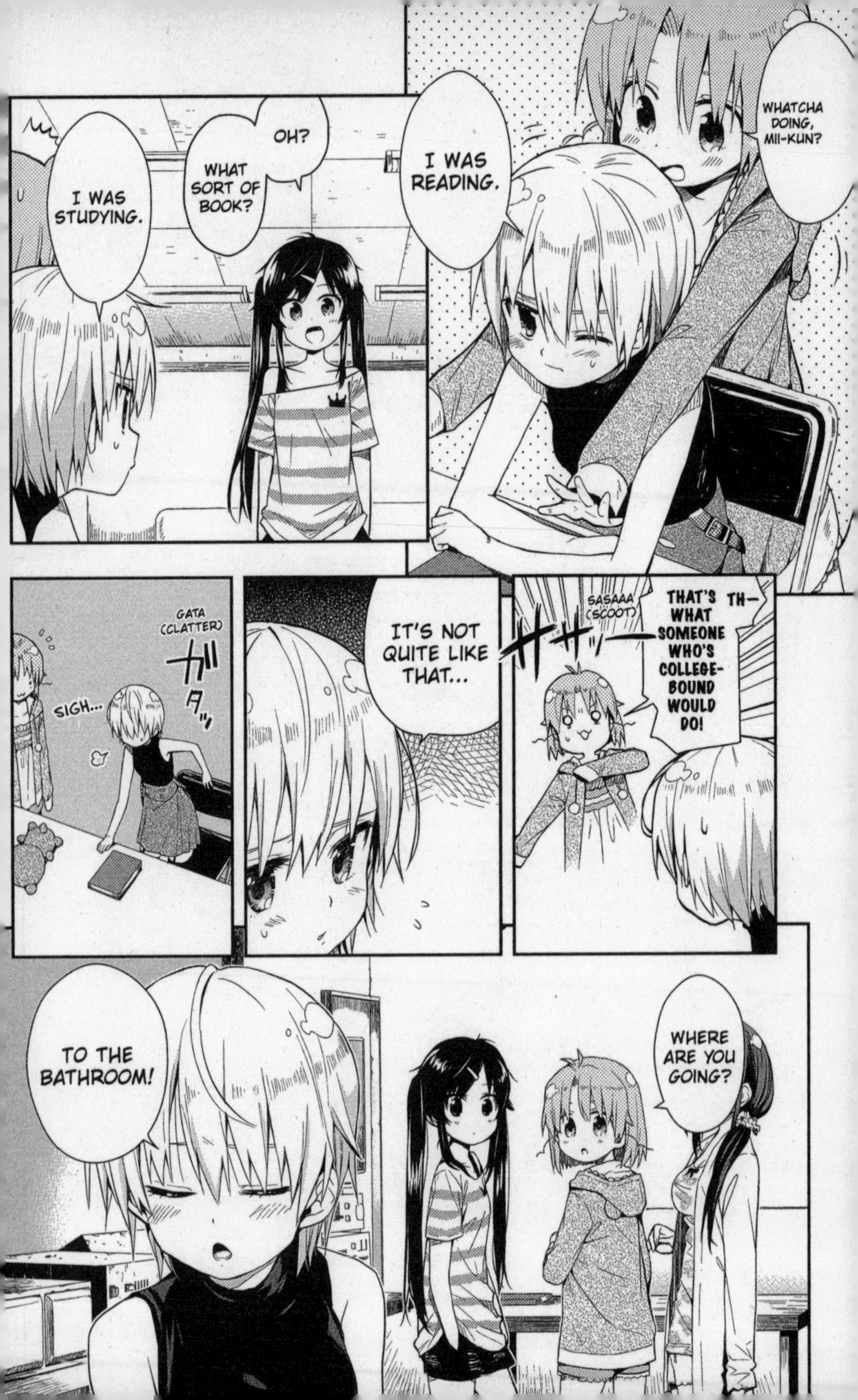
WHATCHA DOING, MII-KUN?
I WAS READING.
OH?
WHAT SORT OF BOOK?
I WAS STUDYING.
TH—
SASAAA (SCOOT)
THAT'S WHAT SOMEONE WHO'S COLLEGE-BOUND WOULD DO!
IT'S NOT QUITE LIKE THAT...
GATA (CLATTER)
SIGH...
WHERE ARE YOU GOING?
TO THE BATHROOM!

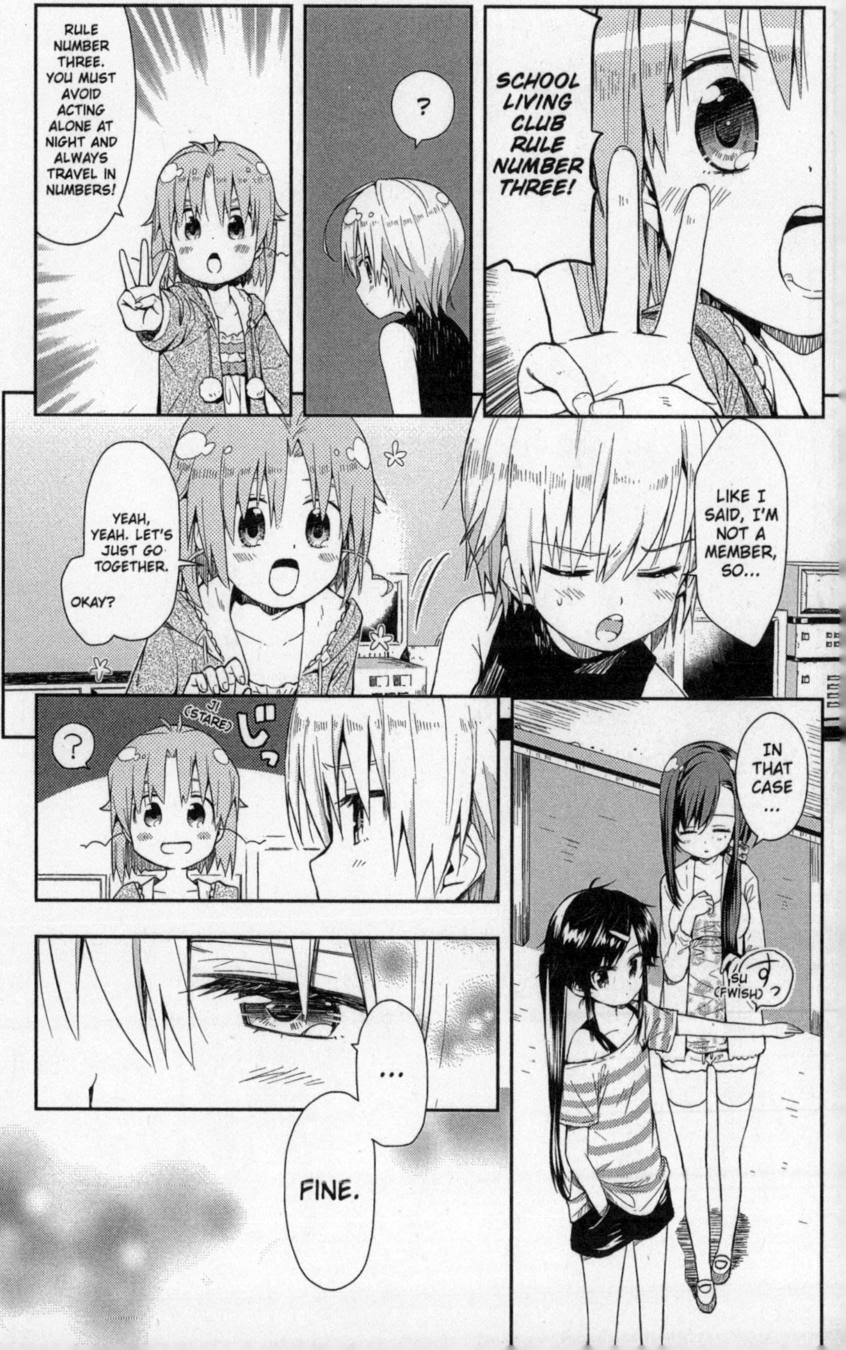
SCHOOL LIVING CLUB RULE NUMBER THREE!
?
RULE NUMBER THREE. YOU MUST AVOID ACTING ALONE AT NIGHT AND ALWAYS TRAVEL IN NUMBERS!
LIKE I SAID, I'M NOT A MEMBER, SO...
YEAH, YEAH. LET'S JUST GO TOGETHER.
OKAY?
IN THAT CASE ...
SU (FWISH)
JI (STARE)
?
...
FINE.

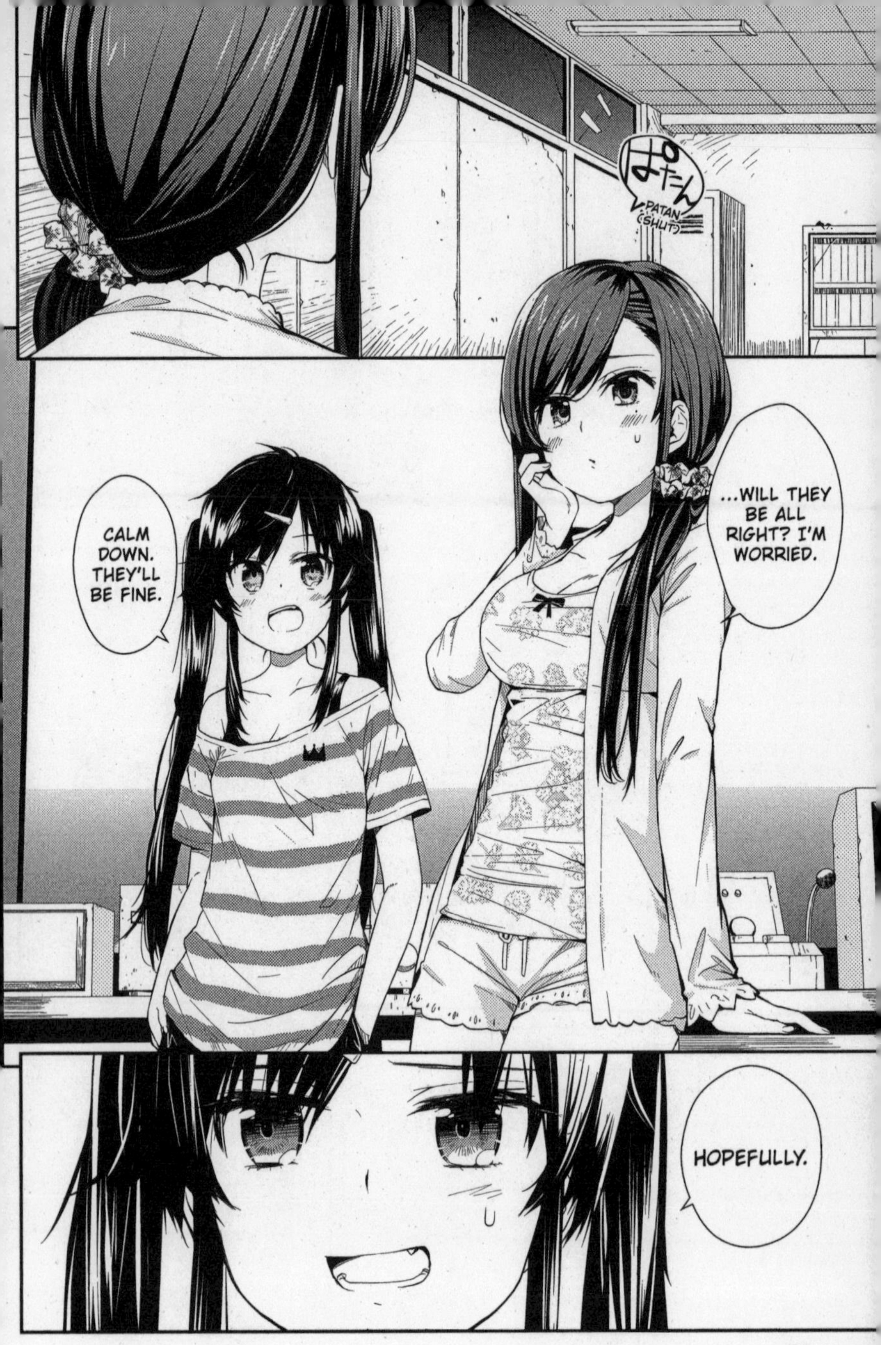
ぱたん
PATAN (SHUT)
...WILL THEY BE ALL RIGHT? I'M WORRIED.
CALM DOWN. THEY'LL BE FINE.
HOPEFULLY.

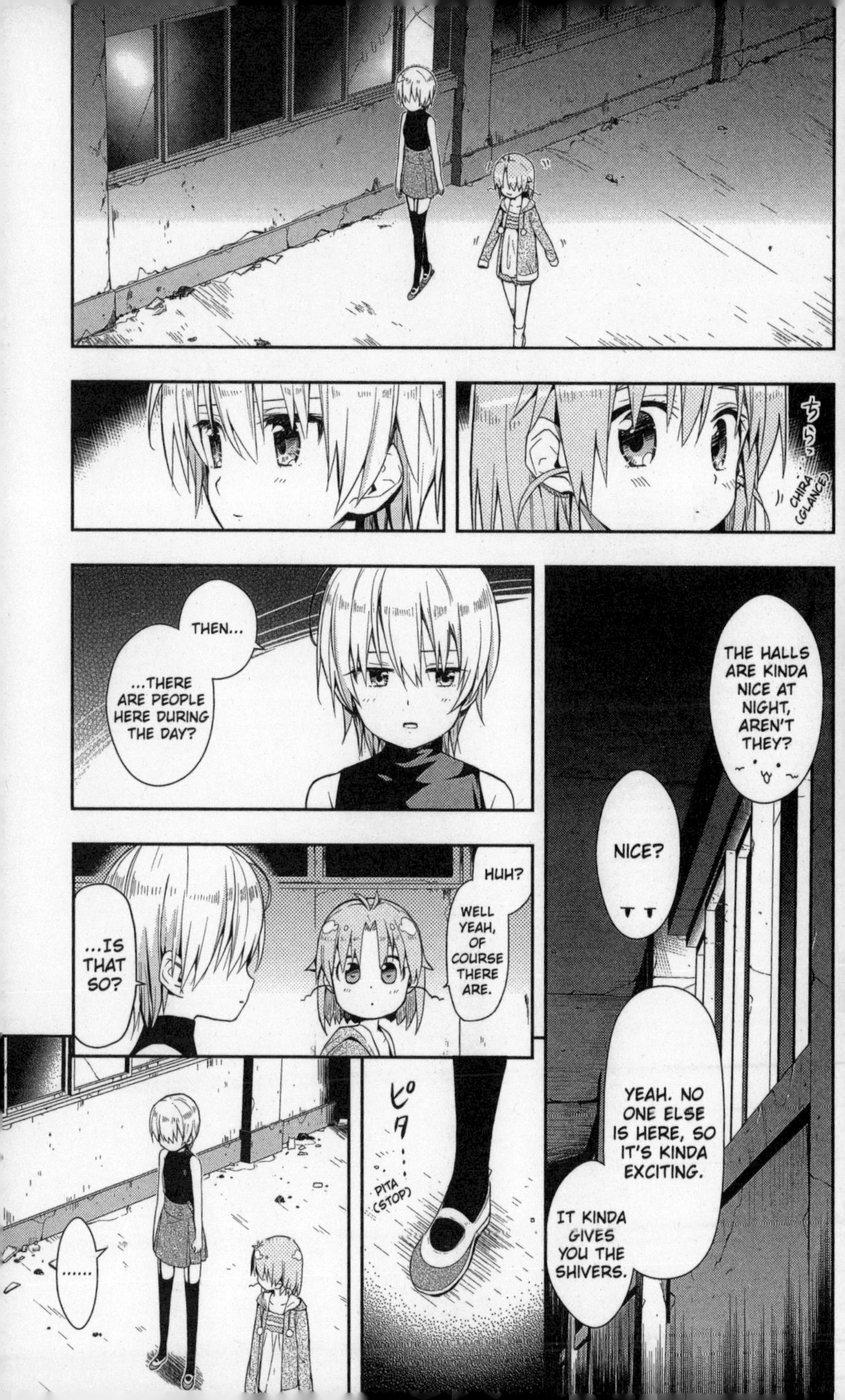
ちらっ
CHIRA (GLANCE)
THE HALLS ARE KINDA NICE AT NIGHT, AREN'T THEY?
NICE?
YEAH. NO ONE ELSE IS HERE, SO IT'S KINDA EXCITING.
IT KINDA GIVES YOU THE SHIVERS.
THEN...
...THERE ARE PEOPLE HERE DURING THE DAY?
HUH?
WELL YEAH, OF COURSE THERE ARE.
...IS THAT SO?
ピタ...
PITA (STOP)
......

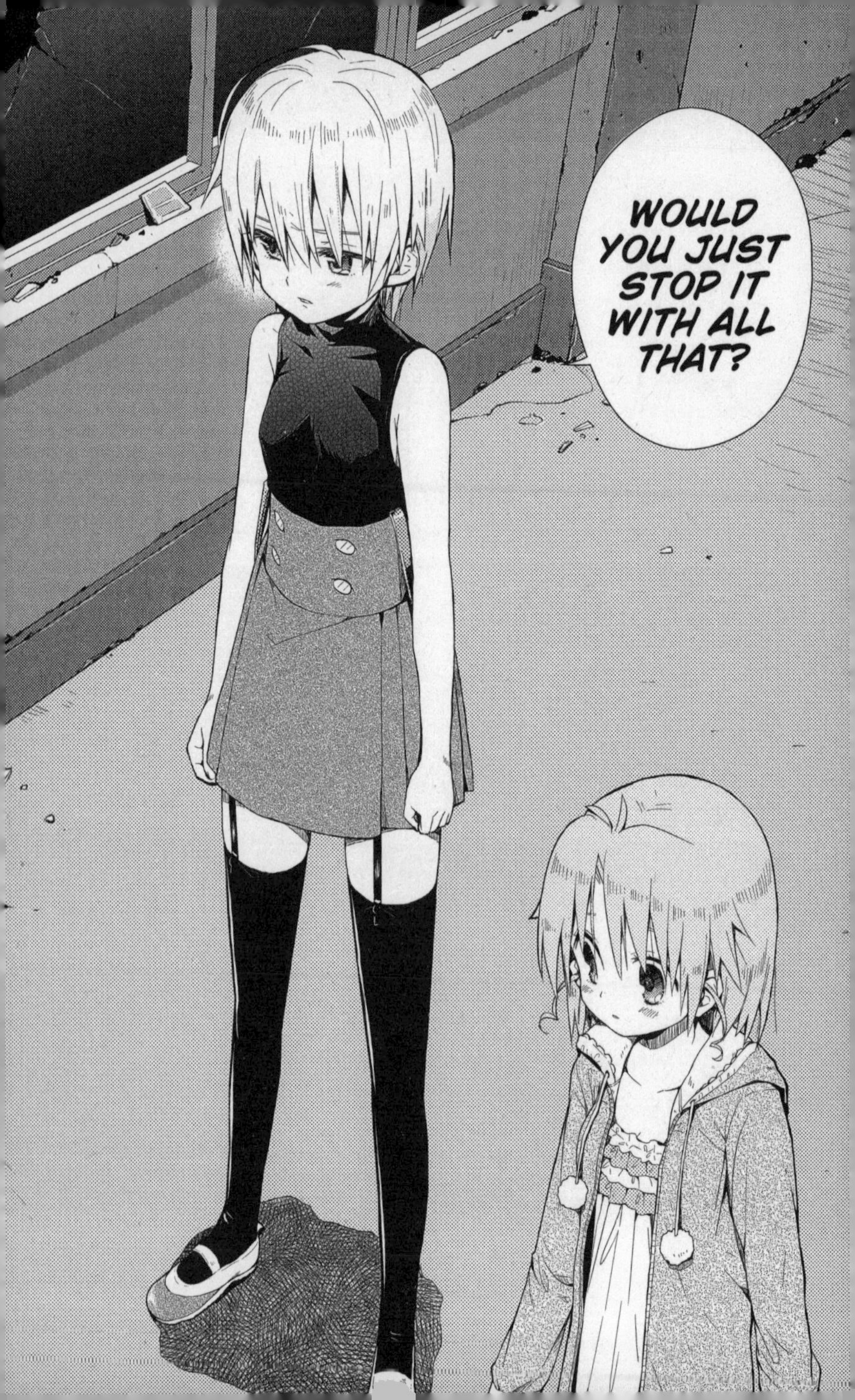
WOULD YOU JUST STOP IT WITH ALL THAT?

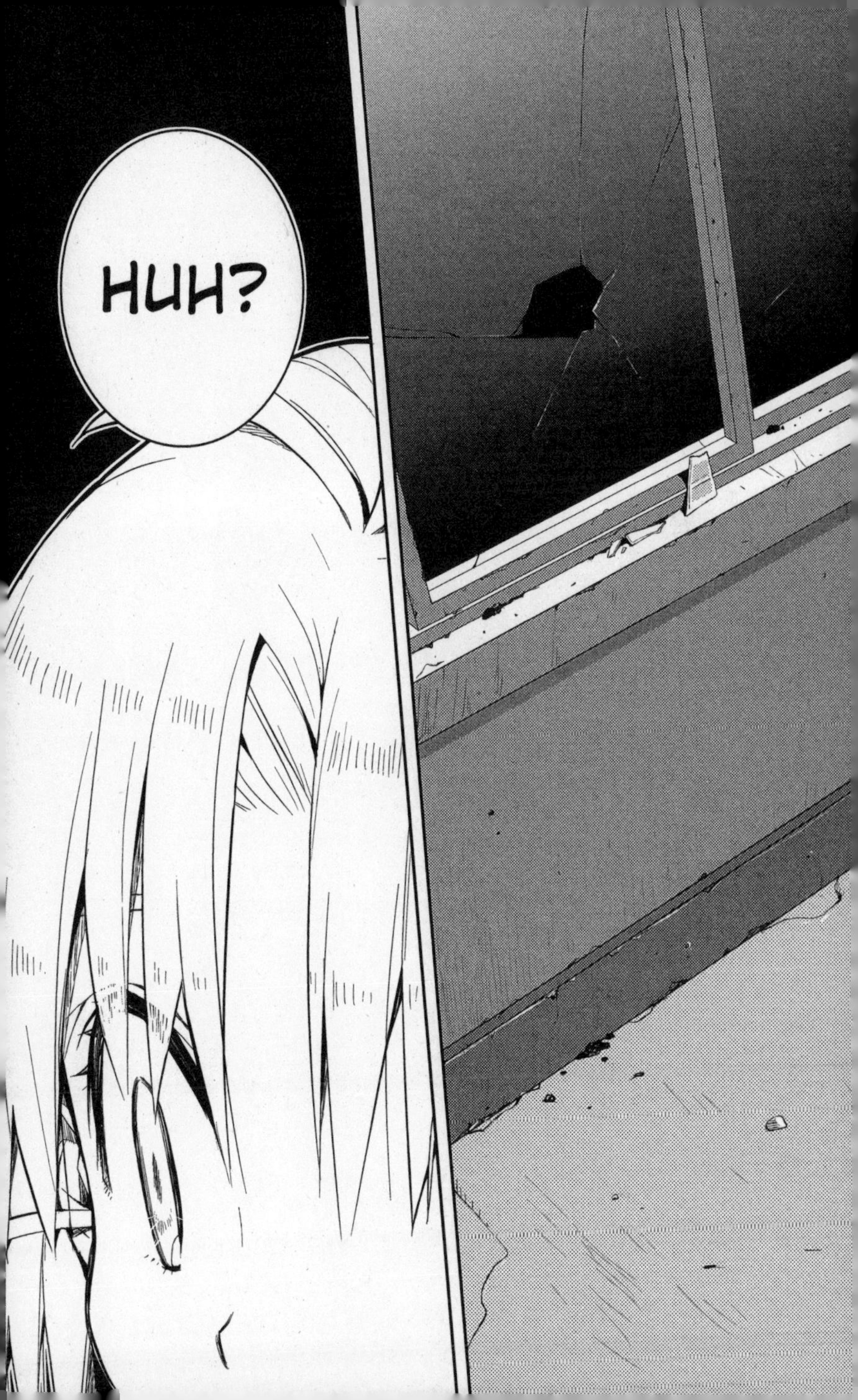
HUH?

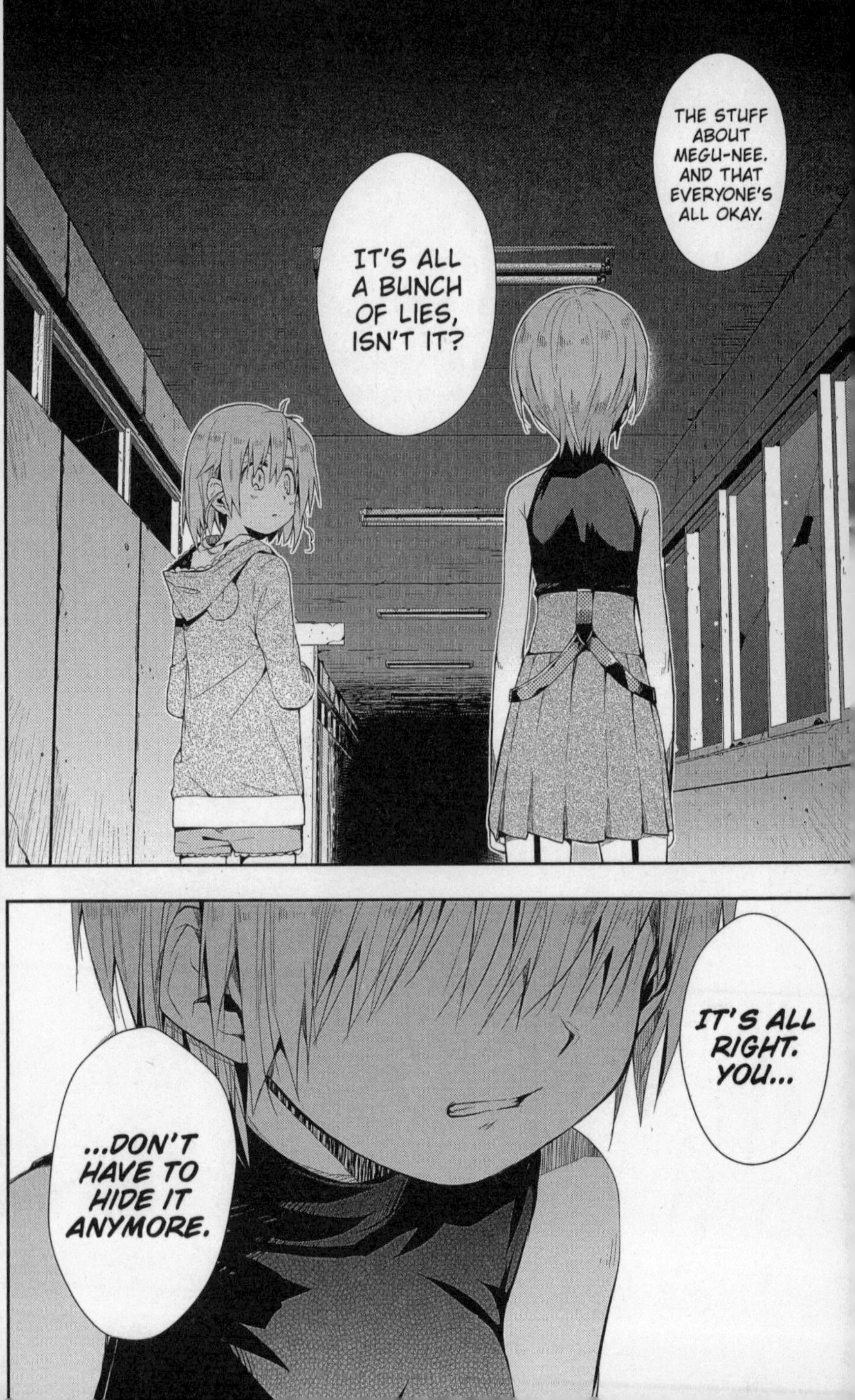
THE STUFF ABOUT MEGU-NEE. AND THAT EVERYONE'S ALL OKAY.
IT'S ALL A BUNCH OF LIES, ISN'T IT?
IT'S ALL RIGHT. YOU...
...DON'T HAVE TO HIDE IT ANYMORE.

SCHOOL-LIVE!

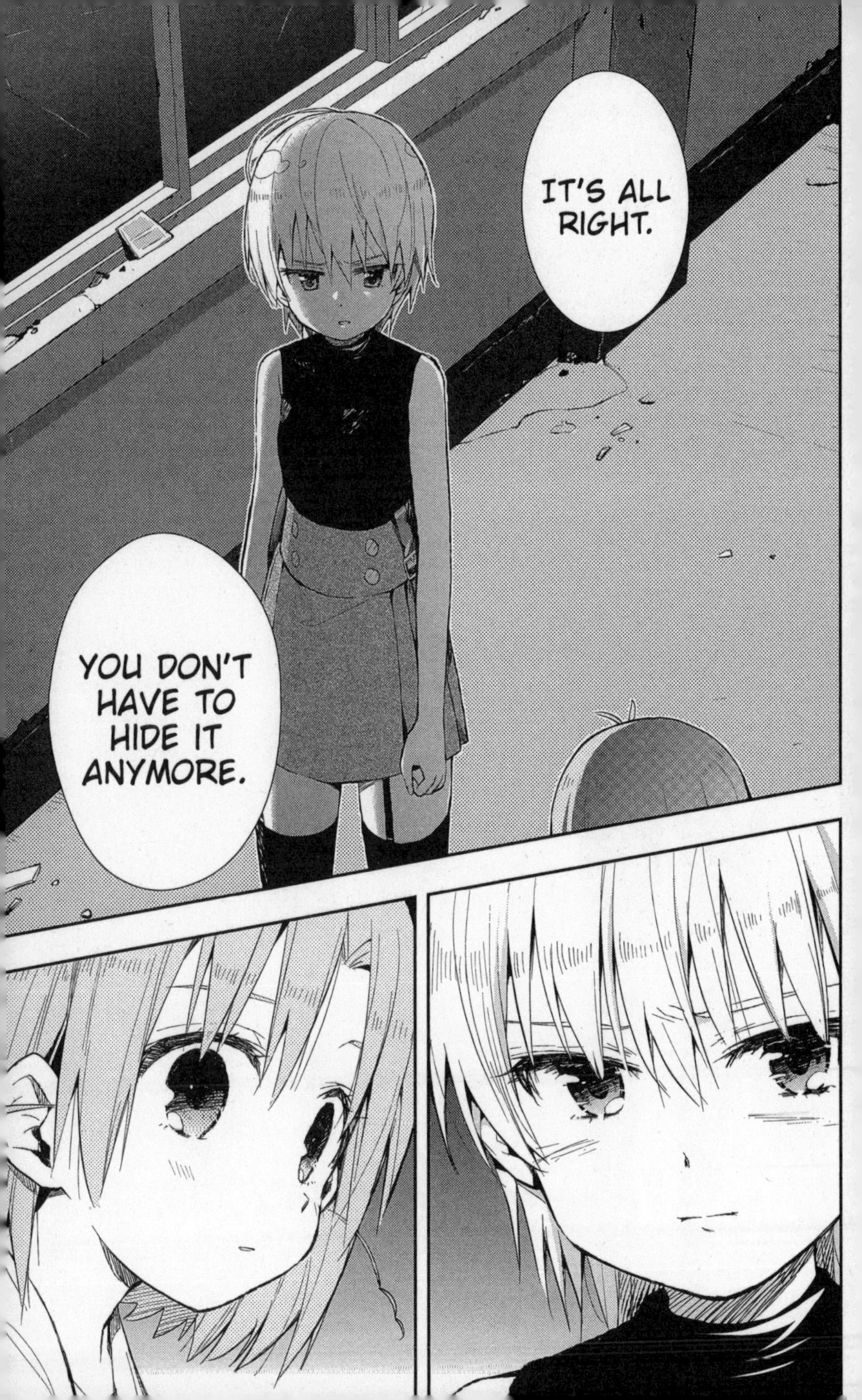
IT'S ALL RIGHT.
YOU DON'T HAVE TO HIDE IT ANYMORE.

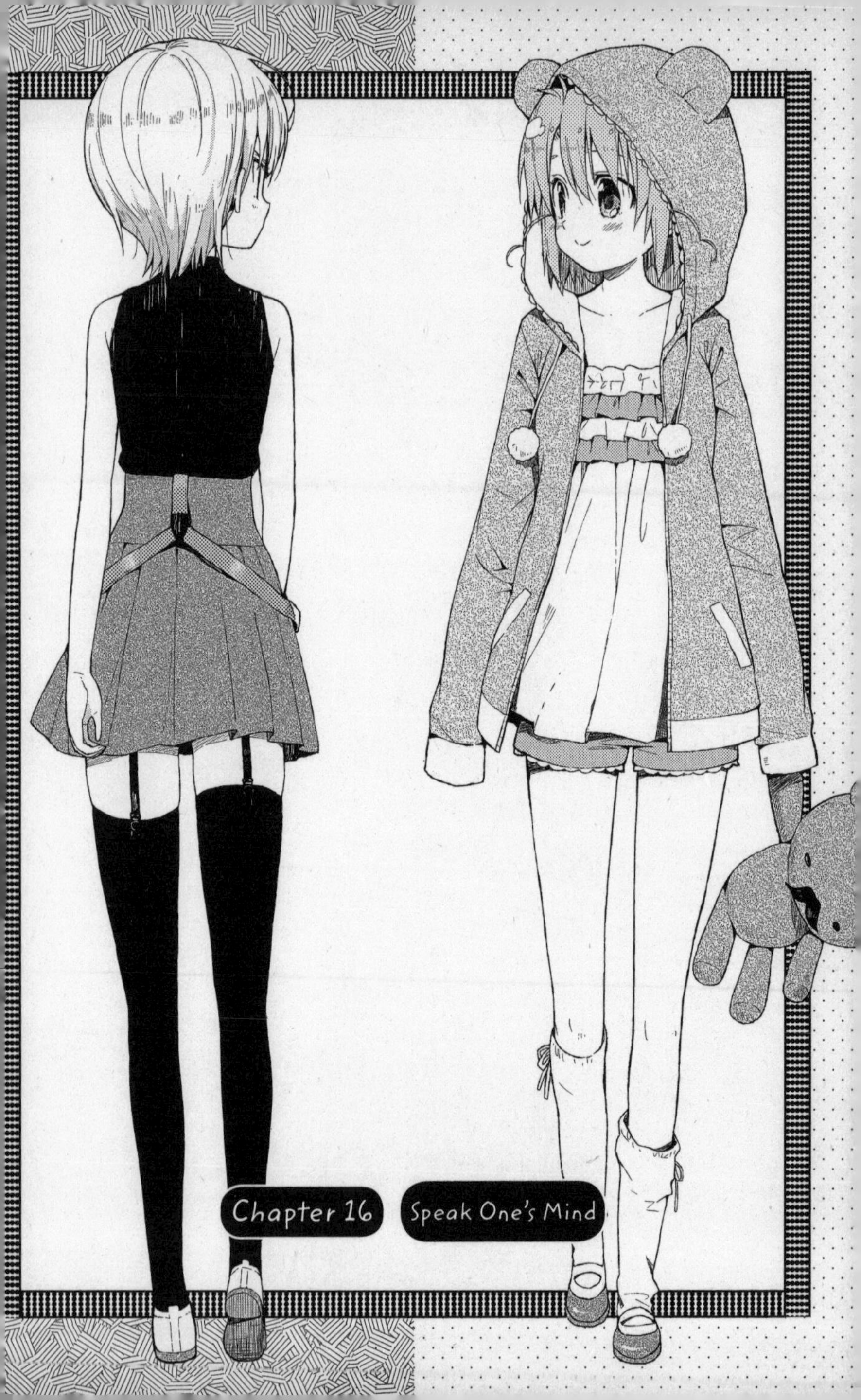
Chapter 16
Speak One's Mind

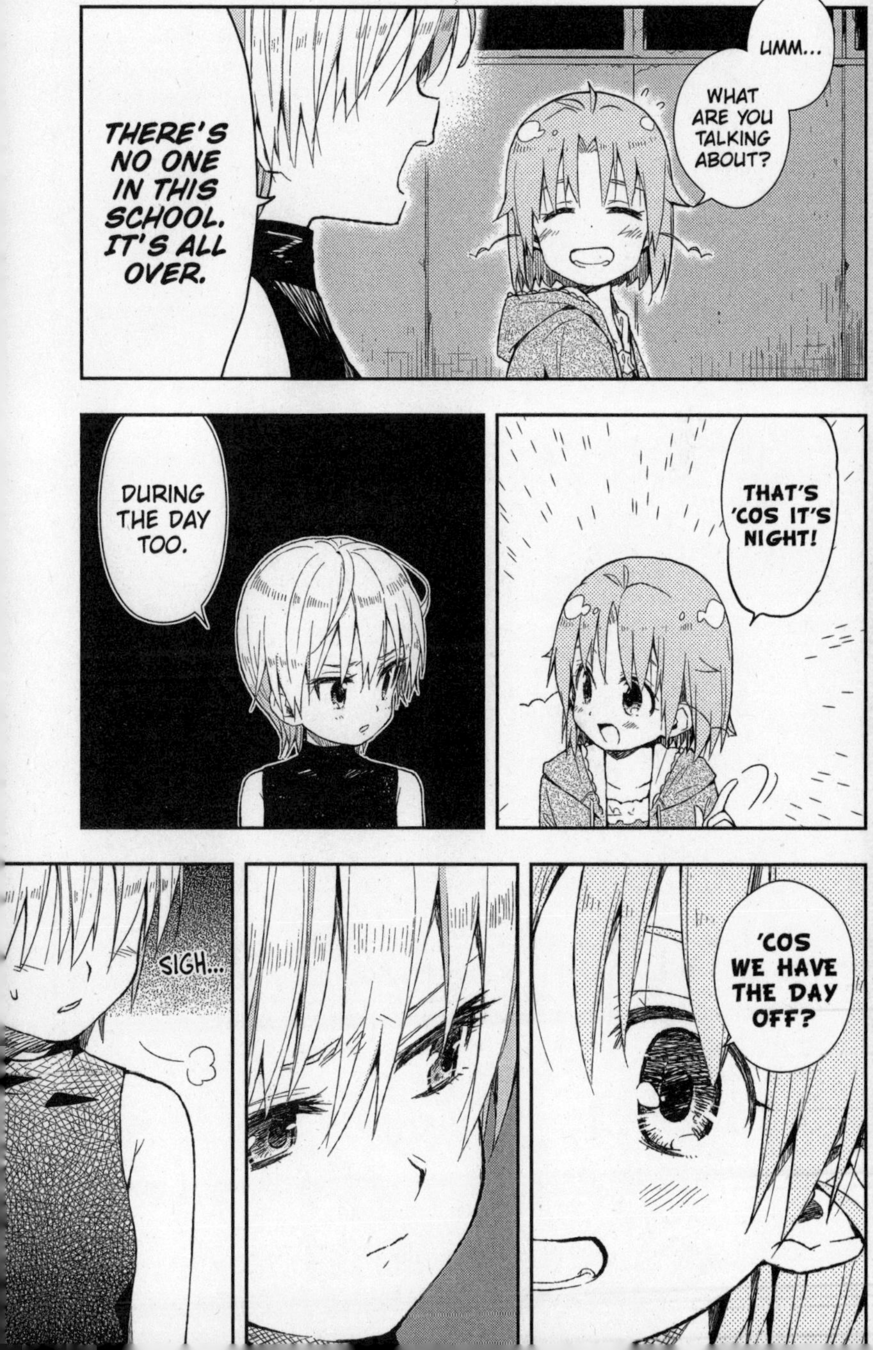
UMM...
WHAT ARE YOU TALKING ABOUT?
THERE'S NO ONE IN THIS SCHOOL. IT'S ALL OVER.
THAT'S 'COS IT'S NIGHT!
DURING THE DAY TOO.
'COS WE HAVE THE DAY OFF?
SIGH...

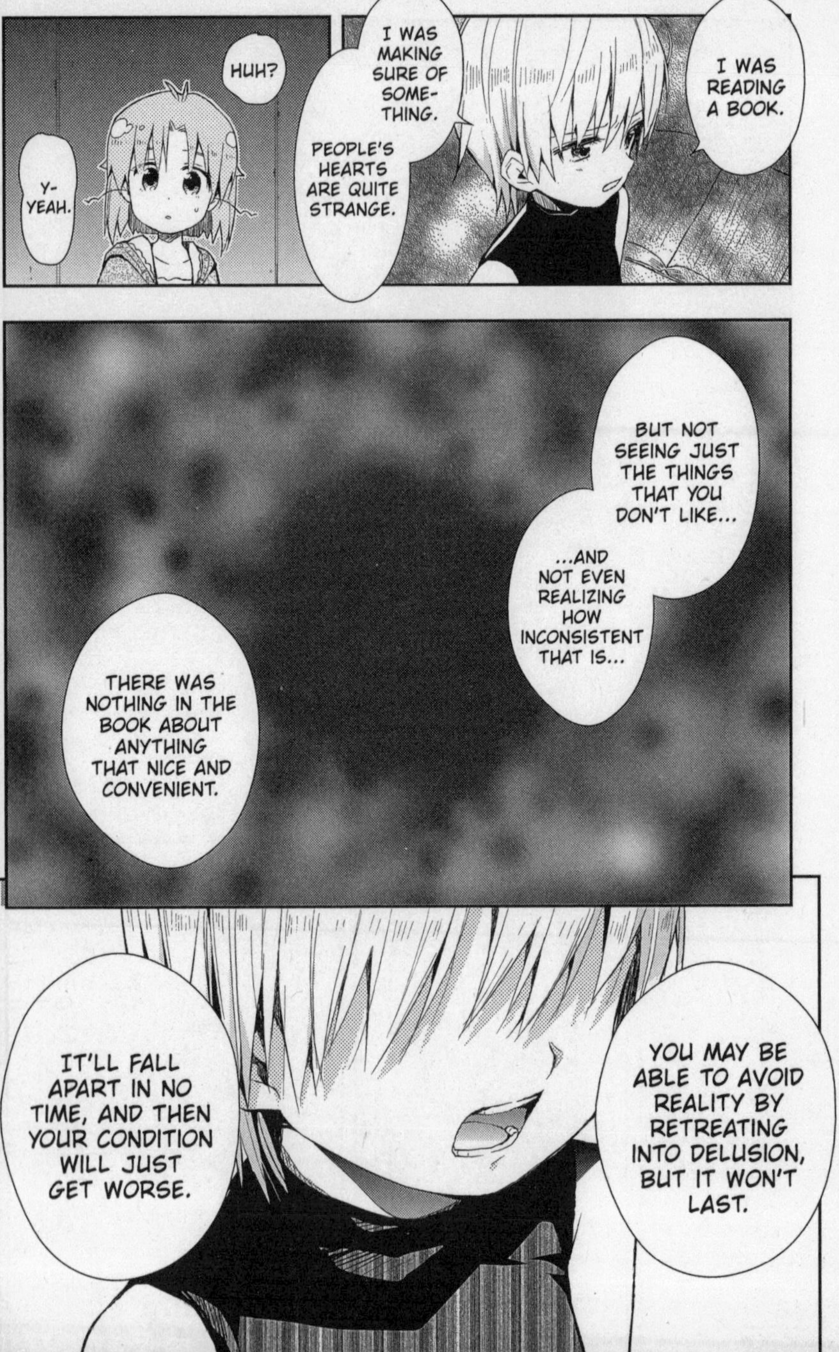
I WAS READING A BOOK.
I WAS MAKING SURE OF SOME-THING.
PEOPLE'S HEARTS ARE QUITE STRANGE.
HUH?
Y-YEAH.
BUT NOT SEEING JUST THE THINGS THAT YOU DON'T LIKE...
...AND NOT EVEN REALIZING HOW INCONSISTENT THAT IS...
THERE WAS NOTHING IN THE BOOK ABOUT ANYTHING THAT NICE AND CONVENIENT.
YOU MAY BE ABLE TO AVOID REALITY BY RETREATING INTO DELUSION, BUT IT WON'T LAST.
IT'LL FALL APART IN NO TIME, AND THEN YOUR CONDITION WILL JUST GET WORSE.

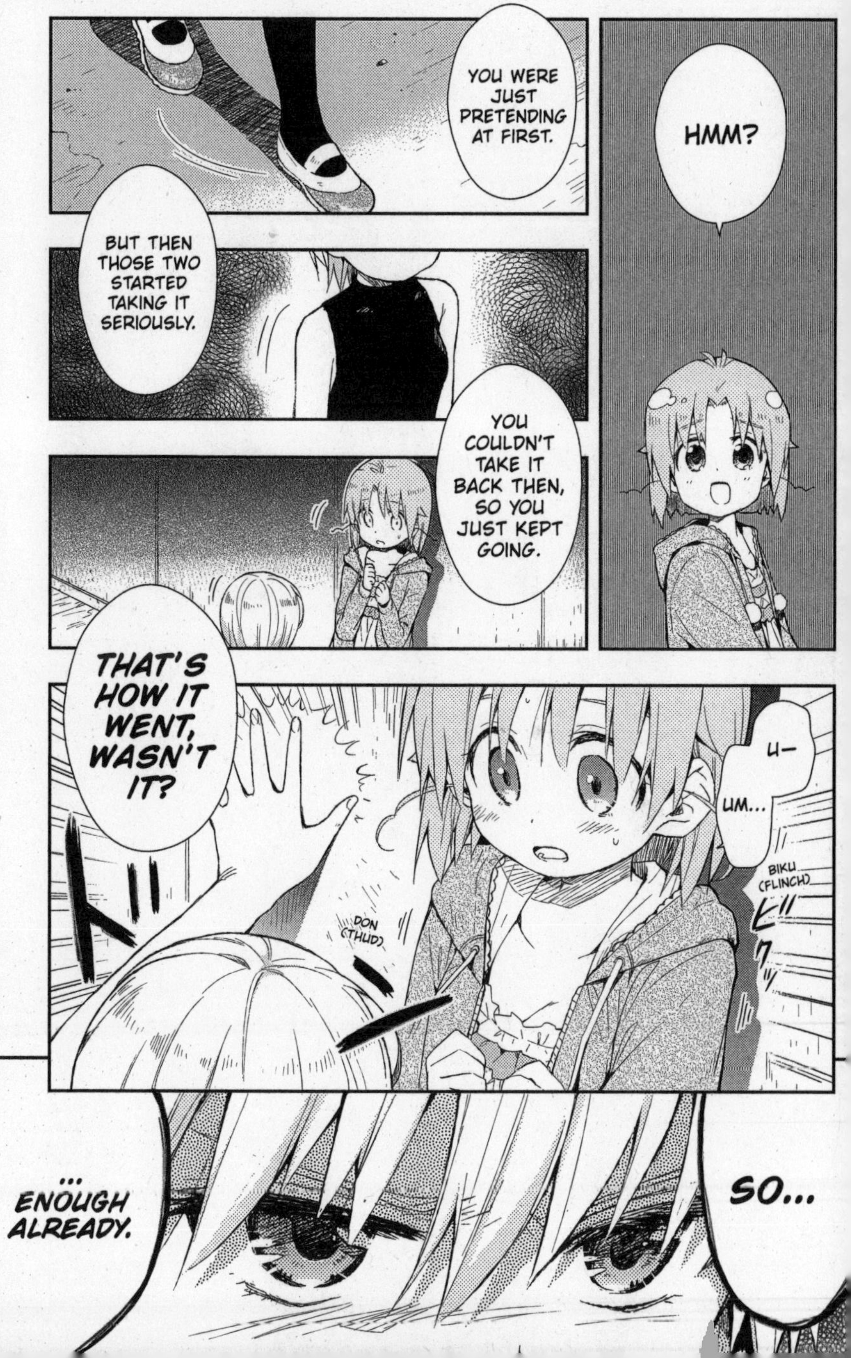
HMM?
YOU WERE JUST PRETENDING AT FIRST.
BUT THEN THOSE TWO STARTED TAKING IT SERIOUSLY.
YOU COULDN'T TAKE IT BACK THEN, SO YOU JUST KEPT GOING.
U— UM...
BIKU (FLINCH)
THAT'S HOW IT WENT, WASN'T IT?
DON (THUD)
SO...
...ENOUGH ALREADY.

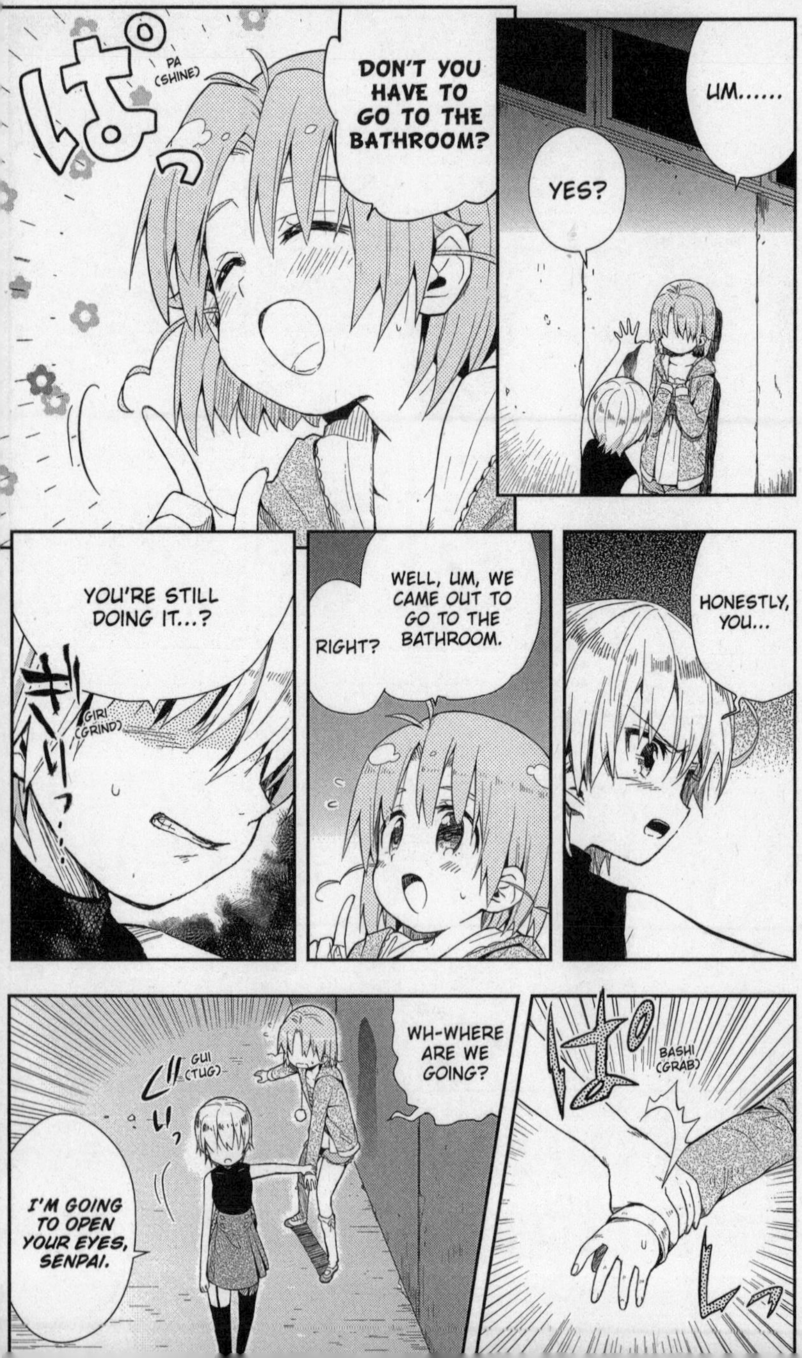
UM......
YES?
DON'T YOU HAVE TO GO TO THE BATHROOM?
PA (SHINE)
HONESTLY, YOU...
WELL, UM, WE CAME OUT TO GO TO THE BATHROOM.
RIGHT?
YOU'RE STILL DOING IT...?
GIRI (GRIND)
BASHI (GRAB)
WH-WHERE ARE WE GOING?
GUI (TUG)
I'M GOING TO OPEN YOUR EYES, SENPAI.

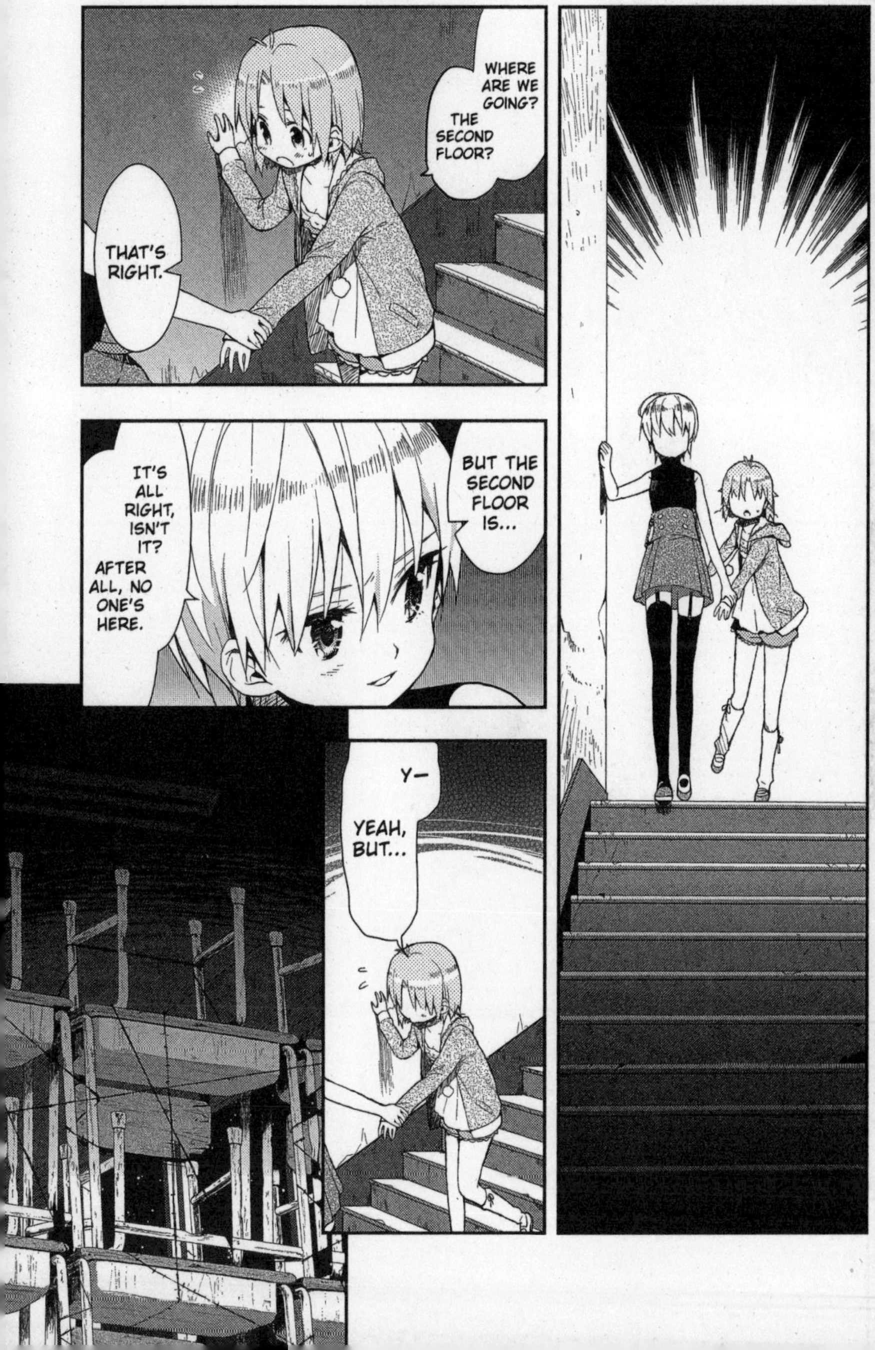
WHERE ARE WE GOING? THE SECOND FLOOR?
THAT'S RIGHT.
BUT THE SECOND FLOOR IS...
IT'S ALL RIGHT, ISN'T IT? AFTER ALL, NO ONE'S HERE.
Y— YEAH, BUT...

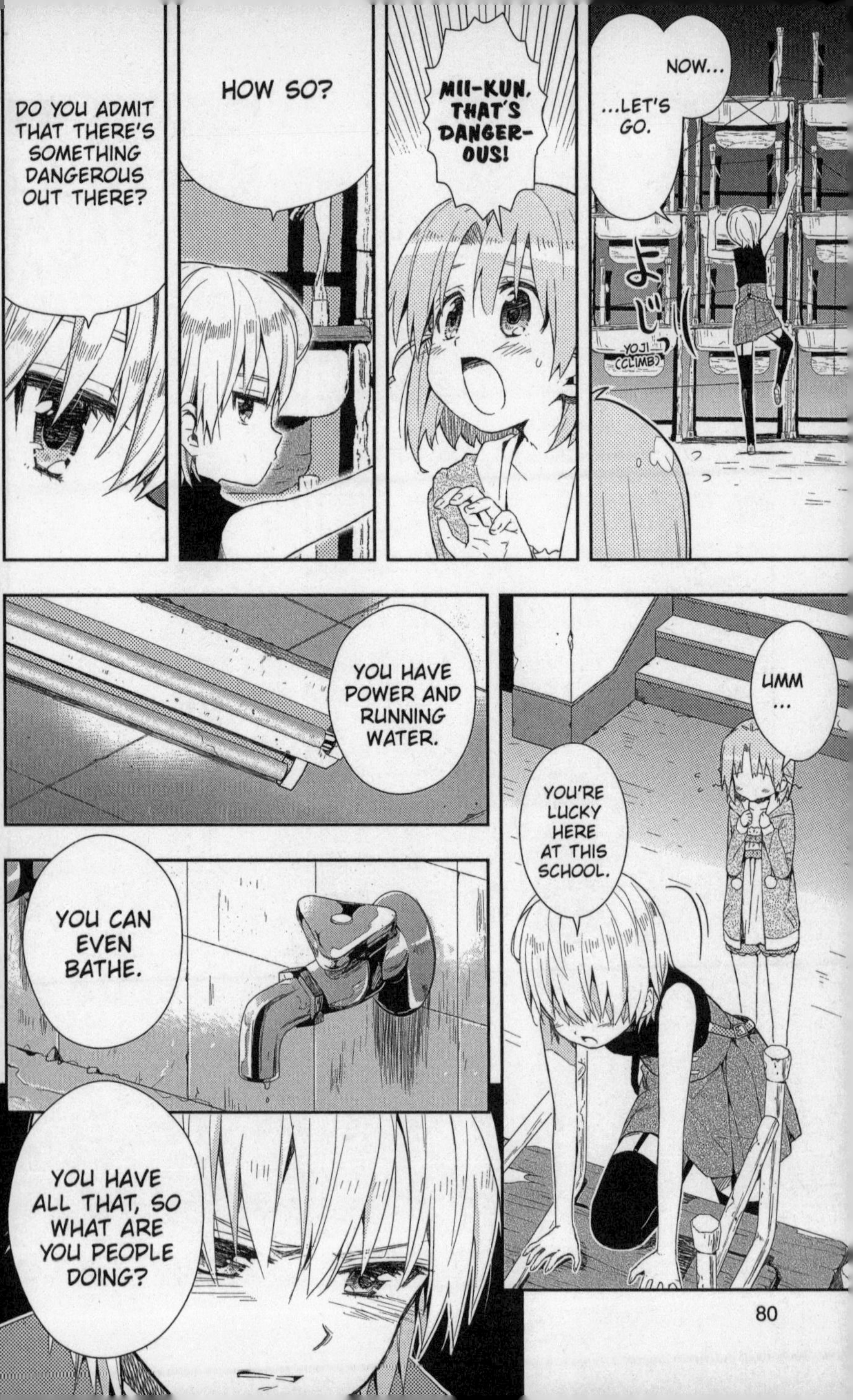
NOW...
...LET'S GO.
よじ
YOJI (CLIMB)
MII-KUN, THAT'S DANGER-OUS!
HOW SO?
DO YOU ADMIT THAT THERE'S SOMETHING DANGEROUS OUT THERE?
UMM ...
YOU'RE LUCKY HERE AT THIS SCHOOL.
YOU HAVE POWER AND RUNNING WATER.
YOU CAN EVEN BATHE.
YOU HAVE ALL THAT, SO WHAT ARE YOU PEOPLE DOING?

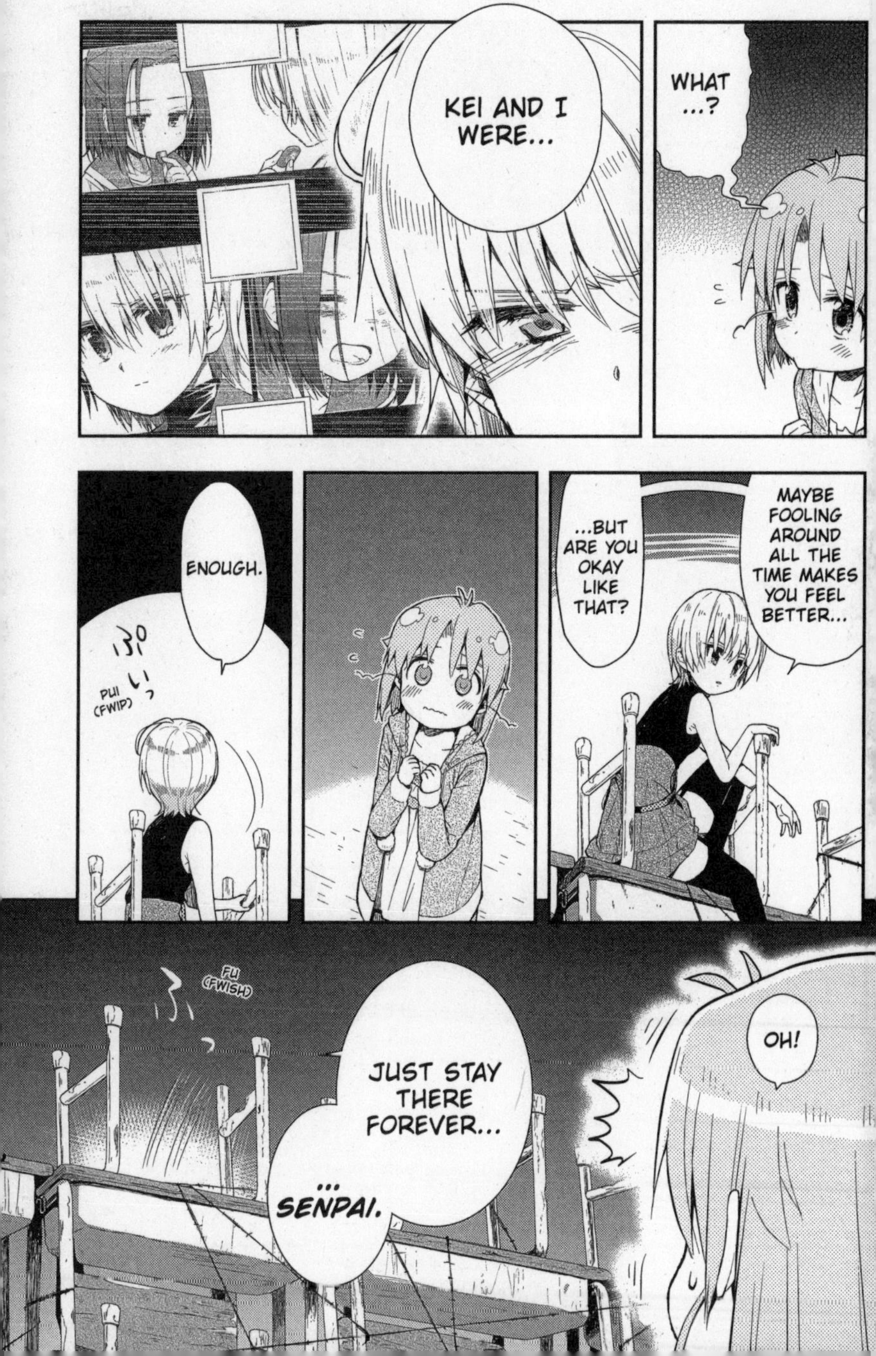
WHAT ...?
KEI AND I WERE...
MAYBE FOOLING AROUND ALL THE TIME MAKES YOU FEEL BETTER...
...BUT ARE YOU OKAY LIKE THAT?
ENOUGH.
ぷいっ
PUI (FWIP)
OH!
ふっ
FU (FWISH)
JUST STAY THERE FOREVER...
... SENPAI.

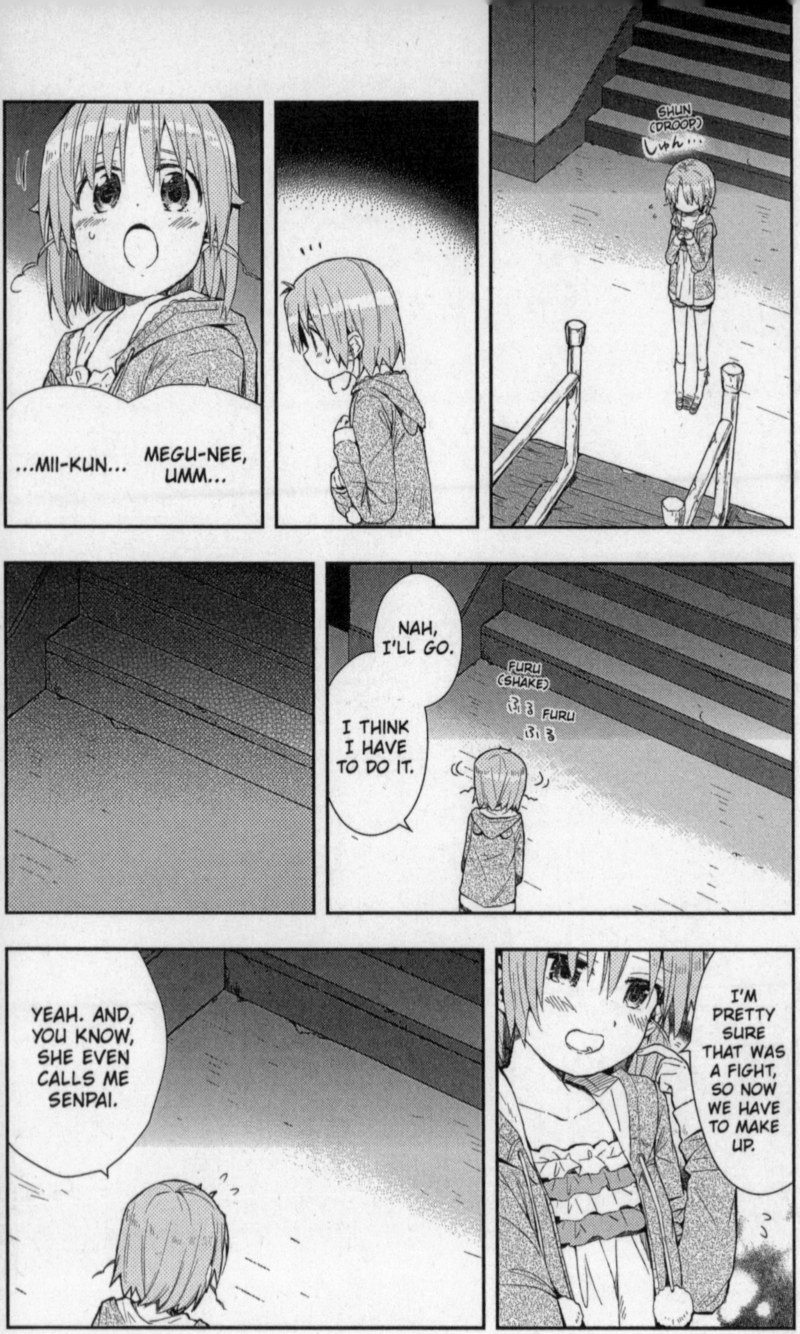
SHUN (DROOP)
しゅん…
MEGU-NEE, UMM...
...MII-KUN...
NAH, I'LL GO.
I THINK I HAVE TO DO IT.
FURU (SHAKE)
ふる FURU ふる
I'M PRETTY SURE THAT WAS A FIGHT, SO NOW WE HAVE TO MAKE UP.
YEAH. AND, YOU KNOW, SHE EVEN CALLS ME SENPAI.

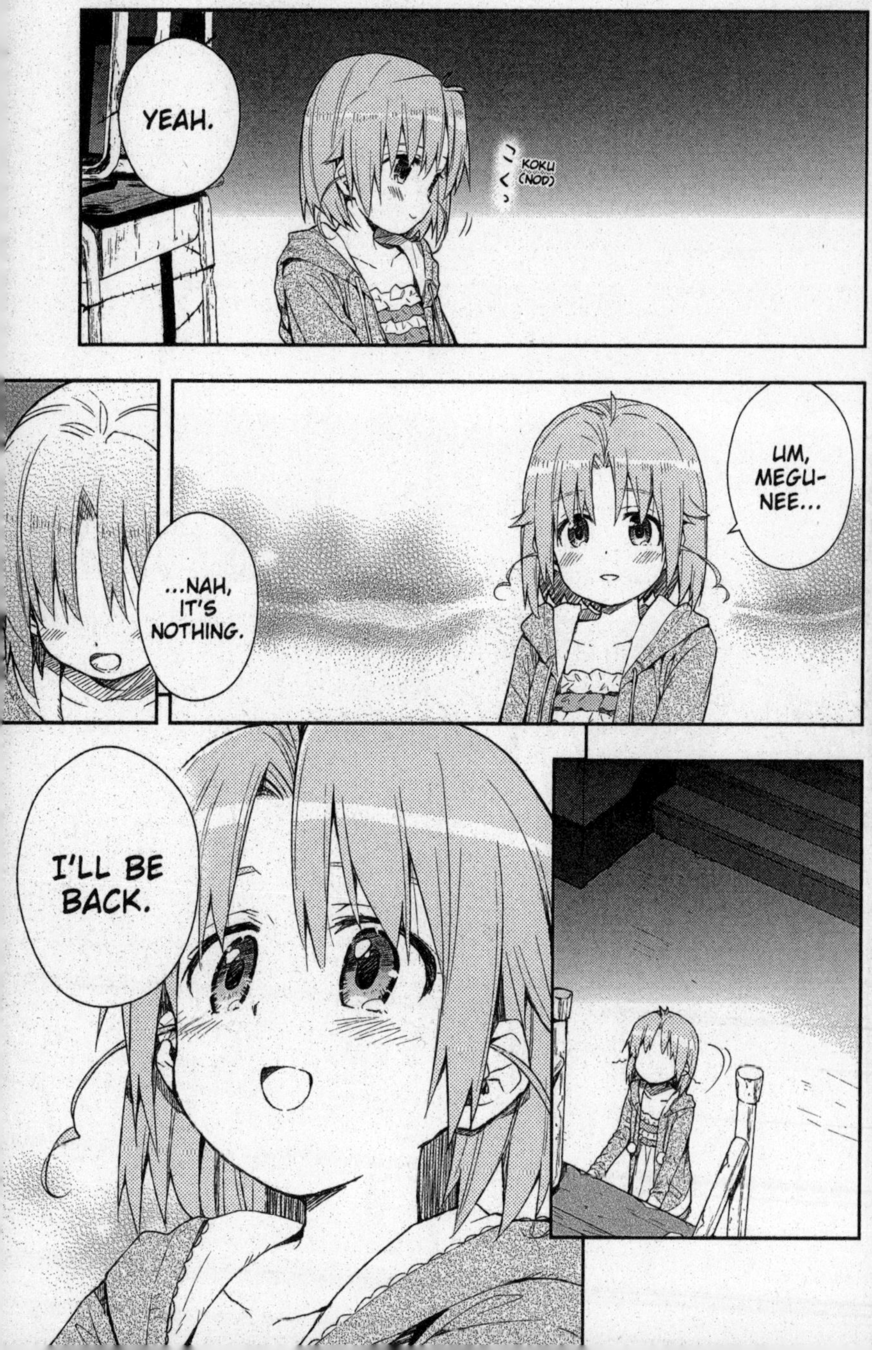
YEAH.
こくっ
KOKU (NOD)
UM, MEGU-NEE...
...NAH, IT'S NOTHING.
I'LL BE BACK.

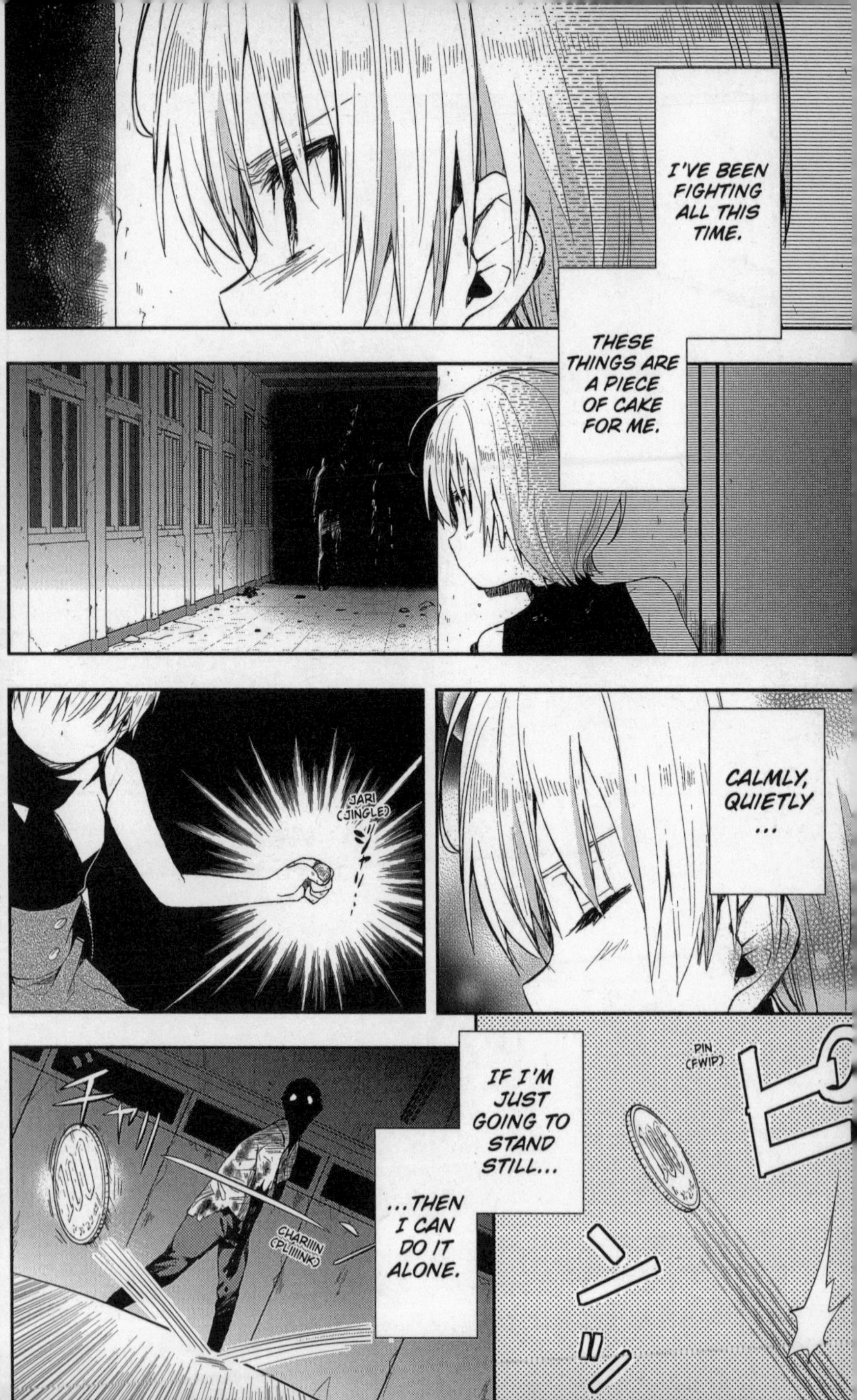
I'VE BEEN FIGHTING ALL THIS TIME.
THESE THINGS ARE A PIECE OF CAKE FOR ME.
CALMLY, QUIETLY ...
JARI (JINGLE)
PIN (FWIP)
IF I'M JUST GOING TO STAND STILL...
...THEN I CAN DO IT ALONE.
CHARIIN (PLIIINK)

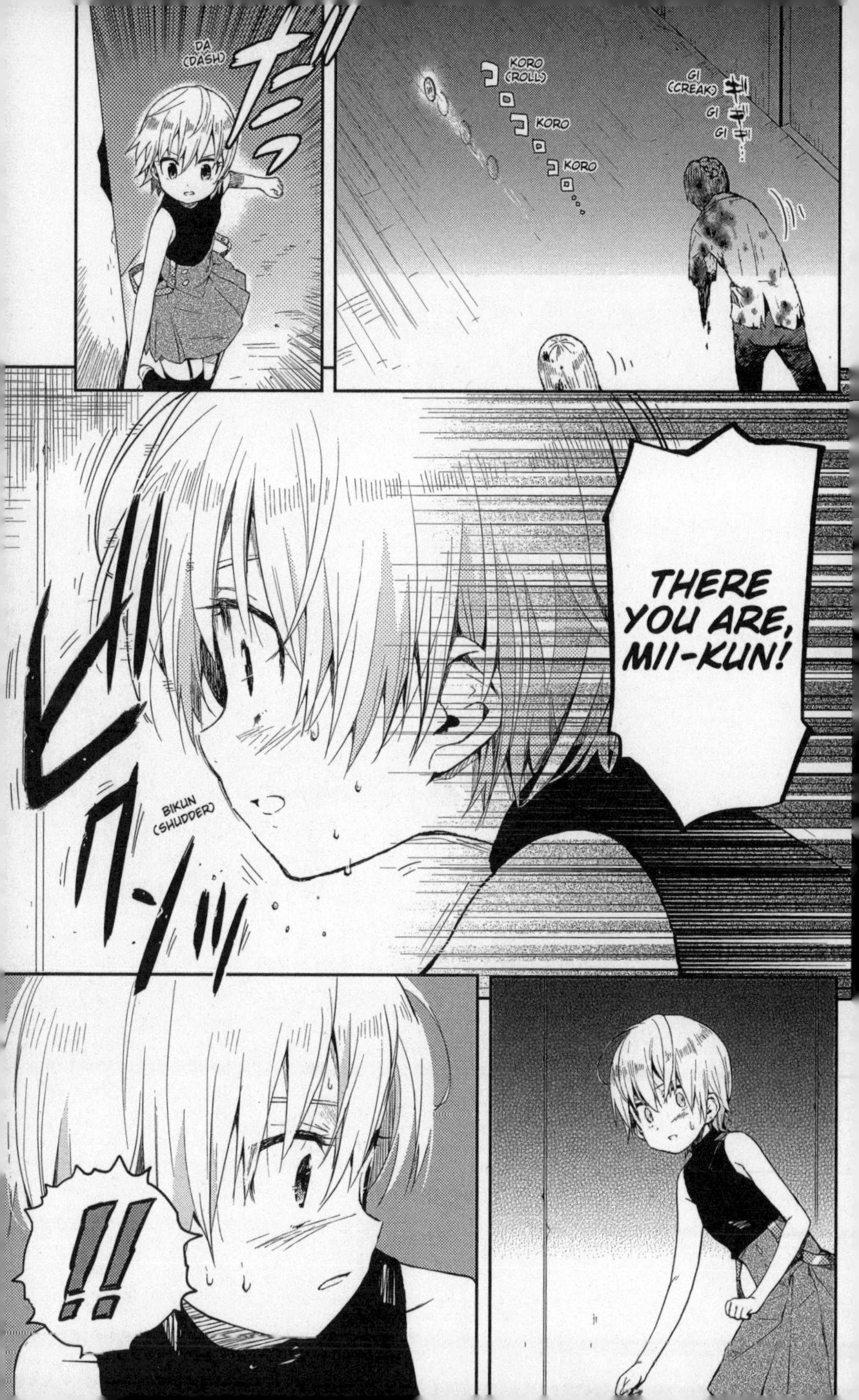
KORO (ROLL)
KORO
KORO
GI (CREAK)
GI
GI
DA (DASH)
THERE YOU ARE, MII-KUN!
BIKUN (SHUDDER)
!!

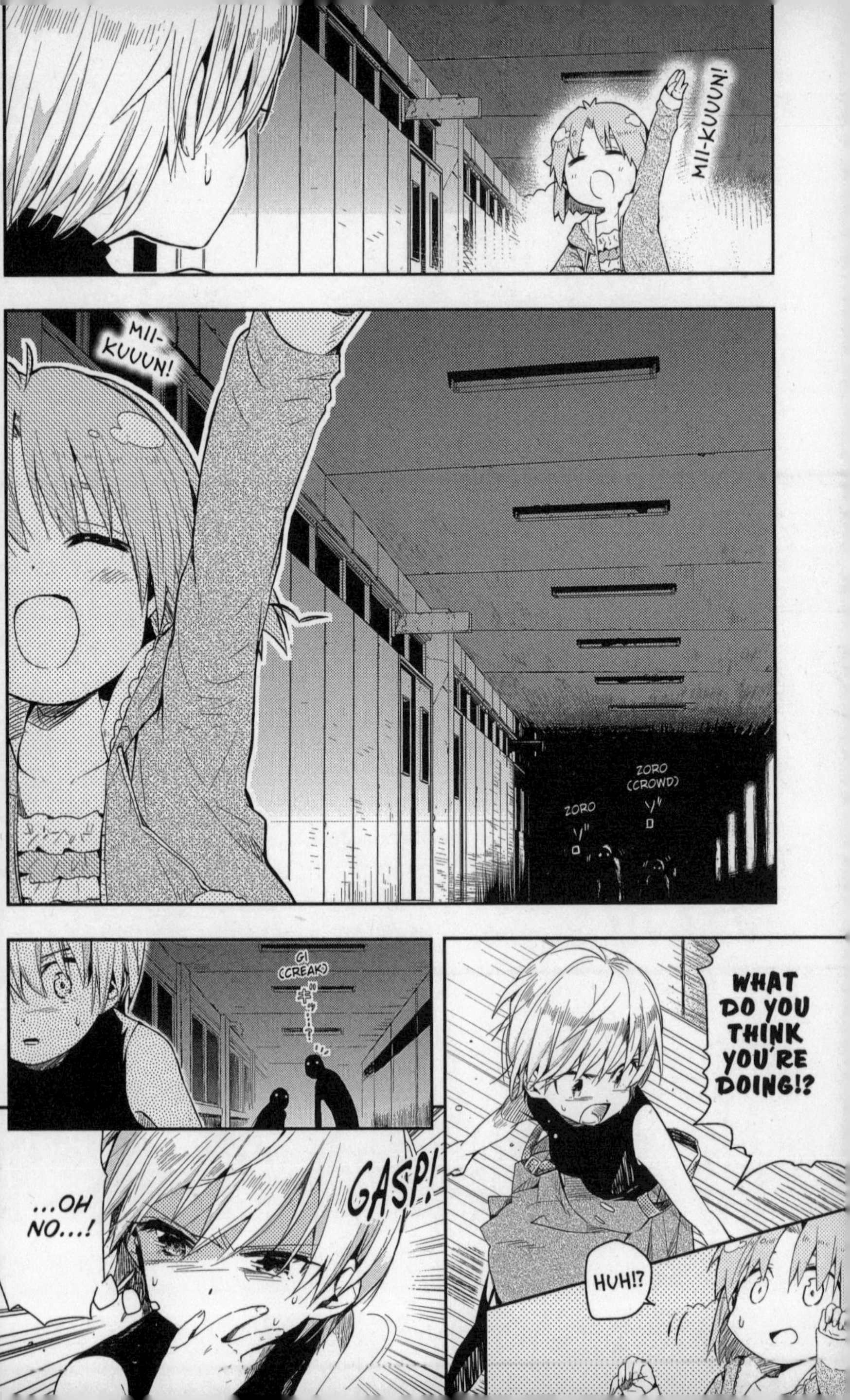
MII-KUUUN!
MII-KUUUN!
ZORO (CROWD)
ZORO
WHAT DO YOU THINK YOU'RE DOING!?
HUH!?
GI (CREAK)
GASP!
...OH NO...!

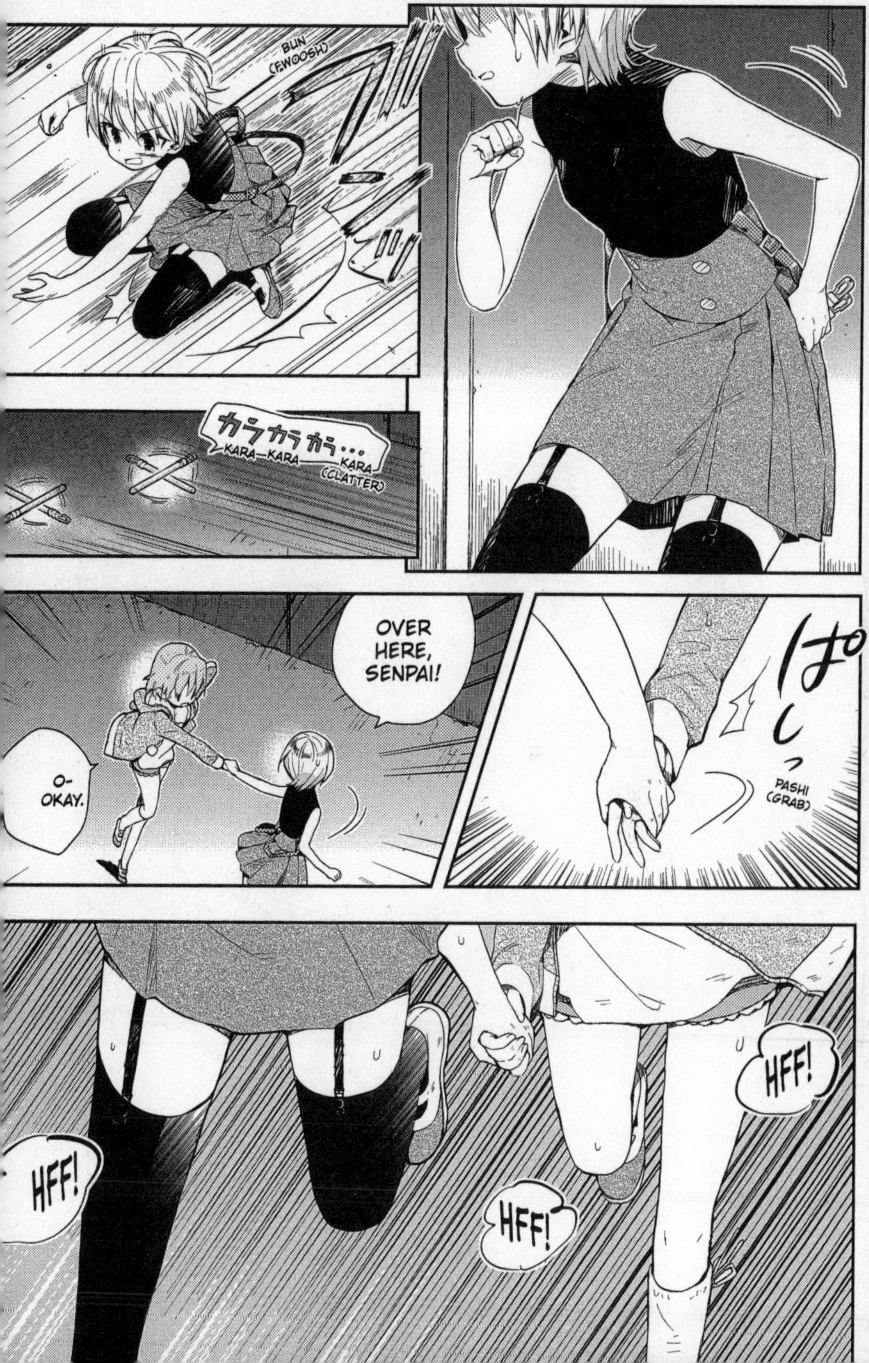
BUN (FWOOSH)
カラカラカラ… KARA-KARA-KARA (CLATTER)
ぱしっ PASHI (GRAB)
OVER HERE, SENPAI!
O-OKAY.
HFF!
HFF!
HFF!

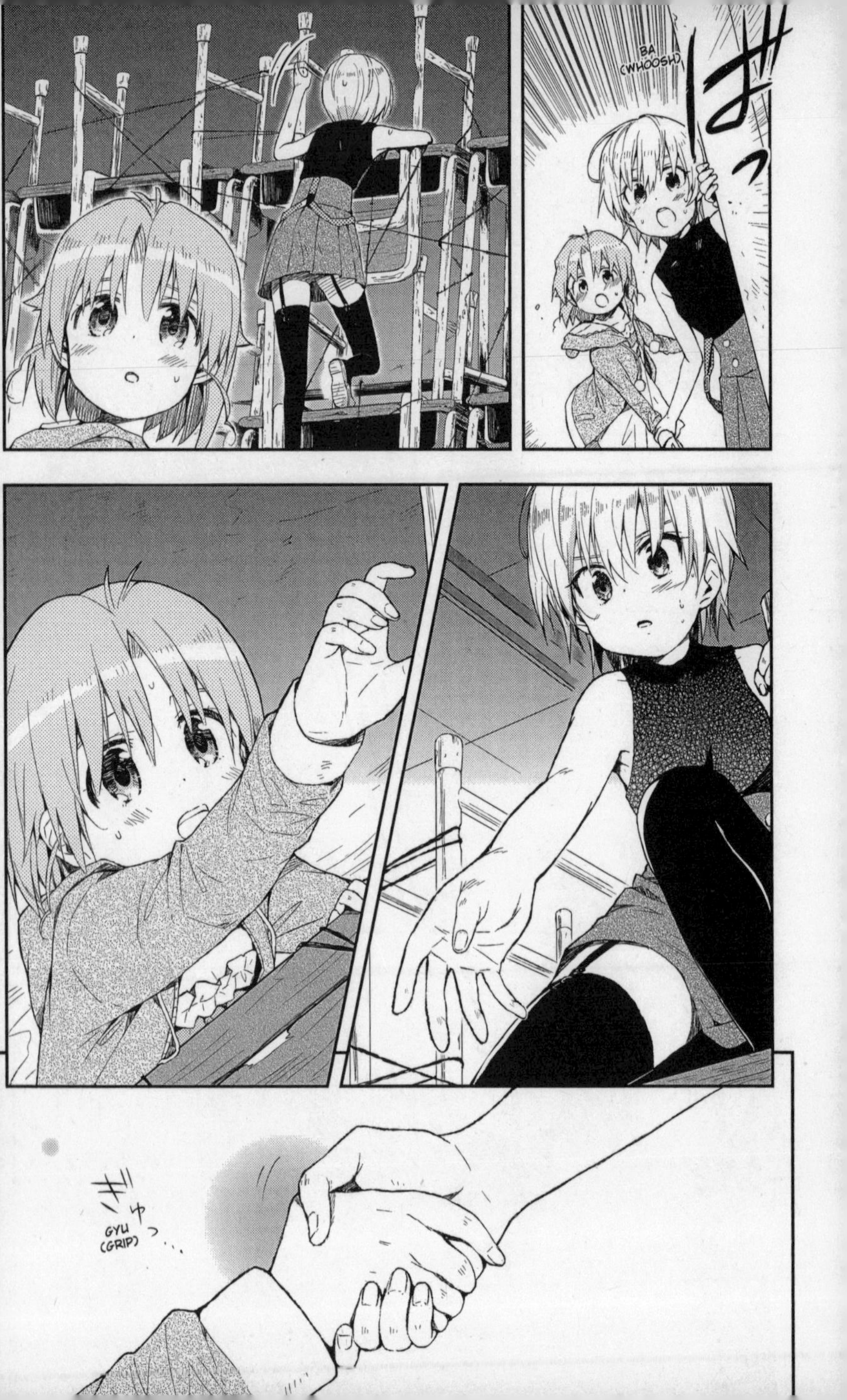
ばっ
BA (WHOOSH)
ぎゅっ…
GYU (GRIP)

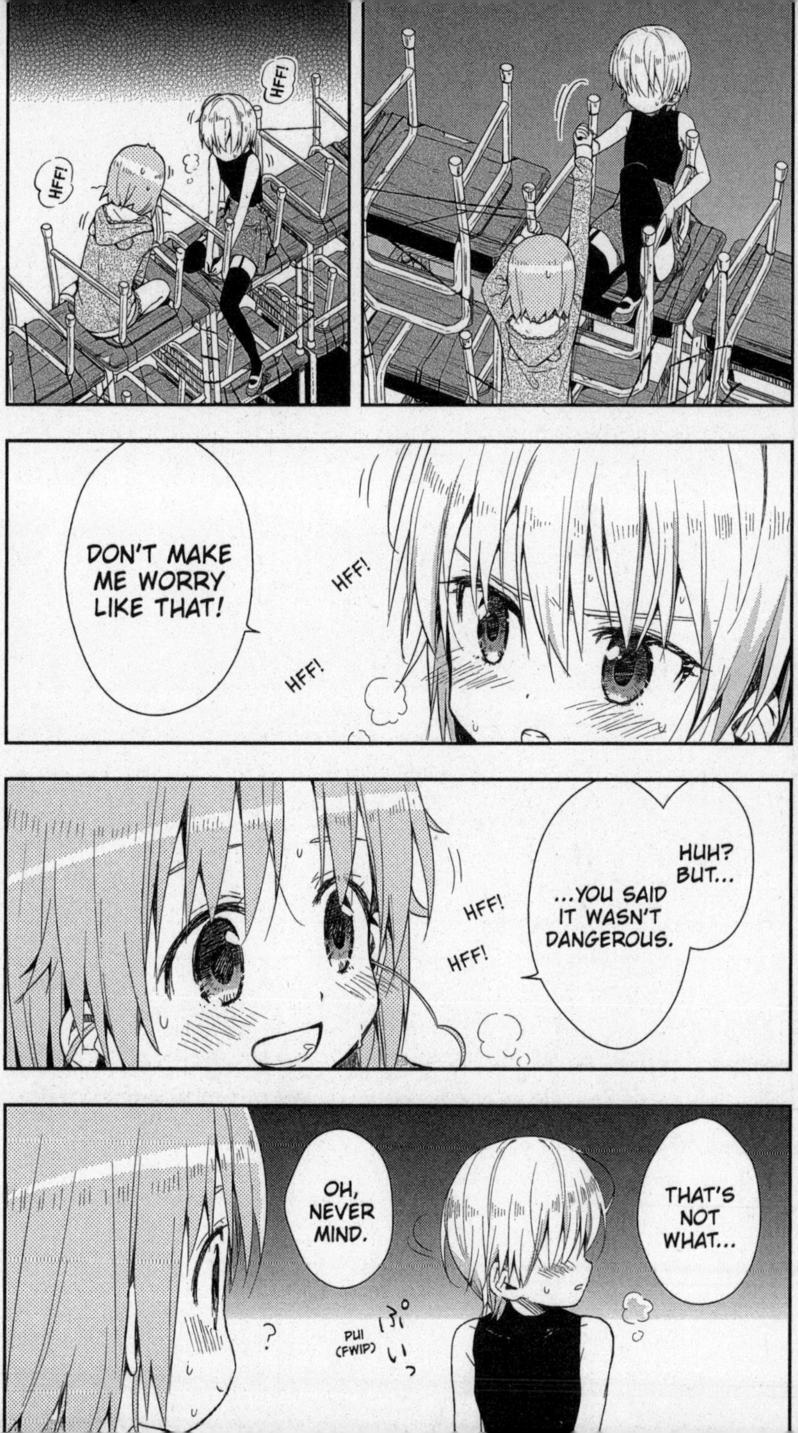
HFF!
HFF!
HFF!
HFF!
DON'T MAKE ME WORRY LIKE THAT!
HUH? BUT...
...YOU SAID IT WASN'T DANGEROUS.
HFF!
HFF!
THAT'S NOT WHAT...
OH, NEVER MIND.
PUI (FWIP)
?

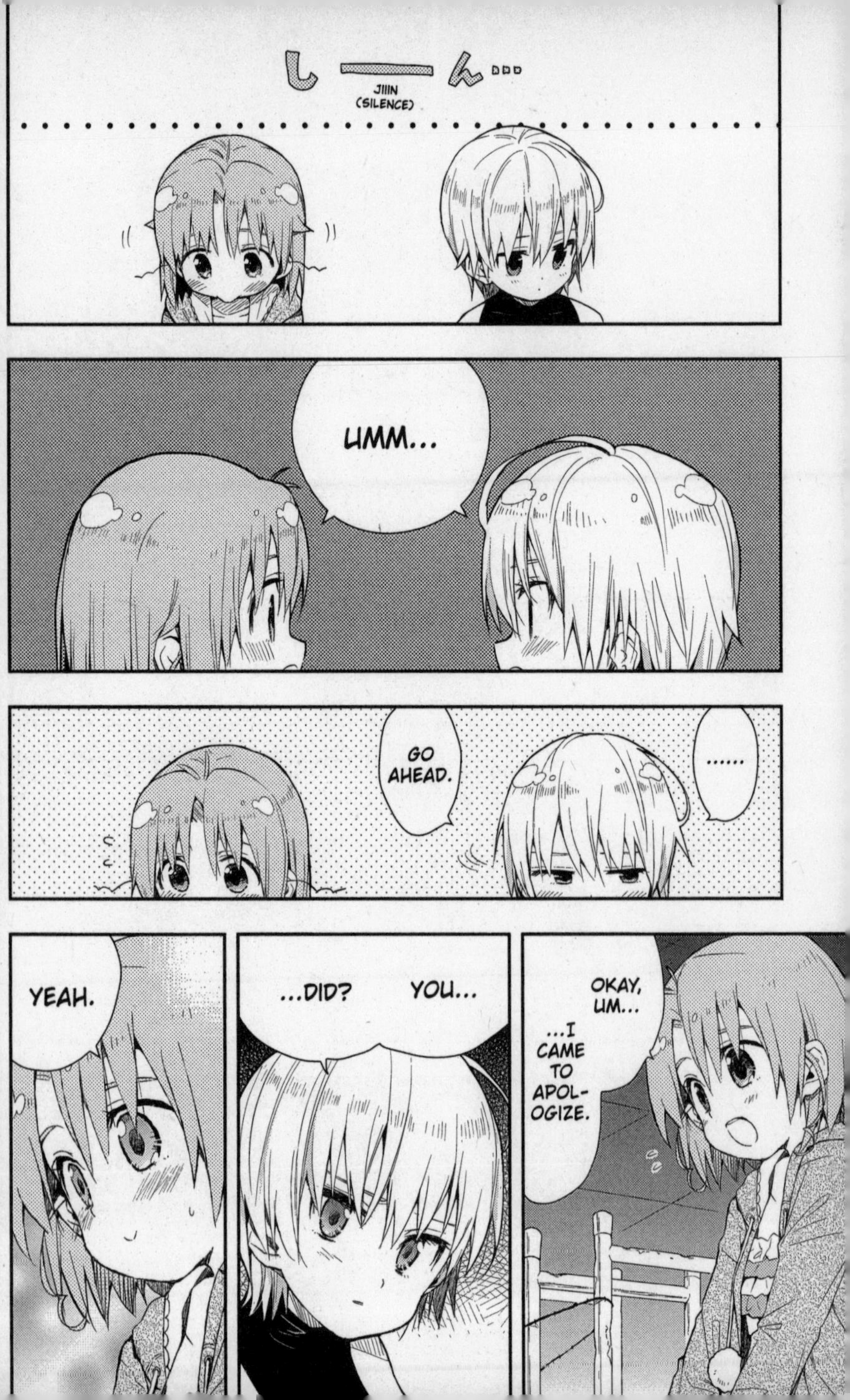
しーーん…
JIIN
(SILENCE)
UMM...
......
GO AHEAD.
OKAY, UM...
...I CAME TO APOLOGIZE.
YOU...
...DID?
YEAH.

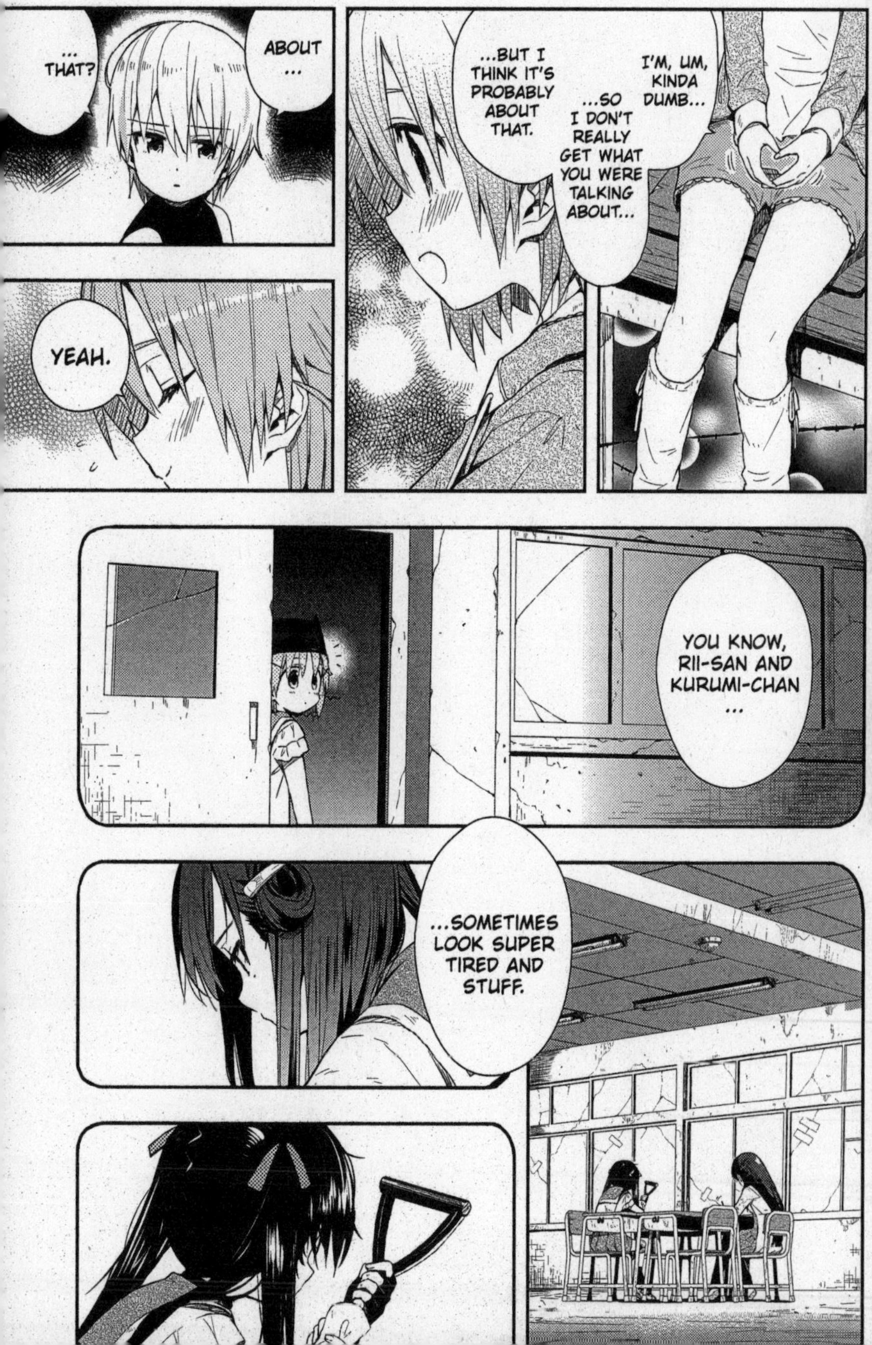
I'M, UM, KINDA DUMB...
...SO I DON'T REALLY GET WHAT YOU WERE TALKING ABOUT...
...BUT I THINK IT'S PROBABLY ABOUT THAT.
ABOUT ...
... THAT?
YEAH.
YOU KNOW, RII-SAN AND KURUMI-CHAN ...
...SOMETIMES LOOK SUPER TIRED AND STUFF.

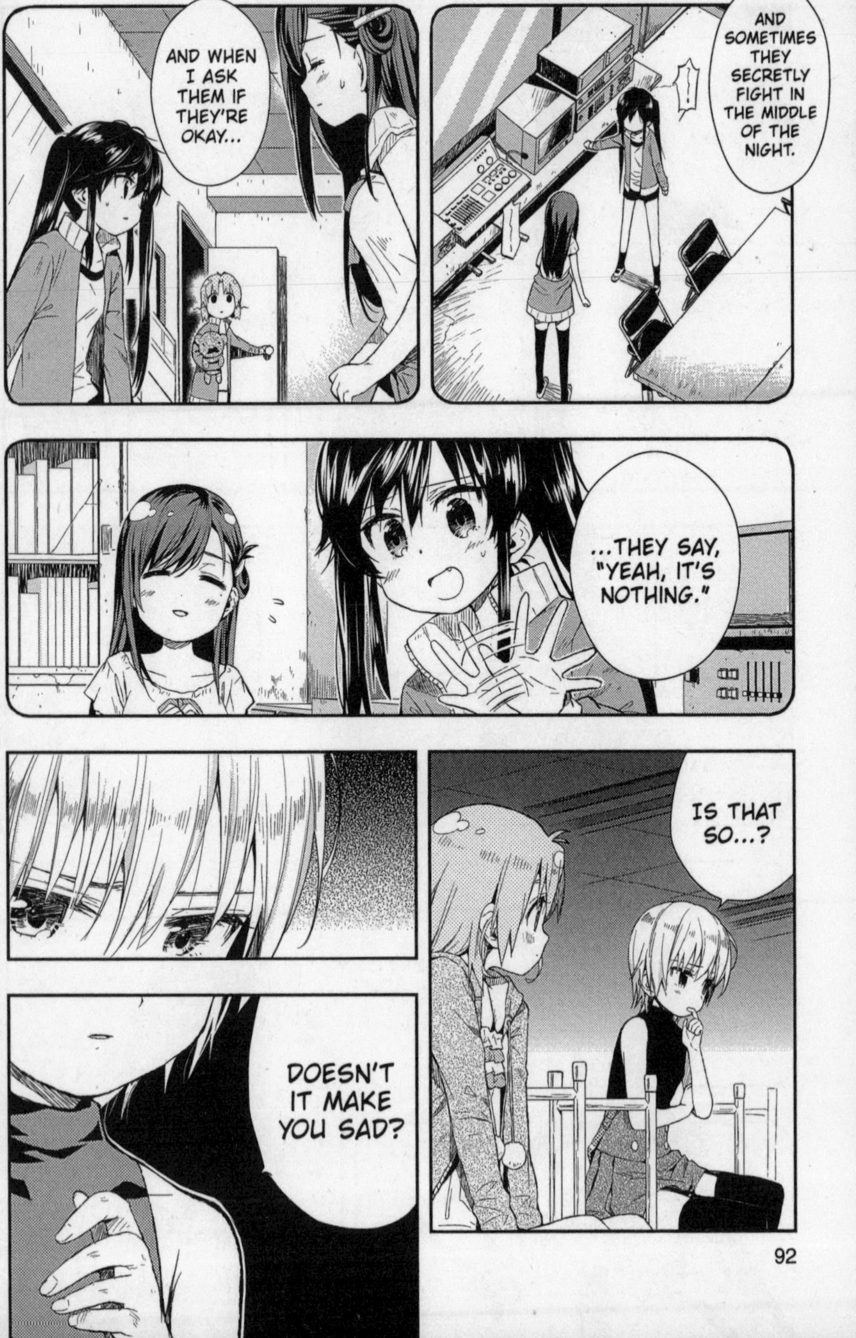
AND SOMETIMES THEY SECRETLY FIGHT IN THE MIDDLE OF THE NIGHT.
!
AND WHEN I ASK THEM IF THEY'RE OKAY...
...THEY SAY, "YEAH, IT'S NOTHING."
IS THAT SO...?
DOESN'T IT MAKE YOU SAD?

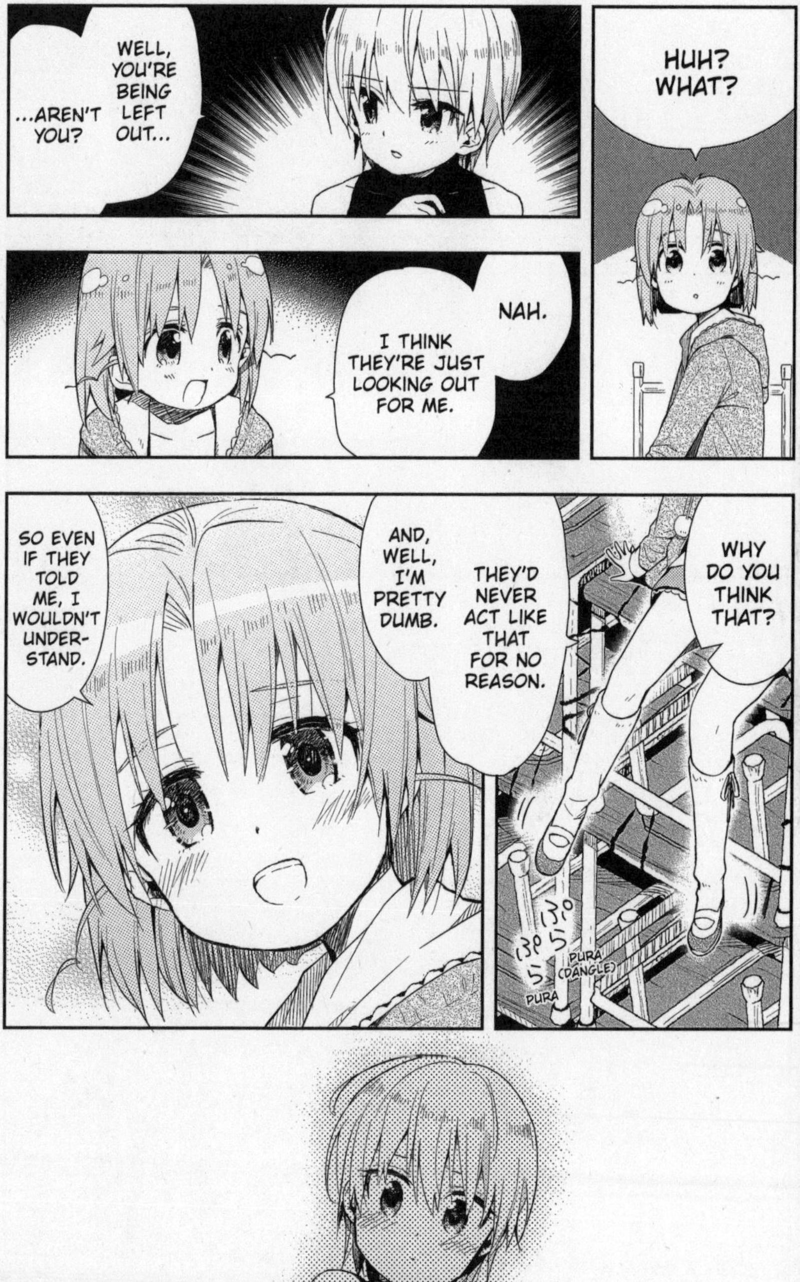
HUH? WHAT?
WELL, YOU'RE BEING LEFT OUT...
...AREN'T YOU?
NAH.
I THINK THEY'RE JUST LOOKING OUT FOR ME.
WHY DO YOU THINK THAT?
THEY'D NEVER ACT LIKE THAT FOR NO REASON.
ぷらぷら
PURA PURA (DANGLE)
AND, WELL, I'M PRETTY DUMB.
SO EVEN IF THEY TOLD ME, I WOULDN'T UNDER-STAND.

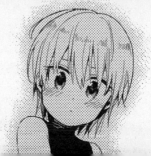

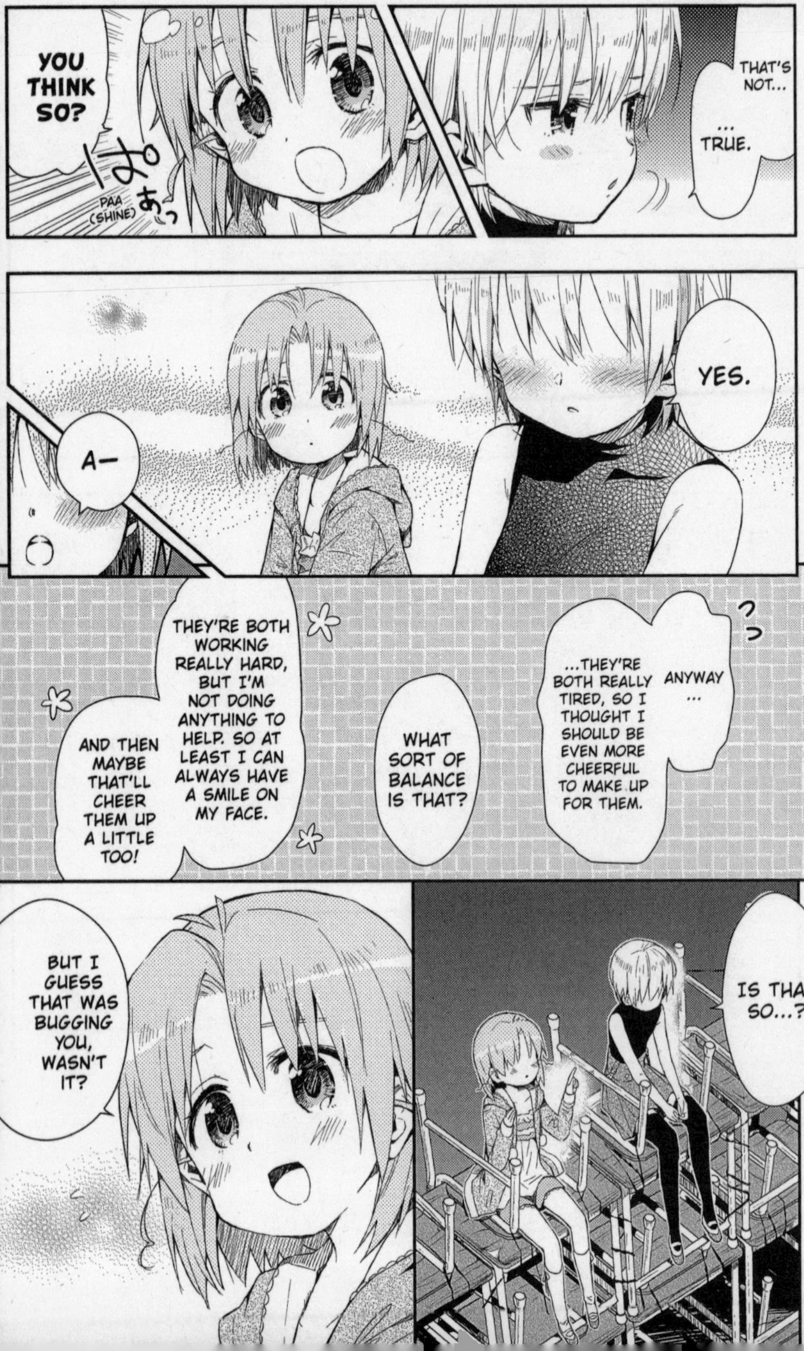
THAT'S NOT...
...TRUE.
YOU THINK SO?
ぱぁっ
PAA (SHINE)
YES.
A—
ANYWAY...
...THEY'RE BOTH REALLY TIRED, SO I THOUGHT I SHOULD BE EVEN MORE CHEERFUL TO MAKE UP FOR THEM.
WHAT SORT OF BALANCE IS THAT?
THEY'RE BOTH WORKING REALLY HARD, BUT I'M NOT DOING ANYTHING TO HELP. SO AT LEAST I CAN ALWAYS HAVE A SMILE ON MY FACE.
AND THEN MAYBE THAT'LL CHEER THEM UP A LITTLE TOO!
IS THAT SO...?
BUT I GUESS THAT WAS BUGGING YOU, WASN'T IT?

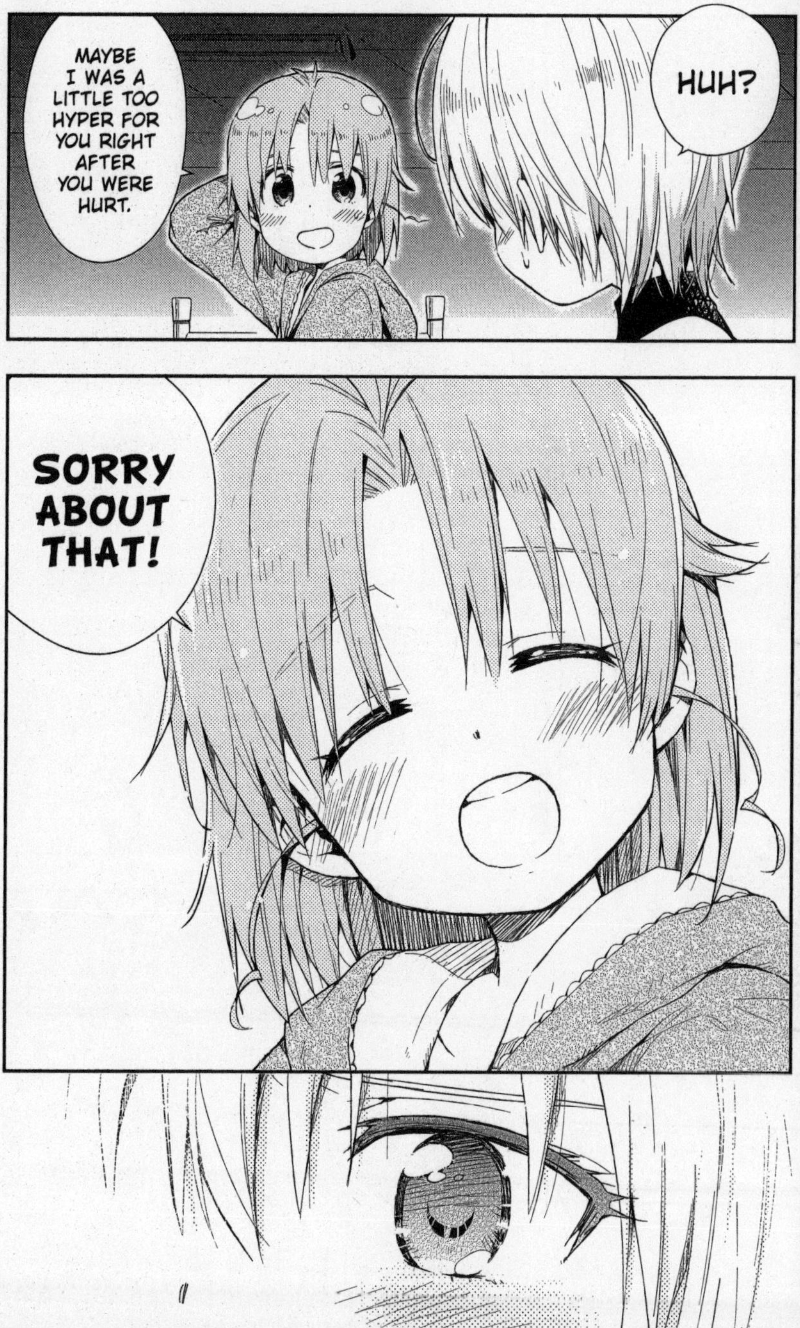
HUH?
MAYBE I WAS A LITTLE TOO HYPER FOR YOU RIGHT AFTER YOU WERE HURT.
SORRY ABOUT THAT!

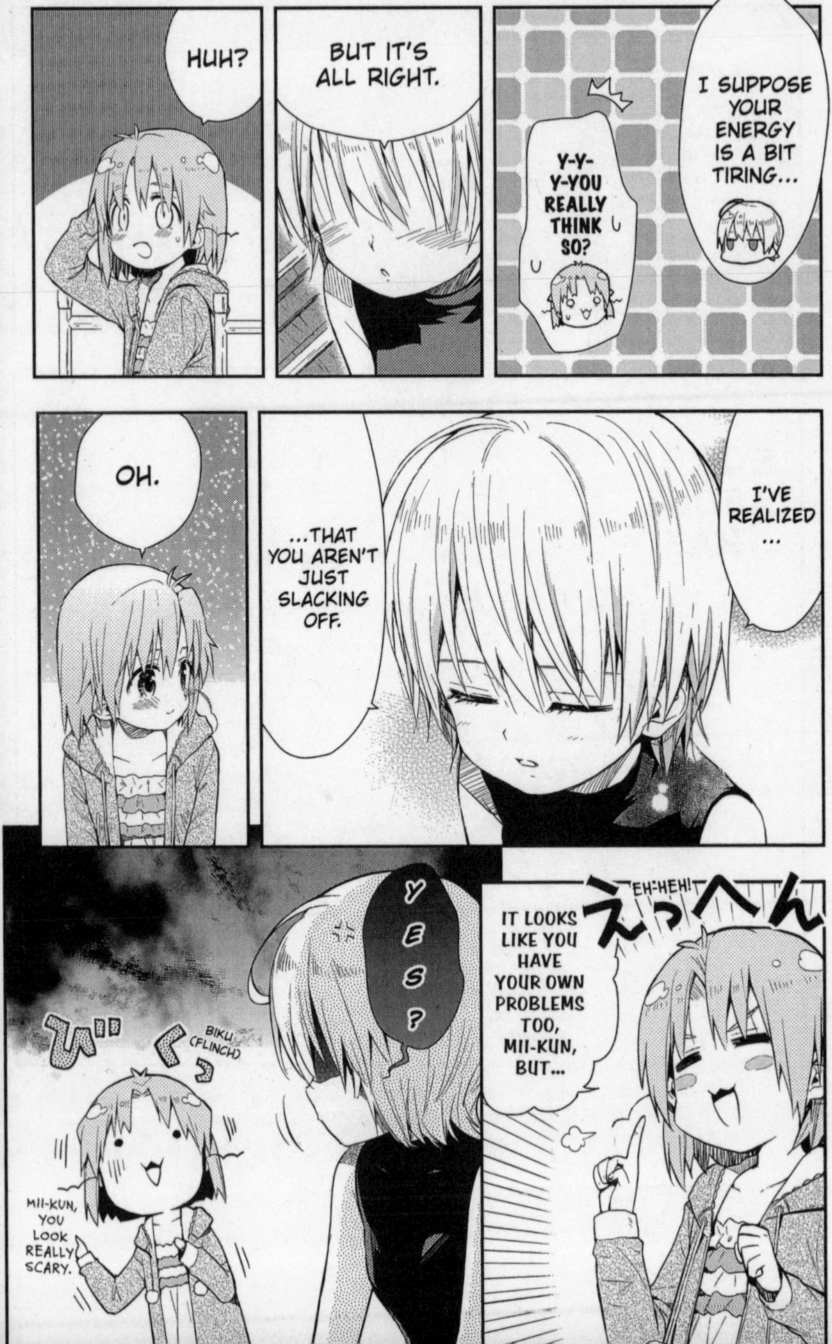
I SUPPOSE YOUR ENERGY IS A BIT TIRING...
Y-Y-Y-YOU REALLY THINK SO?
BUT IT'S ALL RIGHT.
HUH?
I'VE REALIZED ...
...THAT YOU AREN'T JUST SLACKING OFF.
OH.
えっへん
EH-HEH!
IT LOOKS LIKE YOU HAVE YOUR OWN PROBLEMS TOO, MII-KUN, BUT...
YES?
びくっ
BIKU (FLINCH)
MII-KUN, YOU LOOK REALLY SCARY.

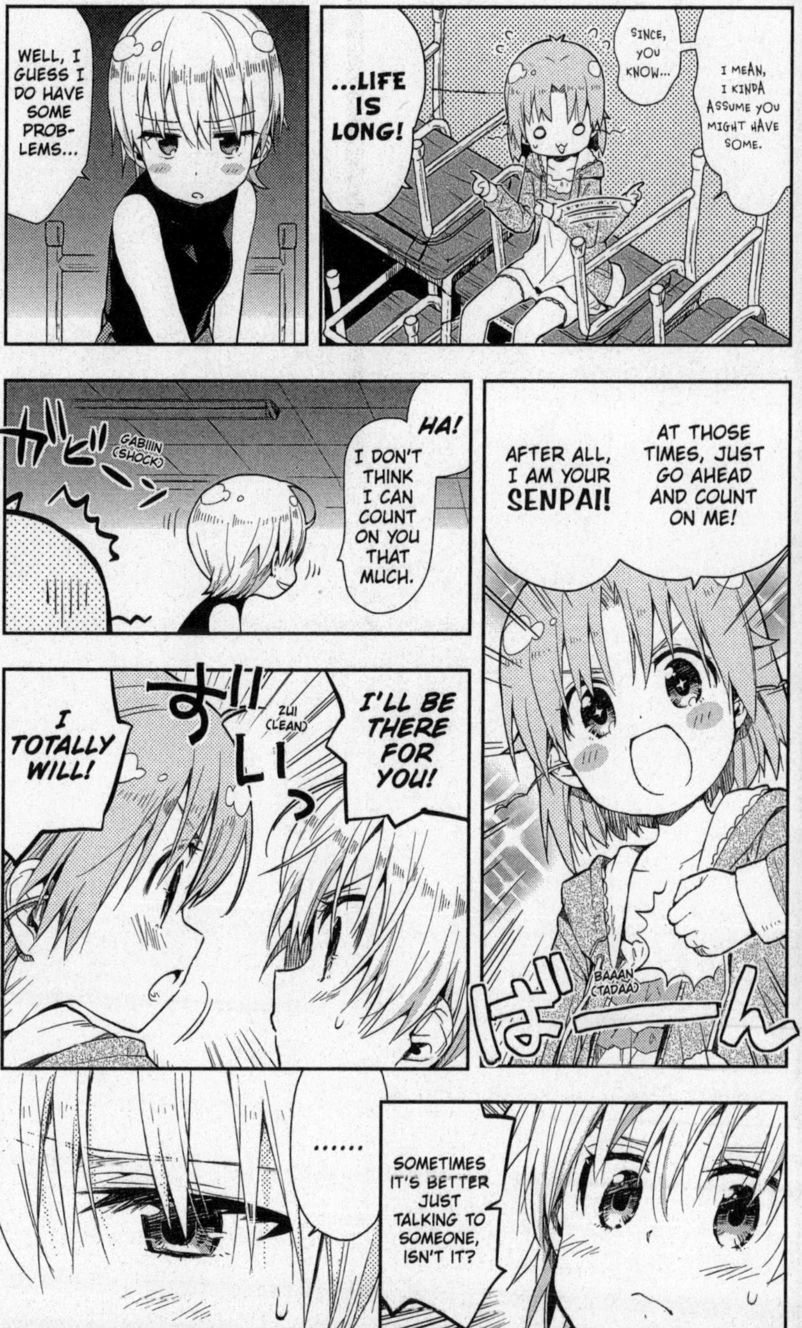
SINCE, YOU KNOW...
I MEAN, I KINDA ASSUME YOU MIGHT HAVE SOME.
...LIFE IS LONG!
WELL, I GUESS I DO HAVE SOME PROB-LEMS...
AT THOSE TIMES, JUST GO AHEAD AND COUNT ON ME!
AFTER ALL, I AM YOUR SENPAI!
ばーん
BAAAN (TADAA)
HA! I DON'T THINK I CAN COUNT ON YOU THAT MUCH.
がびーん
GABIIN (SHOCK)
I'LL BE THERE FOR YOU!
ずいっ
ZUI (LEAN)
I TOTALLY WILL!
SOMETIMES IT'S BETTER JUST TALKING TO SOMEONE, ISN'T IT?
......

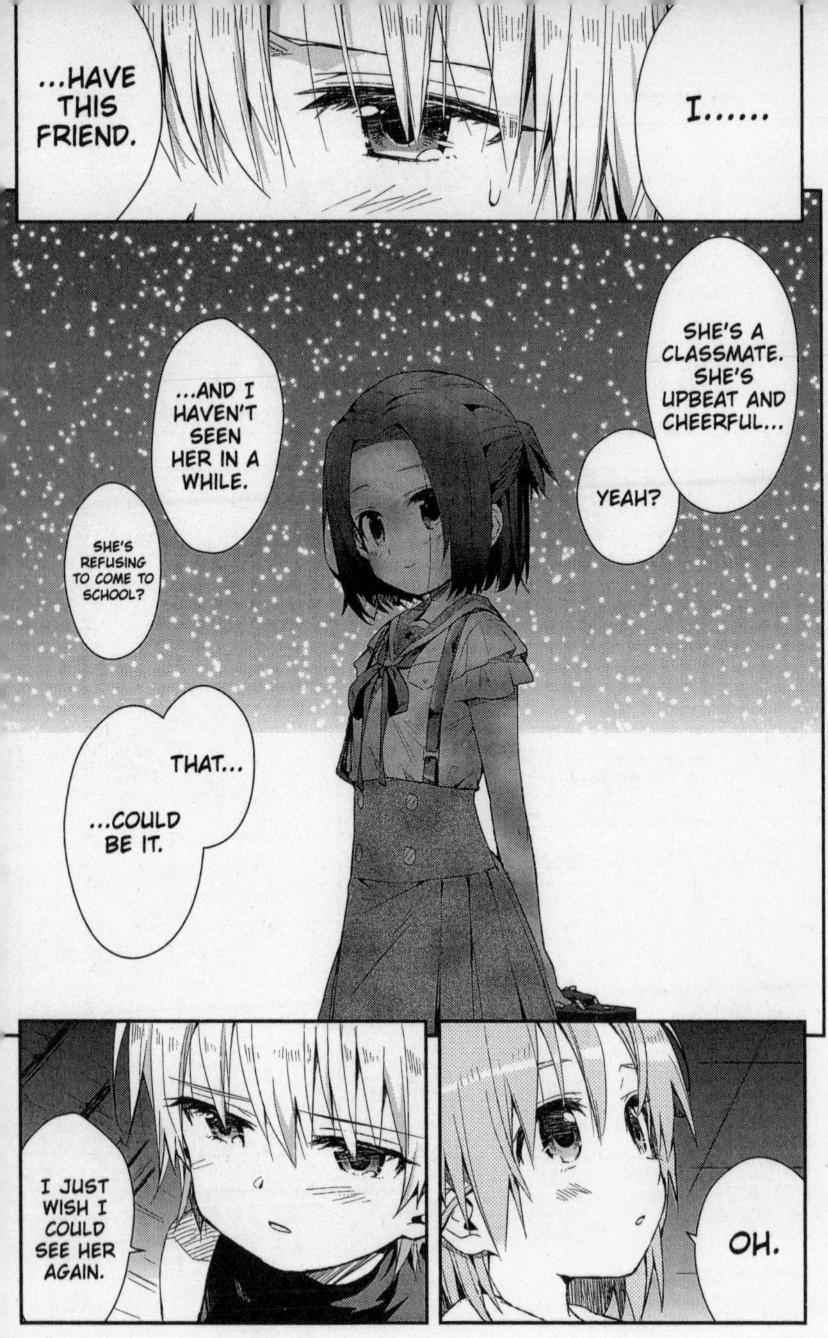
I......
...HAVE THIS FRIEND.
SHE'S A CLASSMATE. SHE'S UPBEAT AND CHEERFUL...
YEAH?
...AND I HAVEN'T SEEN HER IN A WHILE.
SHE'S REFUSING TO COME TO SCHOOL?
THAT...
...COULD BE IT.
OH.
I JUST WISH I COULD SEE HER AGAIN.

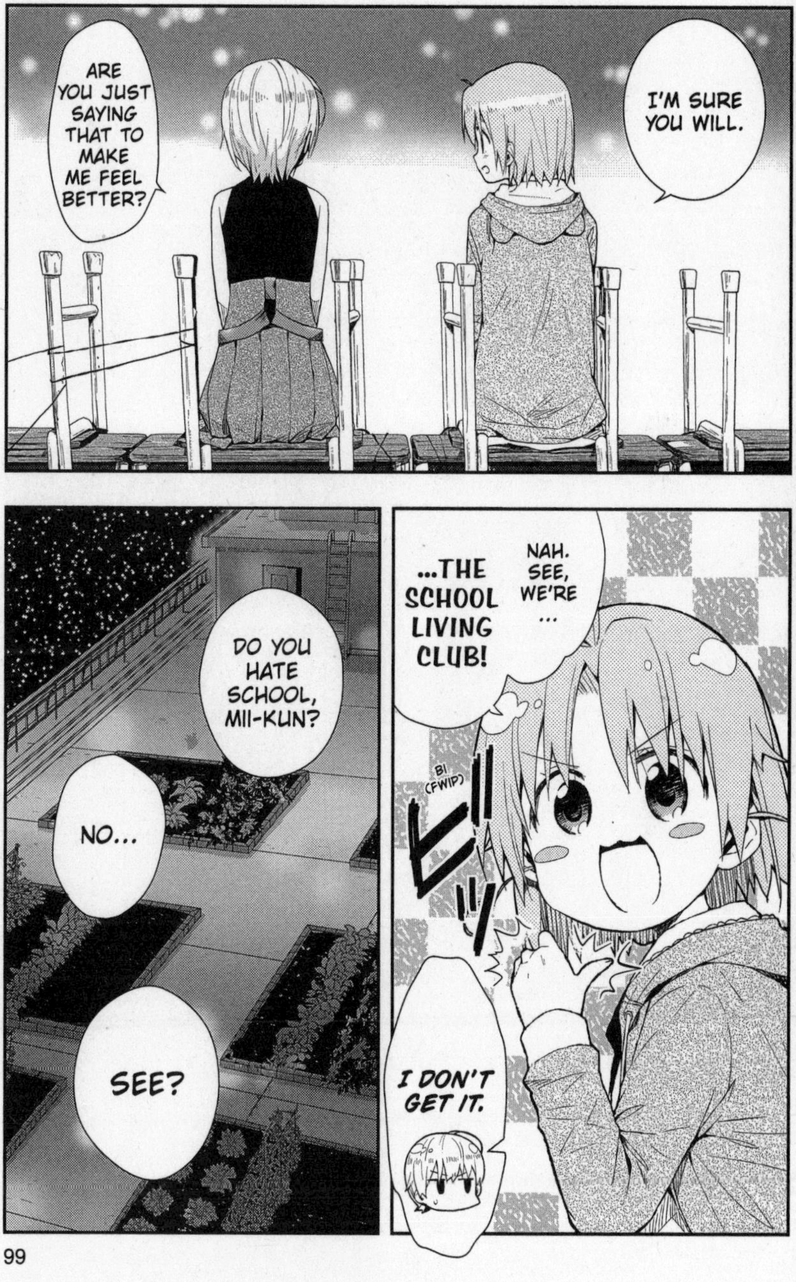
I'M SURE YOU WILL.
ARE YOU JUST SAYING THAT TO MAKE ME FEEL BETTER?
NAH. SEE, WE'RE ...
...THE SCHOOL LIVING CLUB!
BI (FWIP)
I DON'T GET IT.
DO YOU HATE SCHOOL, MII-KUN?
NO...
SEE?

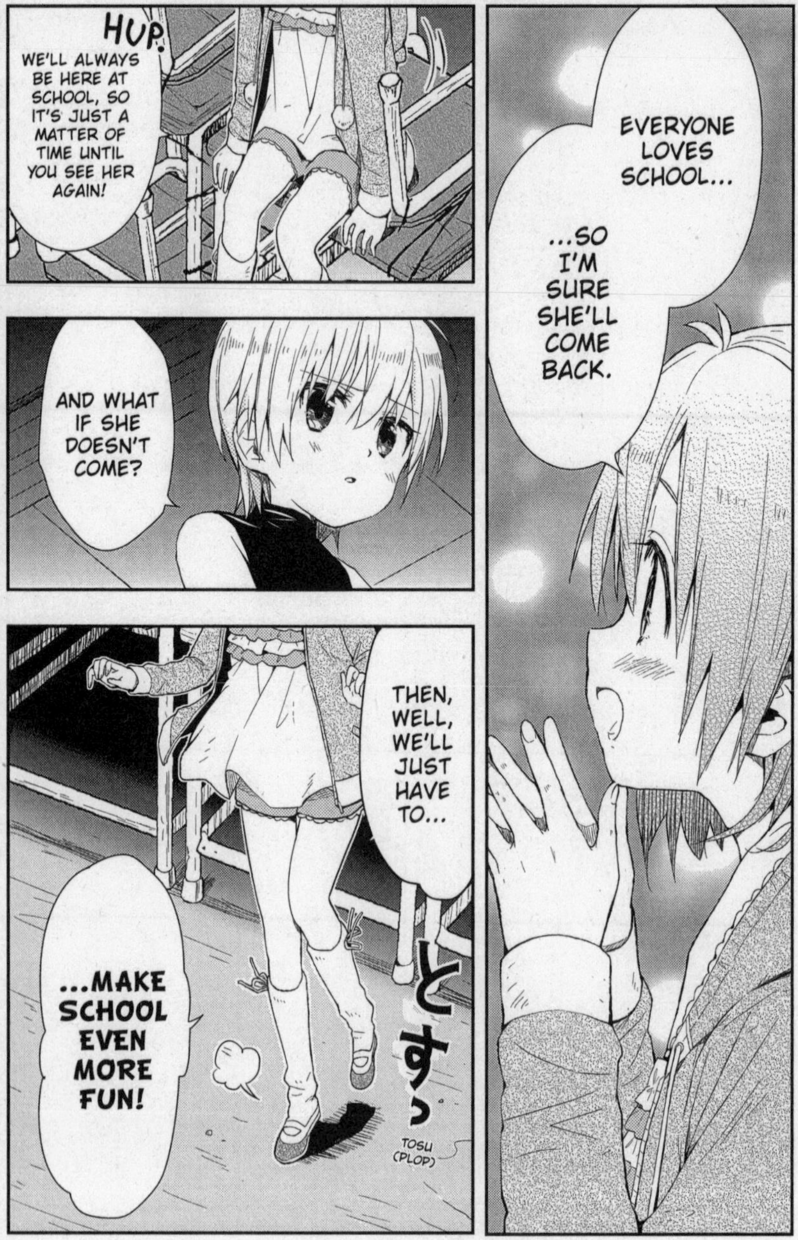
EVERYONE LOVES SCHOOL...
...SO I'M SURE SHE'LL COME BACK.
HUP!
WE'LL ALWAYS BE HERE AT SCHOOL, SO IT'S JUST A MATTER OF TIME UNTIL YOU SEE HER AGAIN!
AND WHAT IF SHE DOESN'T COME?
THEN, WELL, WE'LL JUST HAVE TO...
...MAKE SCHOOL EVEN MORE FUN!
とすっ
TOSU (PLOP)

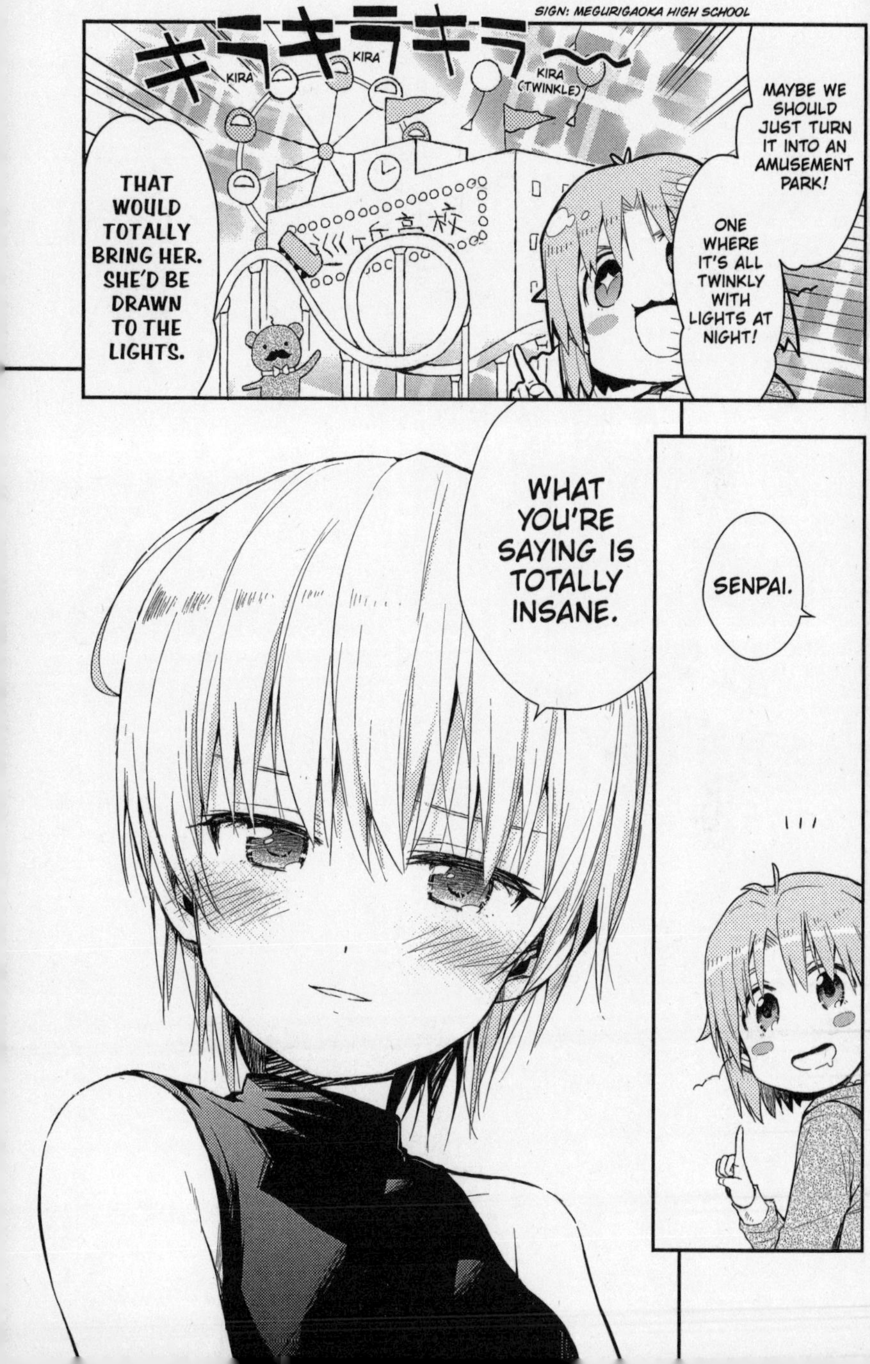
SIGN: MEGURIGAOKA HIGH SCHOOL
MAYBE WE SHOULD JUST TURN IT INTO AN AMUSEMENT PARK!
ONE WHERE IT'S ALL TWINKLY WITH LIGHTS AT NIGHT!
キラキラキラ〜
KIRA KIRA KIRA (TWINKLE)
THAT WOULD TOTALLY BRING HER. SHE'D BE DRAWN TO THE LIGHTS.
SENPAI.
WHAT YOU'RE SAYING IS TOTALLY INSANE.

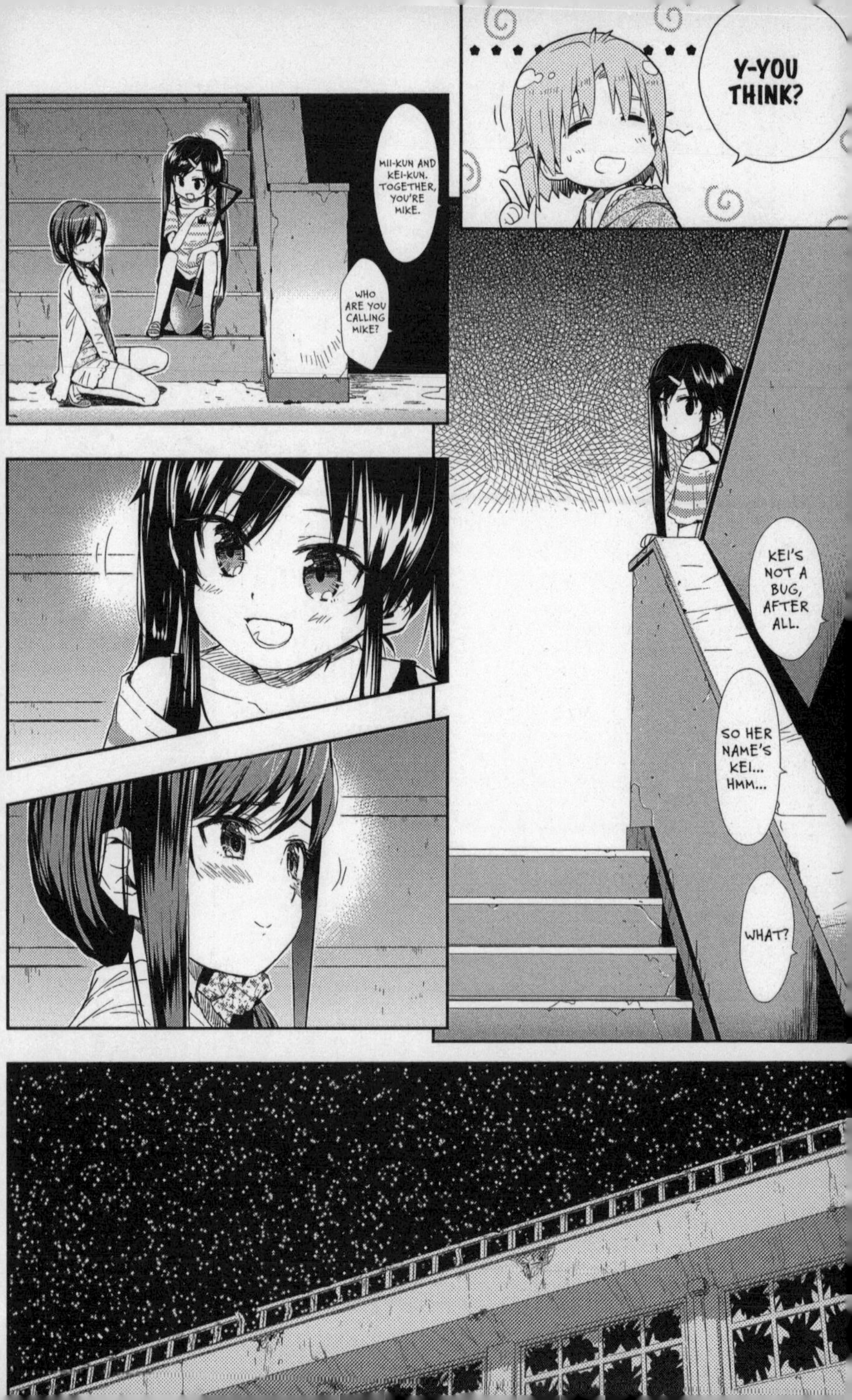

Y-YOU THINK?
MII-KUN AND KEI-KUN. TOGETHER, YOU'RE MIKE.
WHO ARE YOU CALLING MIKE?
KEI'S NOT A BUG, AFTER ALL.
SO HER NAME'S KEI... HMM...
WHAT?

SCHOOL-LIVE!

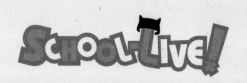

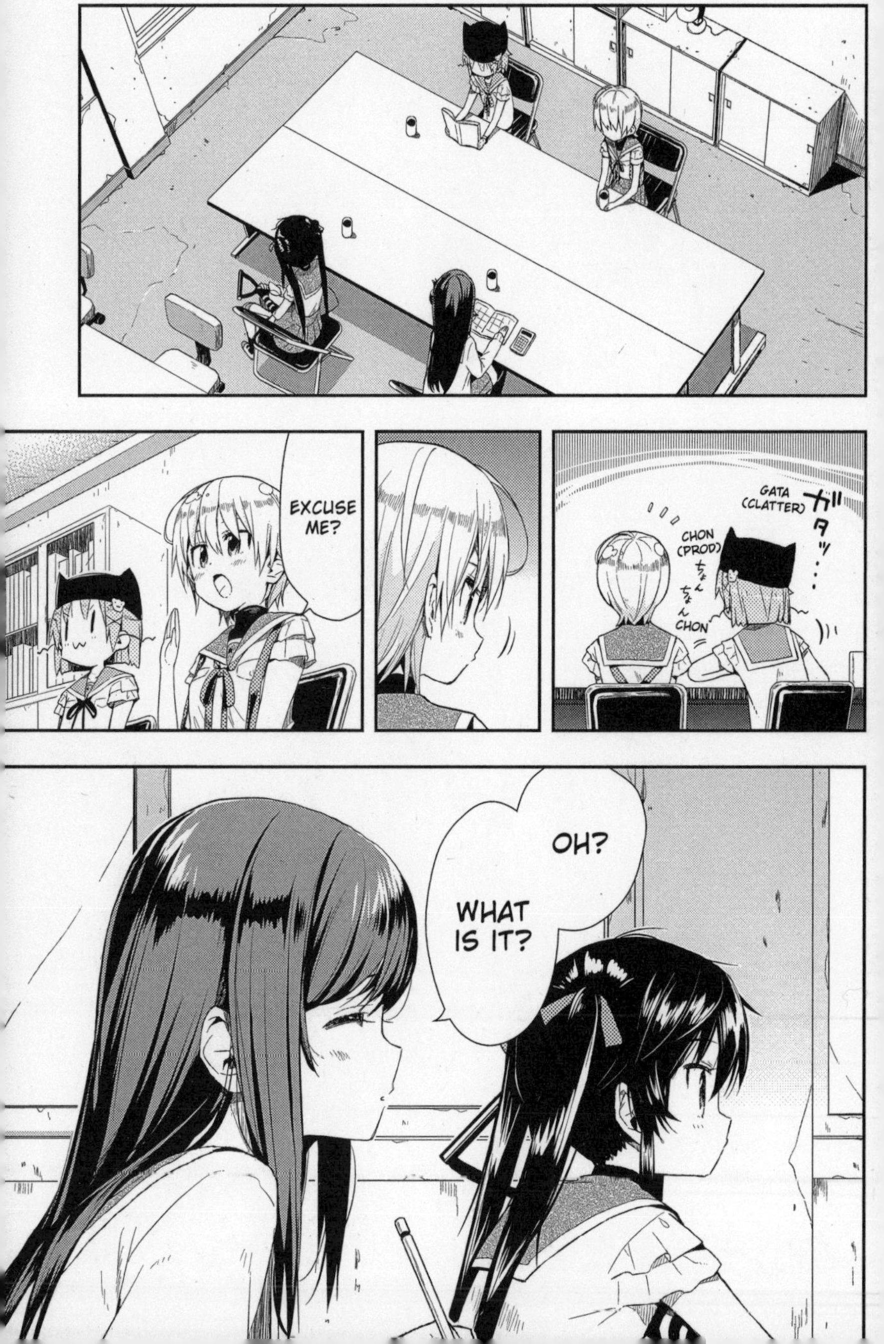
GATA (CLATTER)
ガタッ…
CHON (PROD)
ちょんちょん
CHON
EXCUSE ME?
OH?
WHAT IS IT?

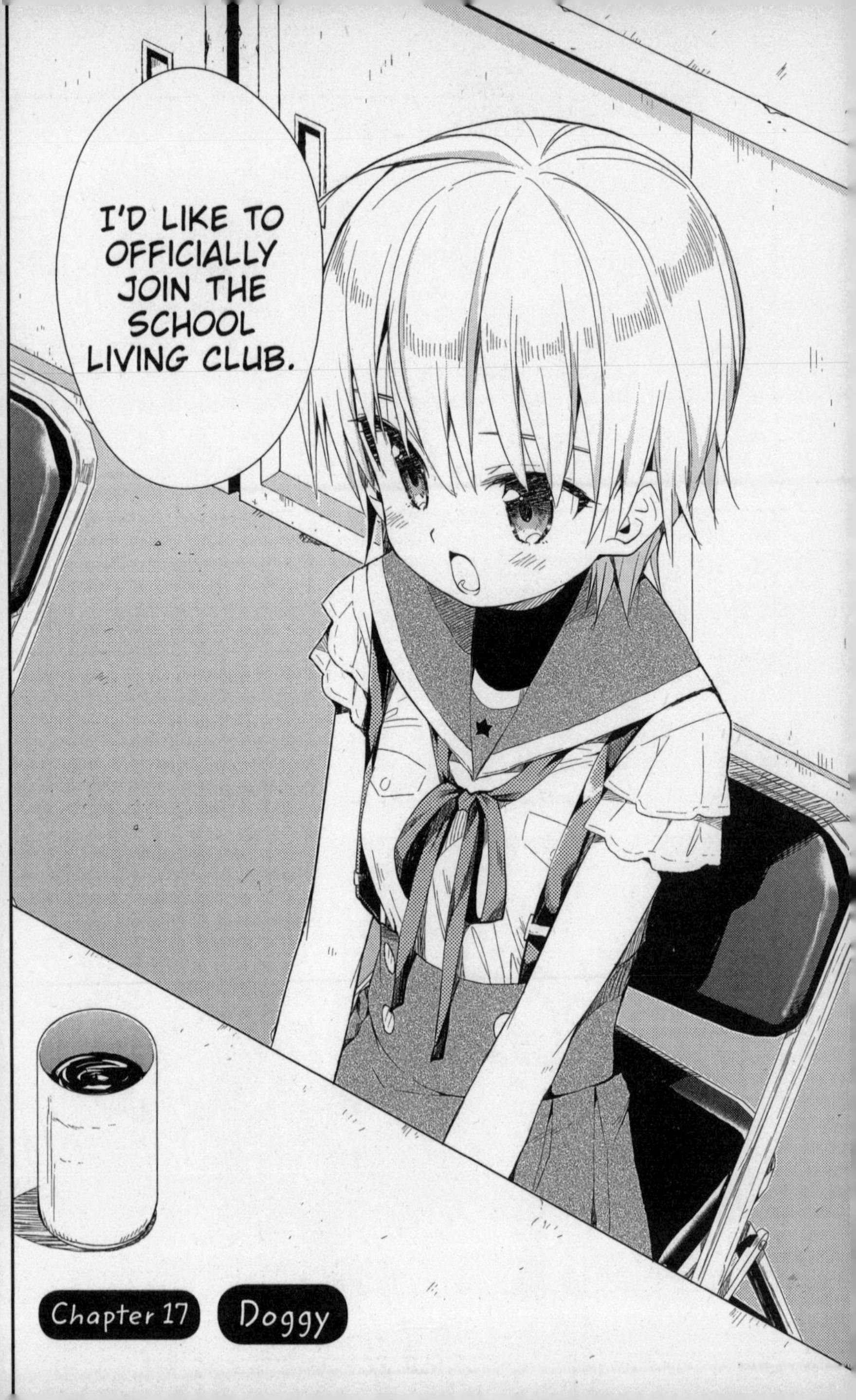
I'D LIKE TO OFFICIALLY JOIN THE SCHOOL LIVING CLUB.
Chapter 17
Doggy

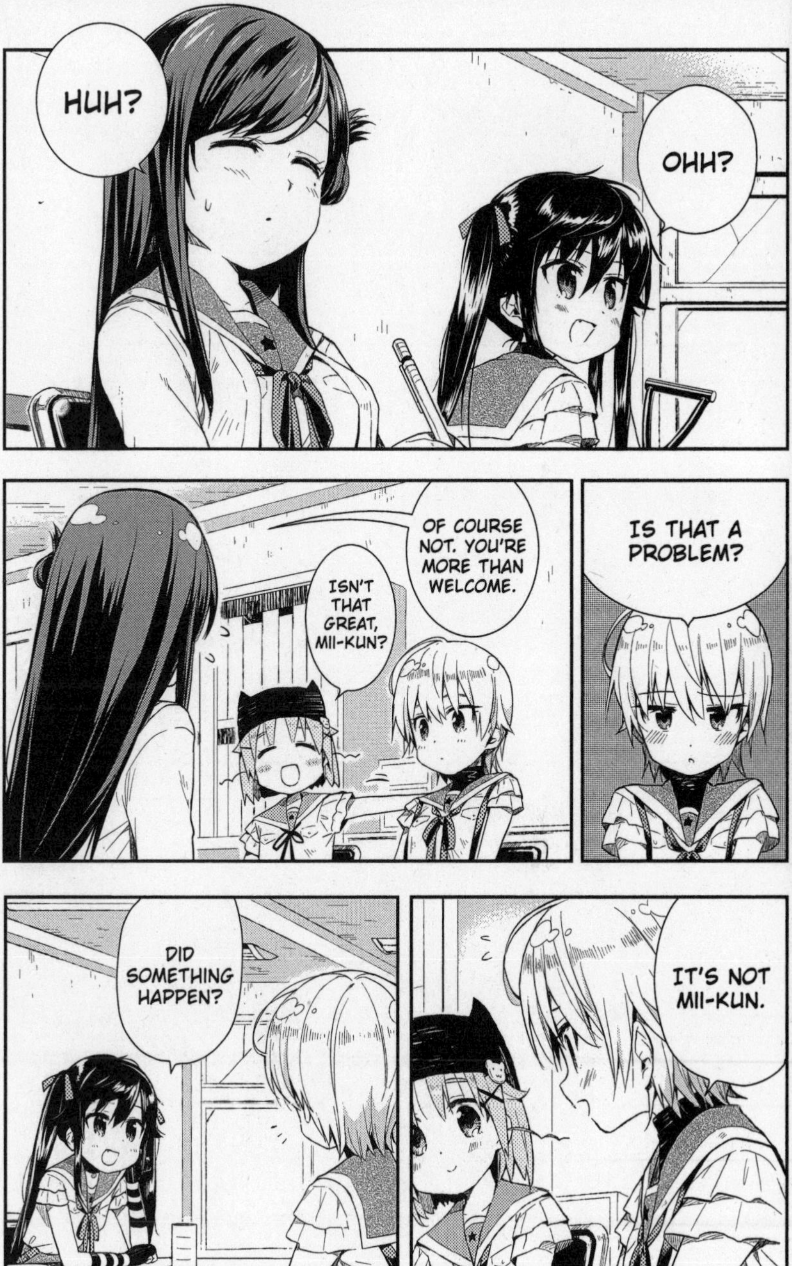
OHH?
HUH?
IS THAT A PROBLEM?
OF COURSE NOT. YOU'RE MORE THAN WELCOME.
ISN'T THAT GREAT, MII-KUN?
IT'S NOT MII-KUN.
DID SOMETHING HAPPEN?

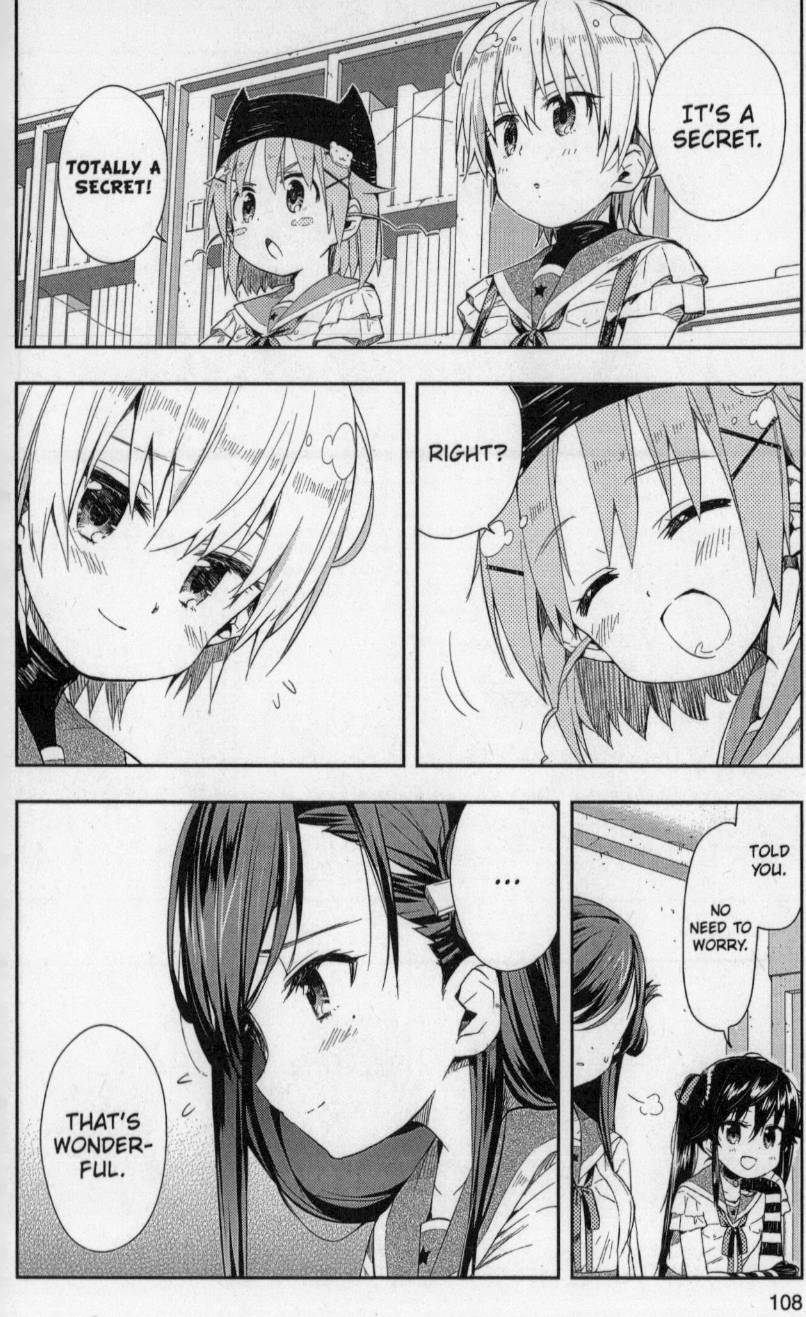
IT'S A SECRET.
TOTALLY A SECRET!
RIGHT?
TOLD YOU.
NO NEED TO WORRY.
...
THAT'S WONDER-FUL.

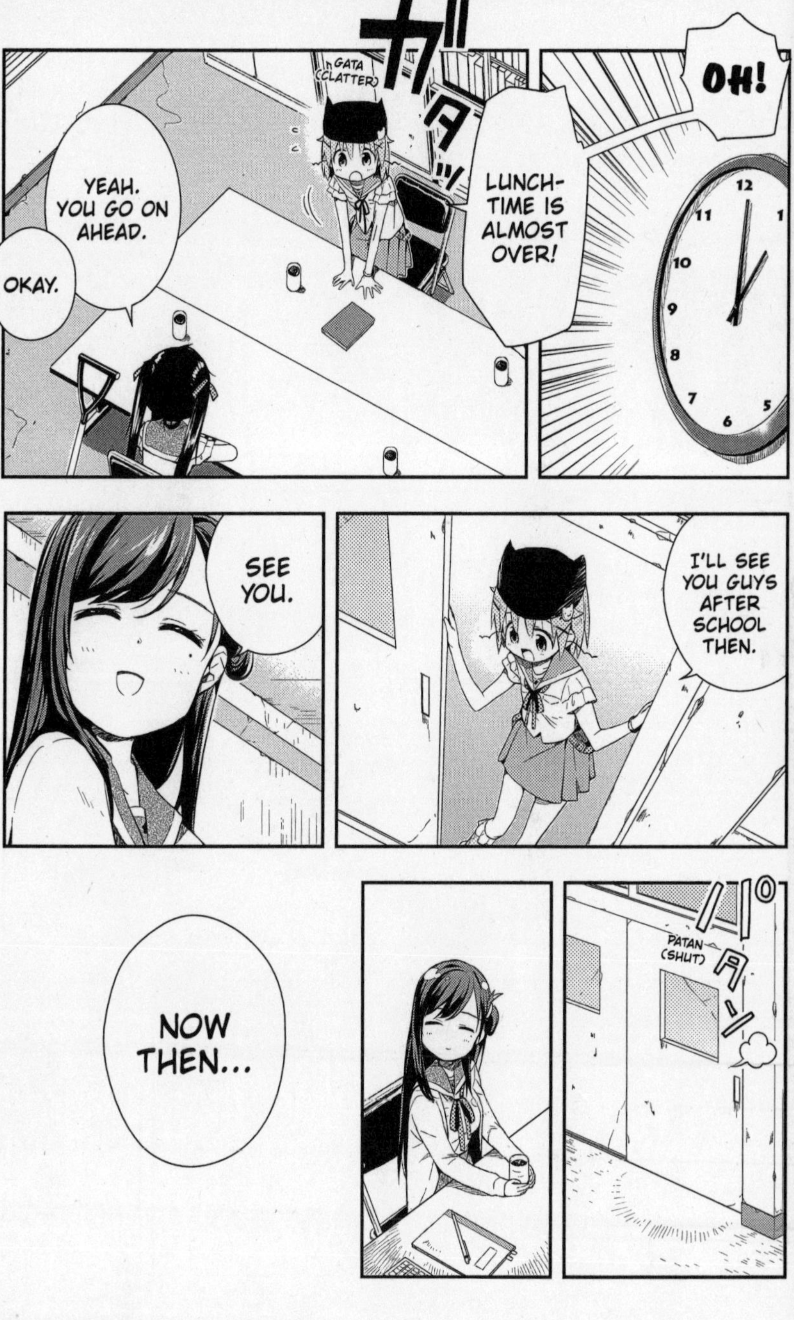
OH!
LUNCH-TIME IS ALMOST OVER!
GATA (CLATTER)
YEAH. YOU GO ON AHEAD.
OKAY.
I'LL SEE YOU GUYS AFTER SCHOOL THEN.
SEE YOU.
PATAN (SHUT)
NOW THEN...

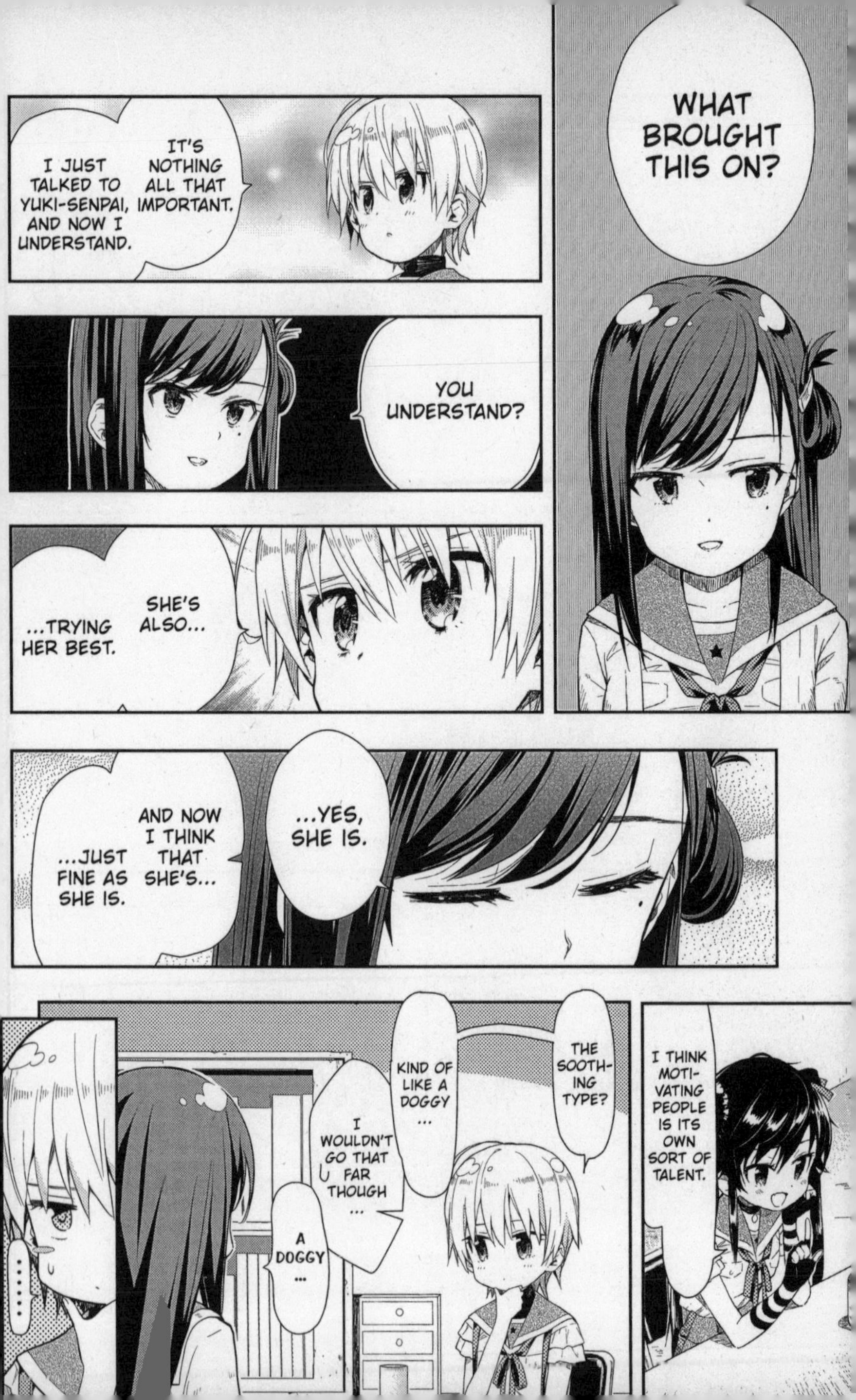
WHAT BROUGHT THIS ON?
IT'S NOTHING ALL THAT IMPORTANT. I JUST TALKED TO YUKI-SENPAI, AND NOW I UNDERSTAND.
YOU UNDERSTAND?
SHE'S ALSO... ...TRYING HER BEST.
...YES, SHE IS.
AND NOW I THINK THAT SHE'S... ...JUST FINE AS SHE IS.
I THINK MOTI-VATING PEOPLE IS ITS OWN SORT OF TALENT.
THE SOOTH-ING TYPE?
KIND OF LIKE A DOGGY ...
I WOULDN'T GO THAT FAR THOUGH ...
A DOGGY ...
......

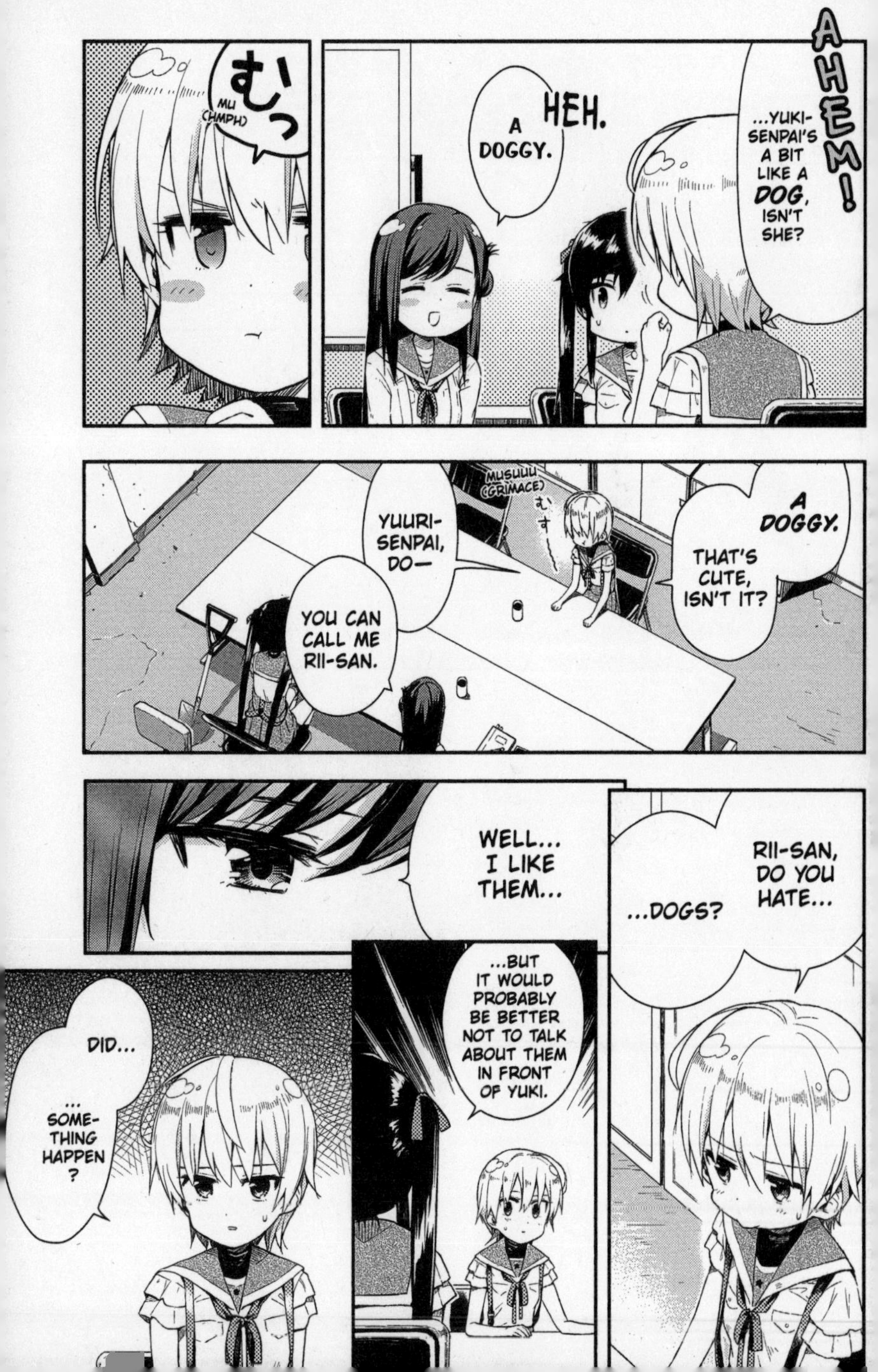
AHEM!
...YUKI-SENPAI'S A BIT LIKE A DOG, ISN'T SHE?
HEH.
A DOGGY.
むっ
MU (HMPH)
A DOGGY. THAT'S CUTE, ISN'T IT?
MUSUUU (GRIMACE)
むすー
YUURI-SENPAI, DO—
YOU CAN CALL ME RII-SAN.
RII-SAN, DO YOU HATE...
...DOGS?
WELL... I LIKE THEM...
...BUT IT WOULD PROBABLY BE BETTER NOT TO TALK ABOUT THEM IN FRONT OF YUKI.
DID...
...SOMETHING HAPPEN?

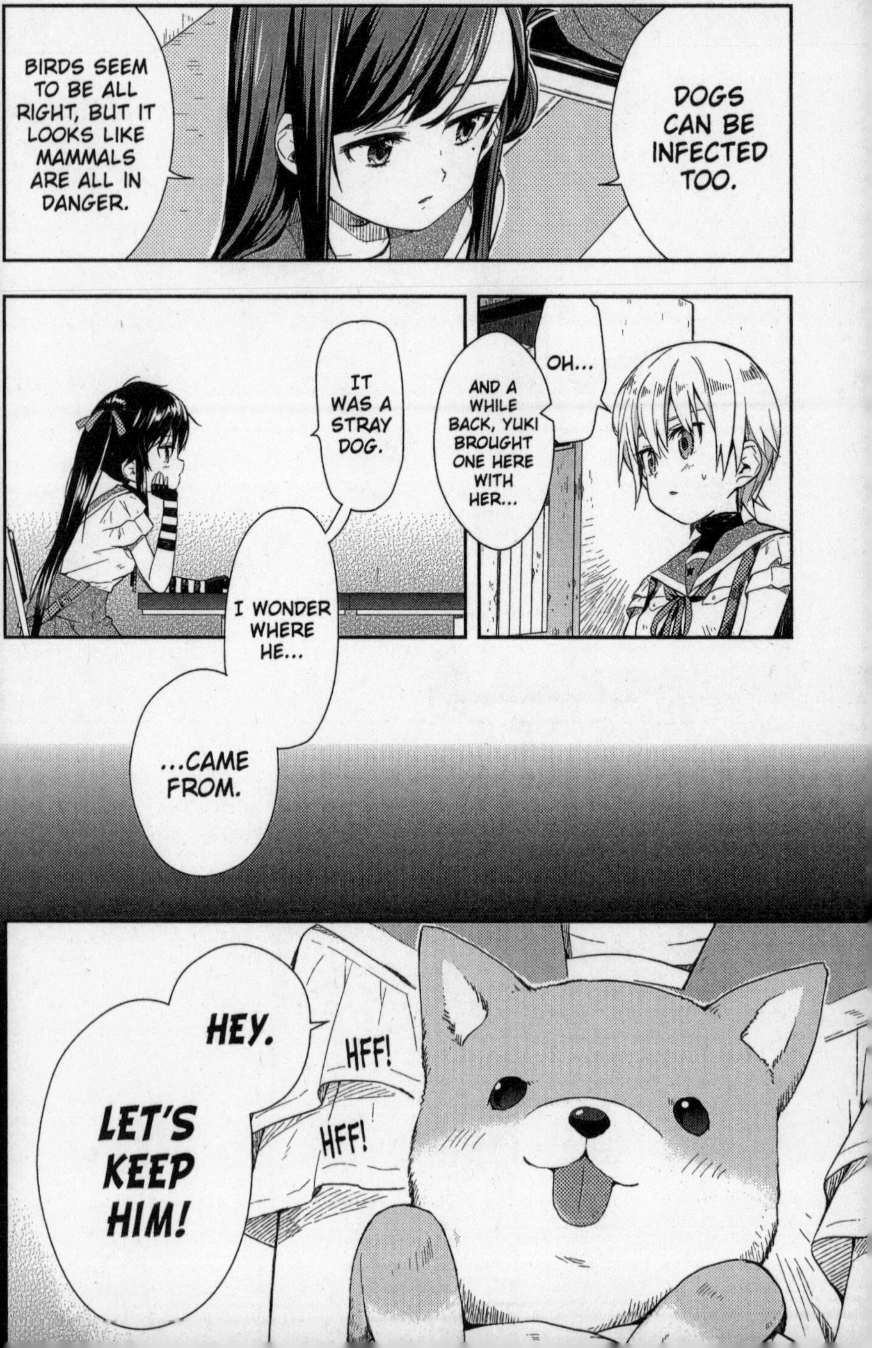
DOGS CAN BE INFECTED TOO.
BIRDS SEEM TO BE ALL RIGHT, BUT IT LOOKS LIKE MAMMALS ARE ALL IN DANGER.
OH...
AND A WHILE BACK, YUKI BROUGHT ONE HERE WITH HER...
IT WAS A STRAY DOG.
I WONDER WHERE HE...
...CAME FROM.
HEY.
HFF!
HFF!
LET'S KEEP HIM!

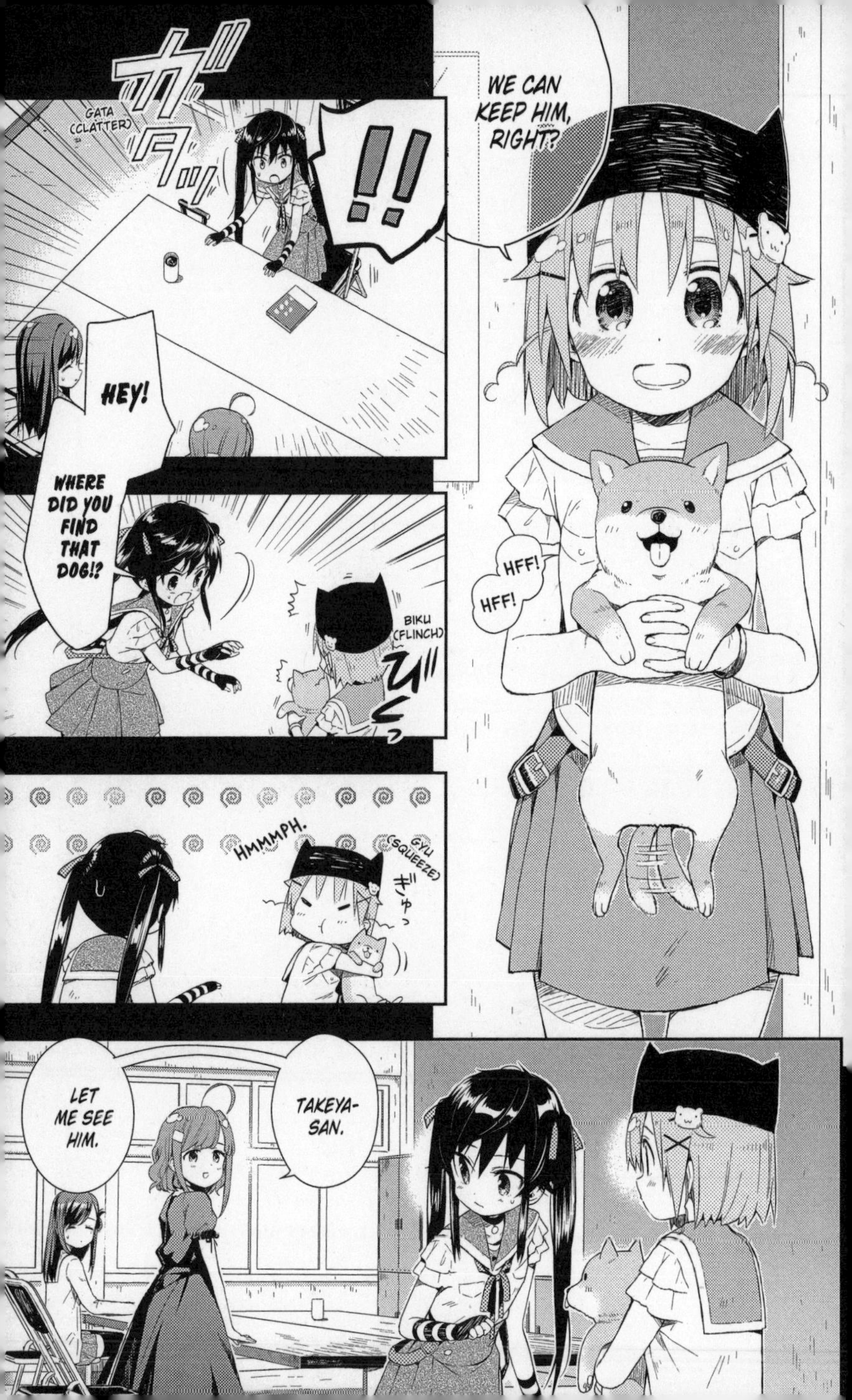
WE CAN KEEP HIM, RIGHT?
HFF!
HFF!
ガタッ
GATA (CLATTER)
!!
HEY!
WHERE DID YOU FIND THAT DOG!?
びくっ
BIKU (FLINCH)
GYU (SQUEEZE)
ぎゅっ
HMMMPH.
TAKEYA-SAN.
LET ME SEE HIM.

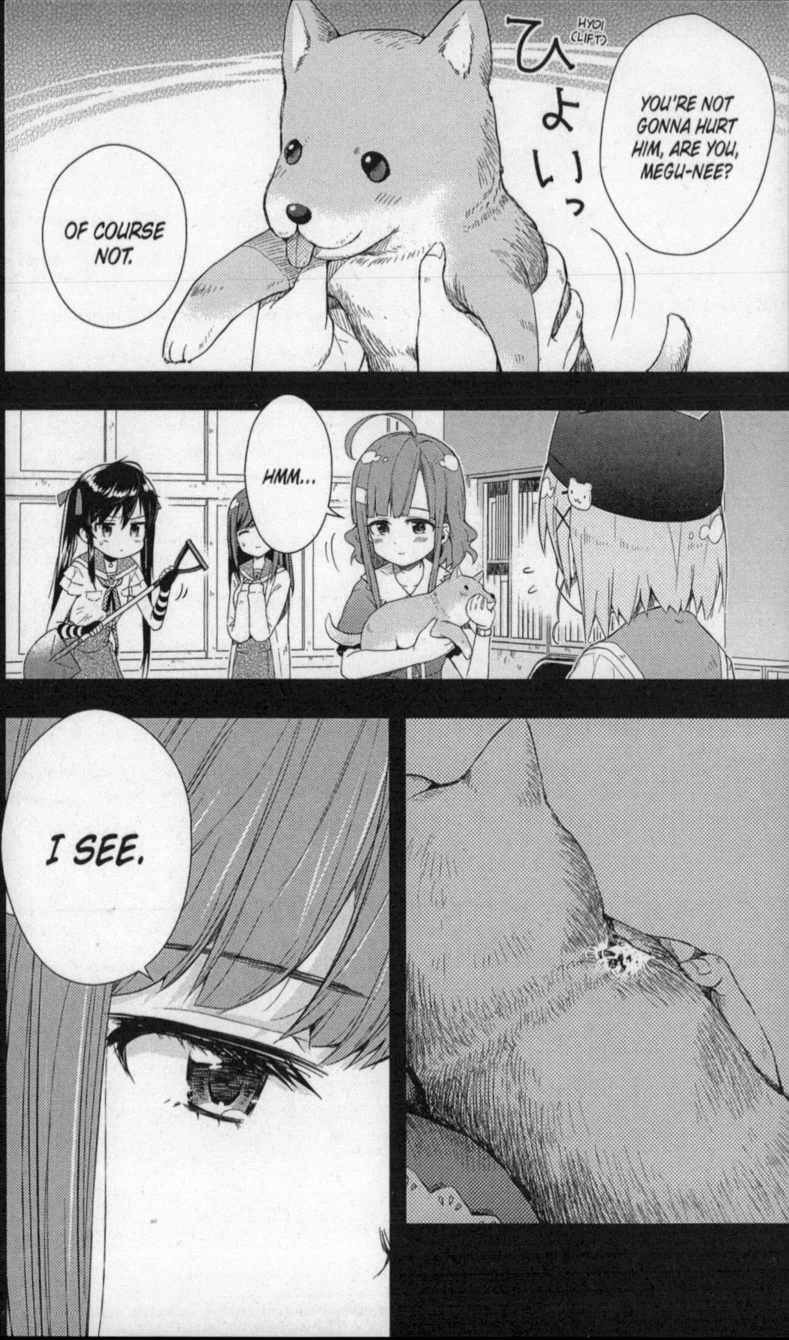

YOU'RE NOT GONNA HURT HIM, ARE YOU, MEGU-NEE?
ひょいっ
HYOI (LIFT)
OF COURSE NOT.
HMM...
I SEE.

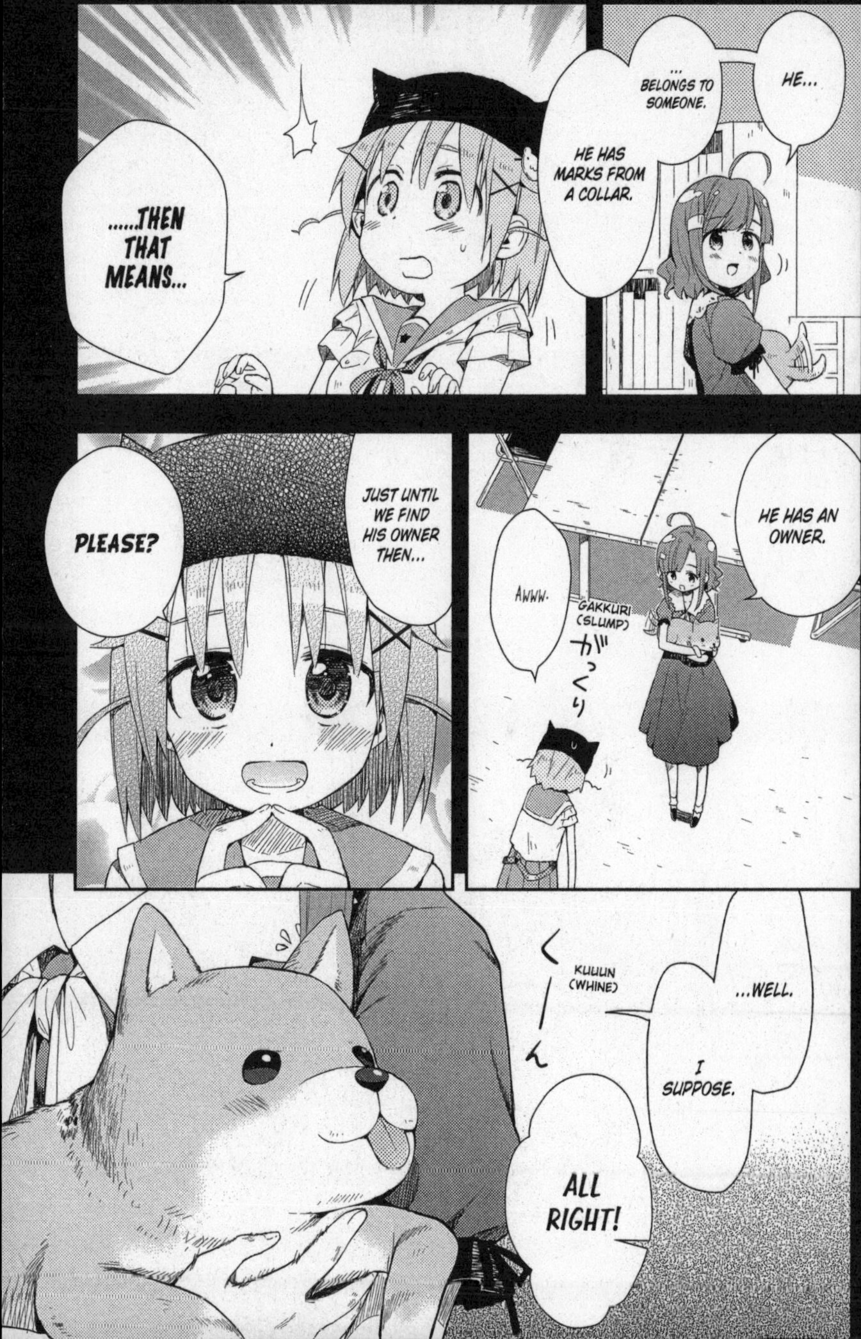
HE...
... BELONGS TO SOMEONE.
HE HAS MARKS FROM A COLLAR.
......THEN THAT MEANS...
HE HAS AN OWNER.
がっくり
GAKKURI (SLUMP)
AWWW.
JUST UNTIL WE FIND HIS OWNER THEN...
PLEASE?
...WELL.
I SUPPOSE.
くーん
KUUUN (WHINE)
ALL RIGHT!

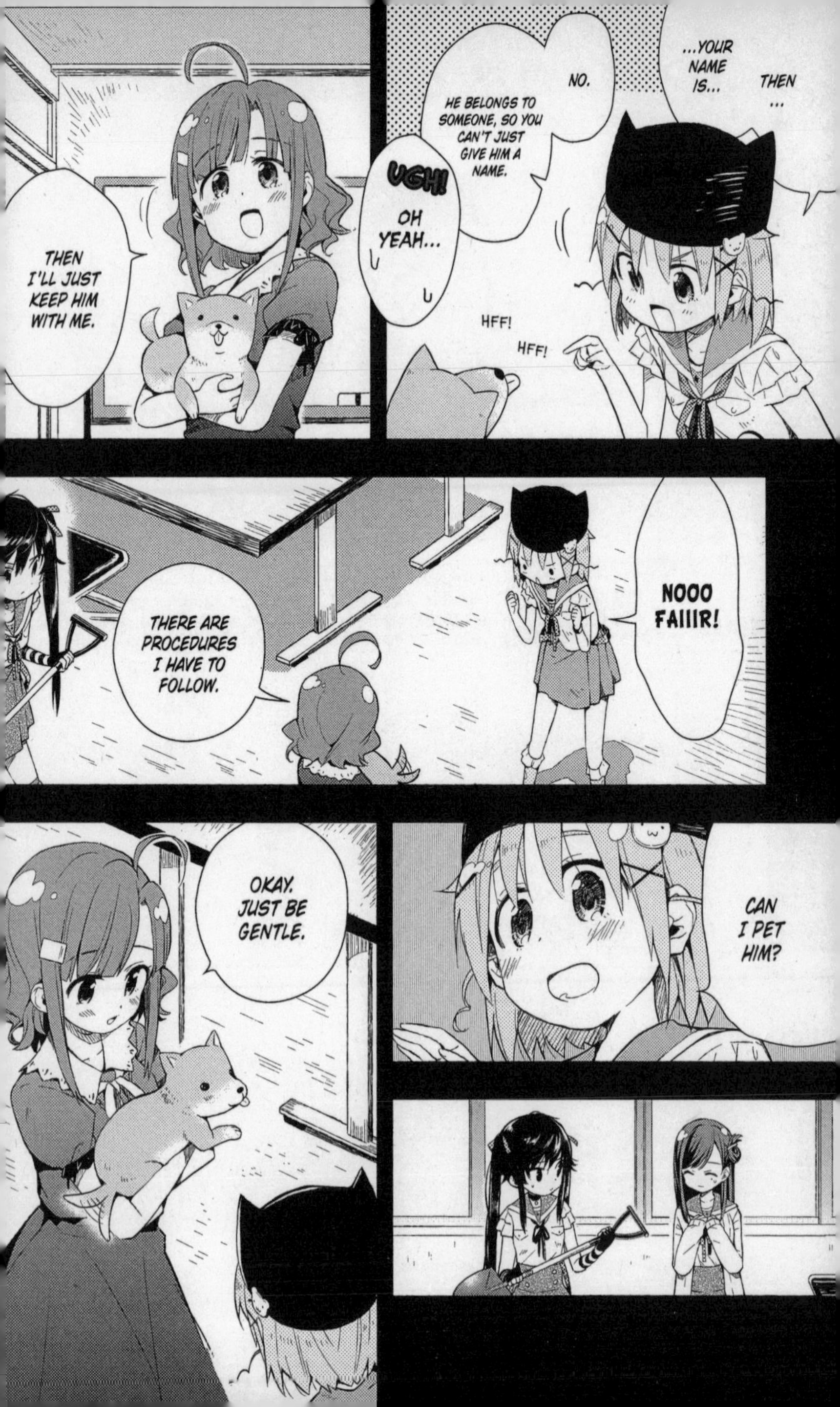
THEN ...
...YOUR NAME IS...
NO.
HE BELONGS TO SOMEONE, SO YOU CAN'T JUST GIVE HIM A NAME.
UGH!
OH YEAH...
HFF!
HFF!
THEN I'LL JUST KEEP HIM WITH ME.
NOOO FAIIIR!
THERE ARE PROCEDURES I HAVE TO FOLLOW.
CAN I PET HIM?
OKAY. JUST BE GENTLE.

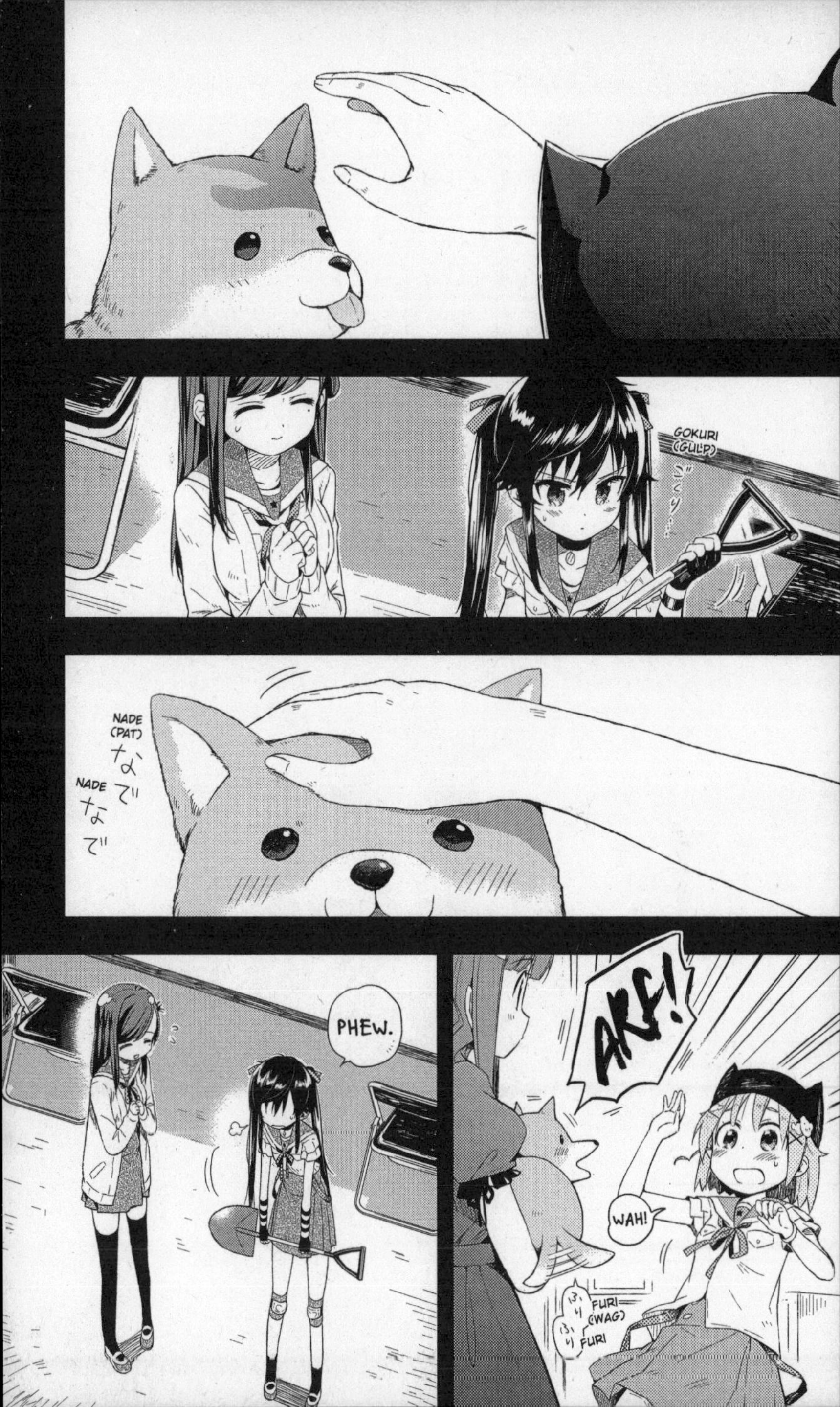
GOKURI (GULP)
ごくり…
NADE (PAT)
なで
NADE
なで
ARF!
WAH!
FURI (WAG)
ふり
ふり
FURI
PHEW.

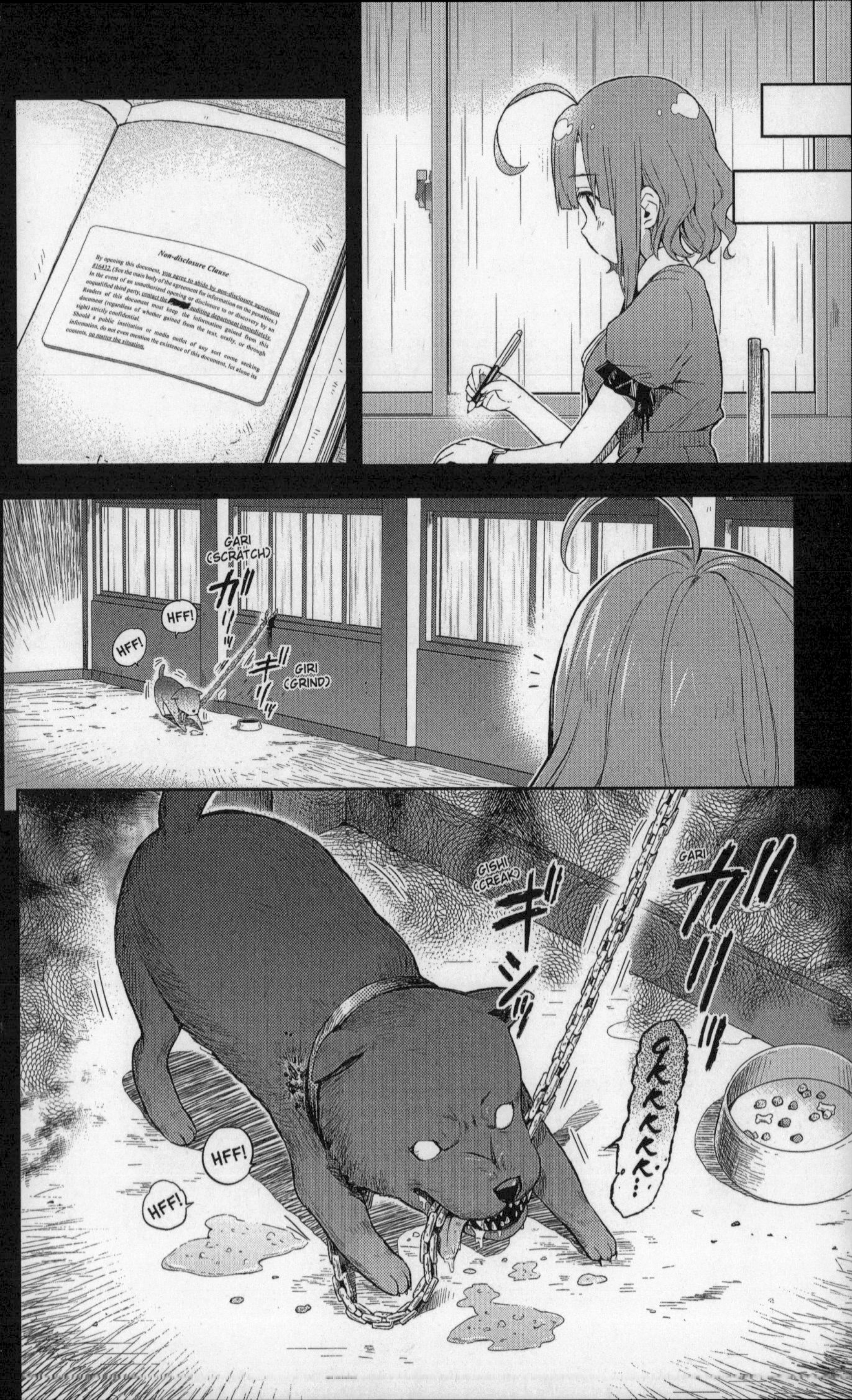
Non-disclosure Clause
By opening this document, you agree to abide by non-disclosure agreement #16432. (See the main body of the agreement for information on the penalties.)
In the event of an unauthorized opening or disclosure to or discovery by an unqualified third party, contact the [redacted] auditing department immediately.
Readers of this document must keep the information gained from this document (regardless of whether gained from the text, orally, or through sight) strictly confidential.
Should a public institution or media outlet of any sort come seeking information, do not even mention the existence of this document, let alone its contents, no matter the situation.
GIRI (GRIND)
GARI (SCRATCH)
HFF!
HFF!
GARI
GISHI (CREAK)
HFF!
HFF!

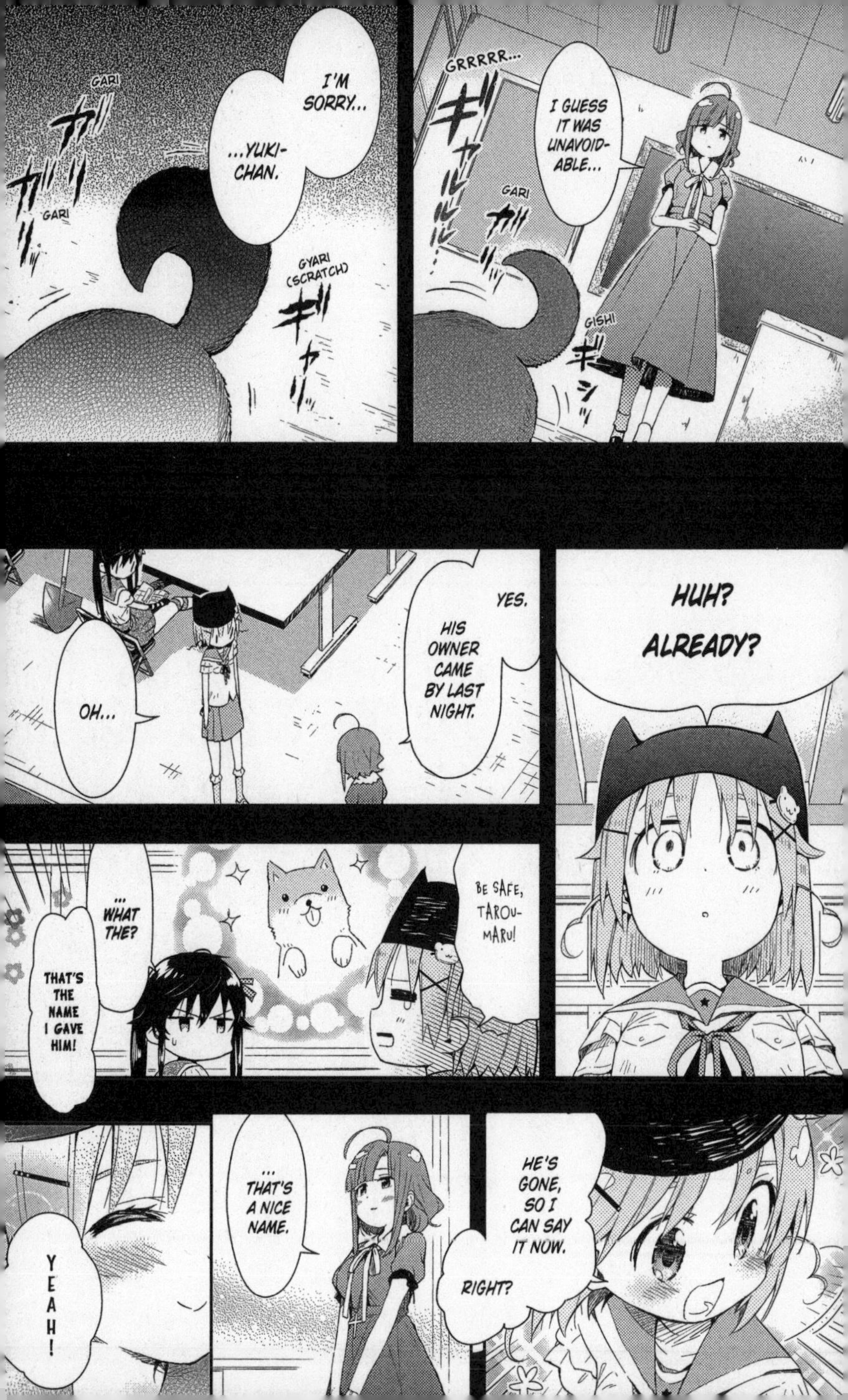
GRRRRR...
I GUESS IT WAS UNAVOIDABLE...
GARI
GISHI
I'M SORRY... ...YUKI-CHAN.
GARI
GARI
GYARI (SCRATCH)
HUH? ALREADY?
YES. HIS OWNER CAME BY LAST NIGHT.
OH...
BE SAFE, TAROU-MARU!
... WHAT THE?
THAT'S THE NAME I GAVE HIM!
HE'S GONE, SO I CAN SAY IT NOW.
RIGHT?
... THAT'S A NICE NAME.
YEAH!

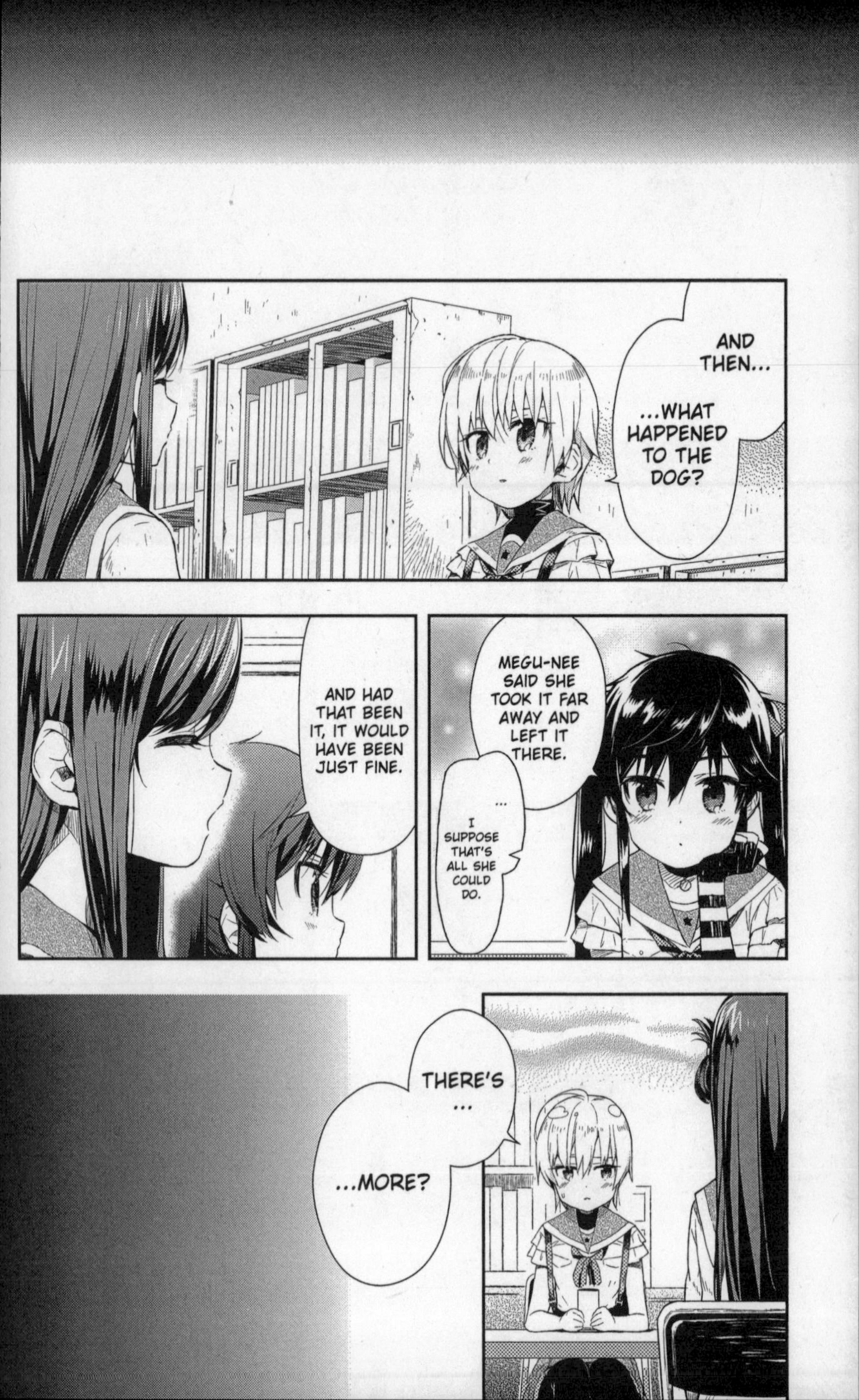
AND THEN...
...WHAT HAPPENED TO THE DOG?
MEGU-NEE SAID SHE TOOK IT FAR AWAY AND LEFT IT THERE.
...
I SUPPOSE THAT'S ALL SHE COULD DO.
AND HAD THAT BEEN IT, IT WOULD HAVE BEEN JUST FINE.
THERE'S ...
...MORE?

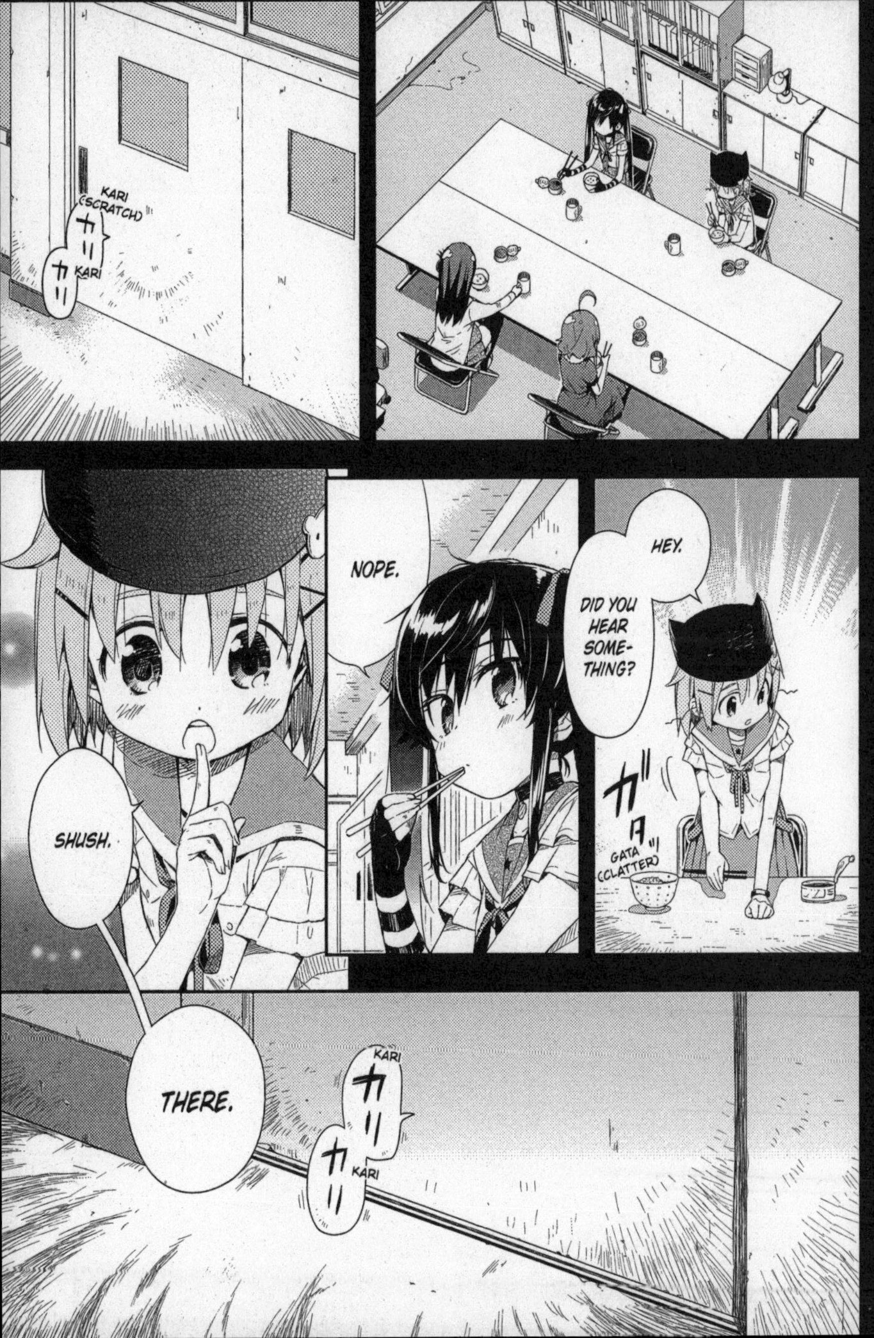

KARI (SCRATCH)
カリ
KARI
カリ
HEY.
DID YOU HEAR SOMETHING?
ガタッ
GATA (CLATTER)
NOPE.
SHUSH.
THERE.
KARI
カリ
KARI
カリ

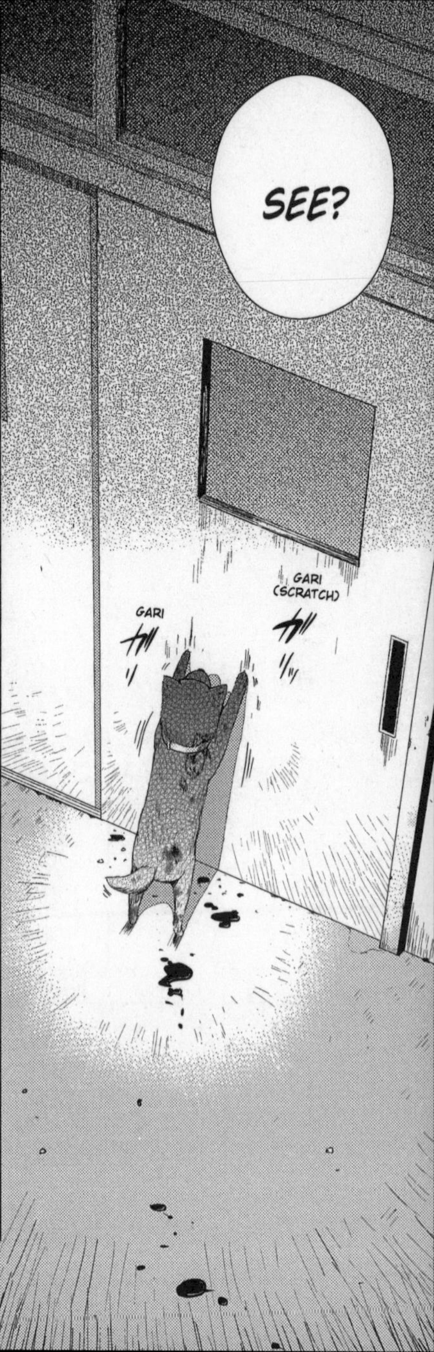
SEE?
GARI (SCRATCH)
GARI

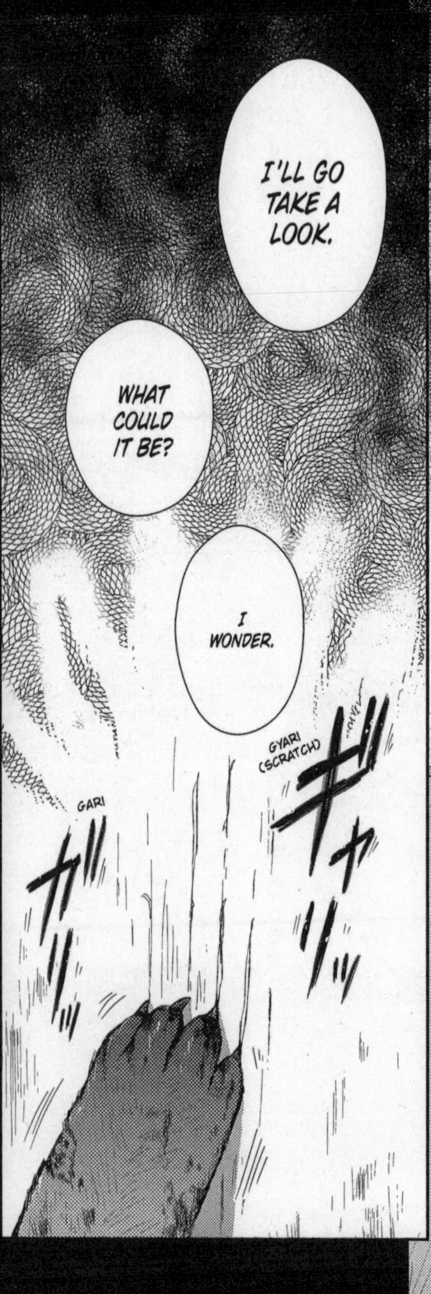
I'LL GO TAKE A LOOK.
WHAT COULD IT BE?
I WONDER.
GYARI (SCRATCH)
GARI

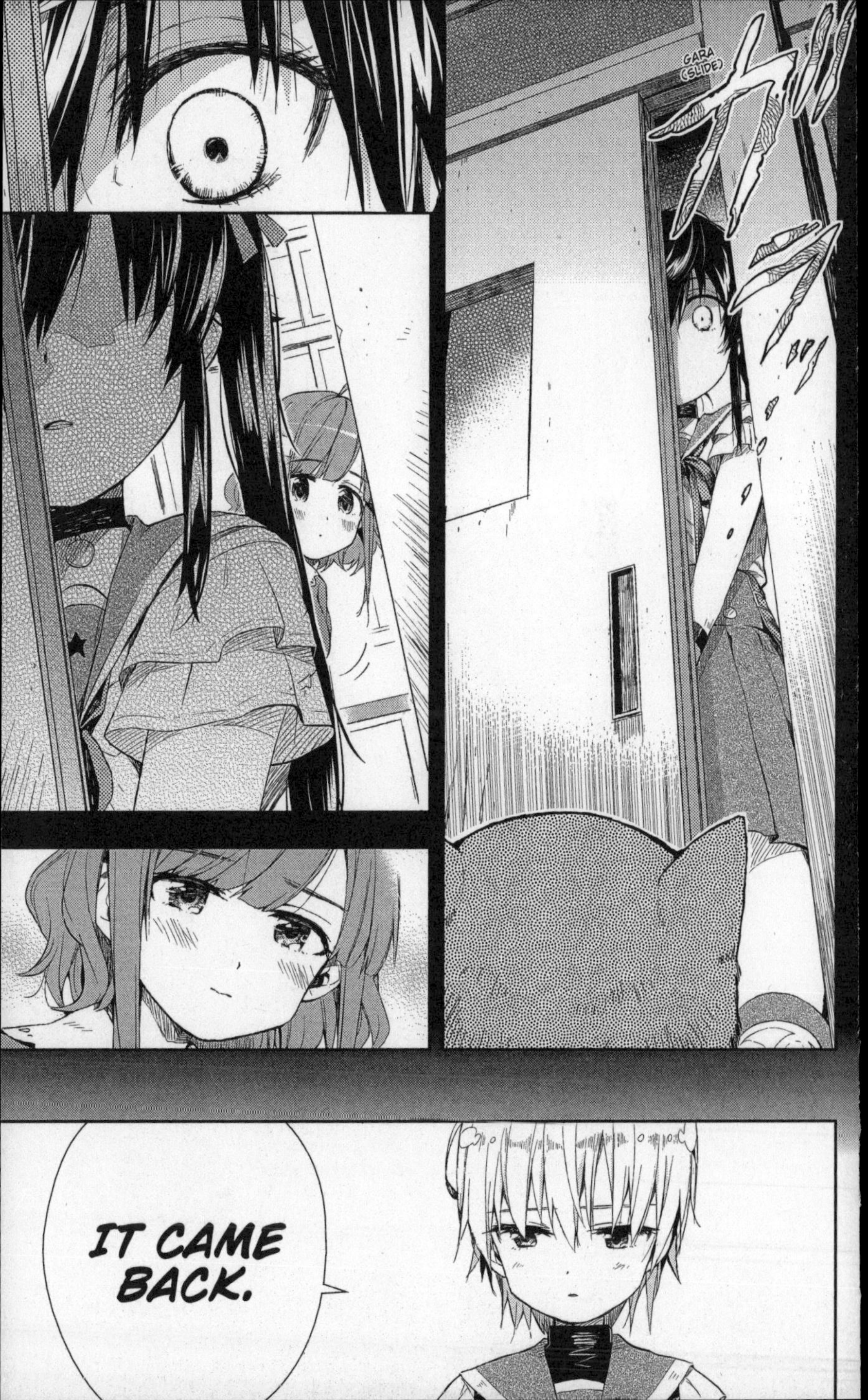
GARA (SLIDE)
IT CAME BACK.

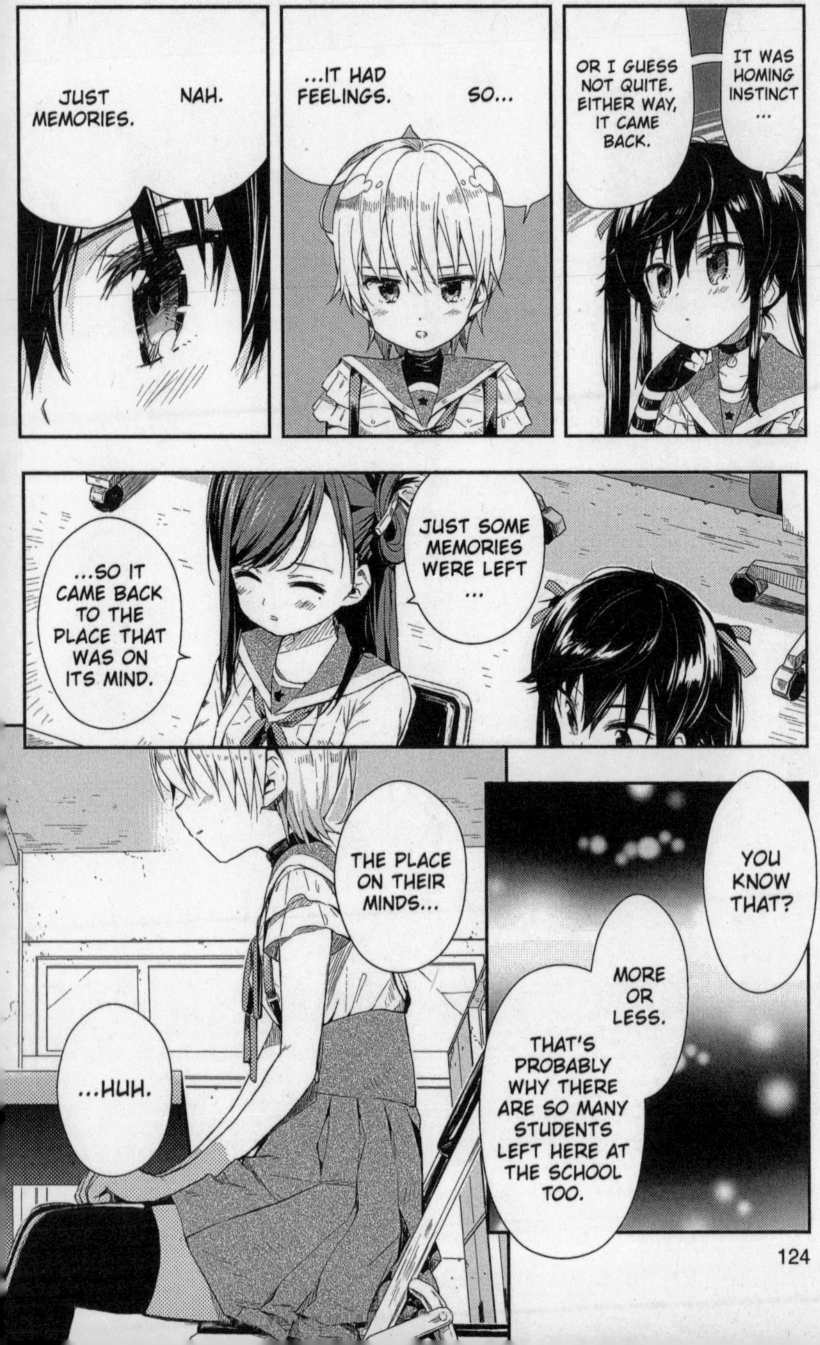
IT WAS HOMING INSTINCT ...
OR I GUESS NOT QUITE. EITHER WAY, IT CAME BACK.
SO...
...IT HAD FEELINGS.
NAH.
JUST MEMORIES.
JUST SOME MEMORIES WERE LEFT ...
...SO IT CAME BACK TO THE PLACE THAT WAS ON ITS MIND.
YOU KNOW THAT?
MORE OR LESS.
THAT'S PROBABLY WHY THERE ARE SO MANY STUDENTS LEFT HERE AT THE SCHOOL TOO.
THE PLACE ON THEIR MINDS...
...HUH.

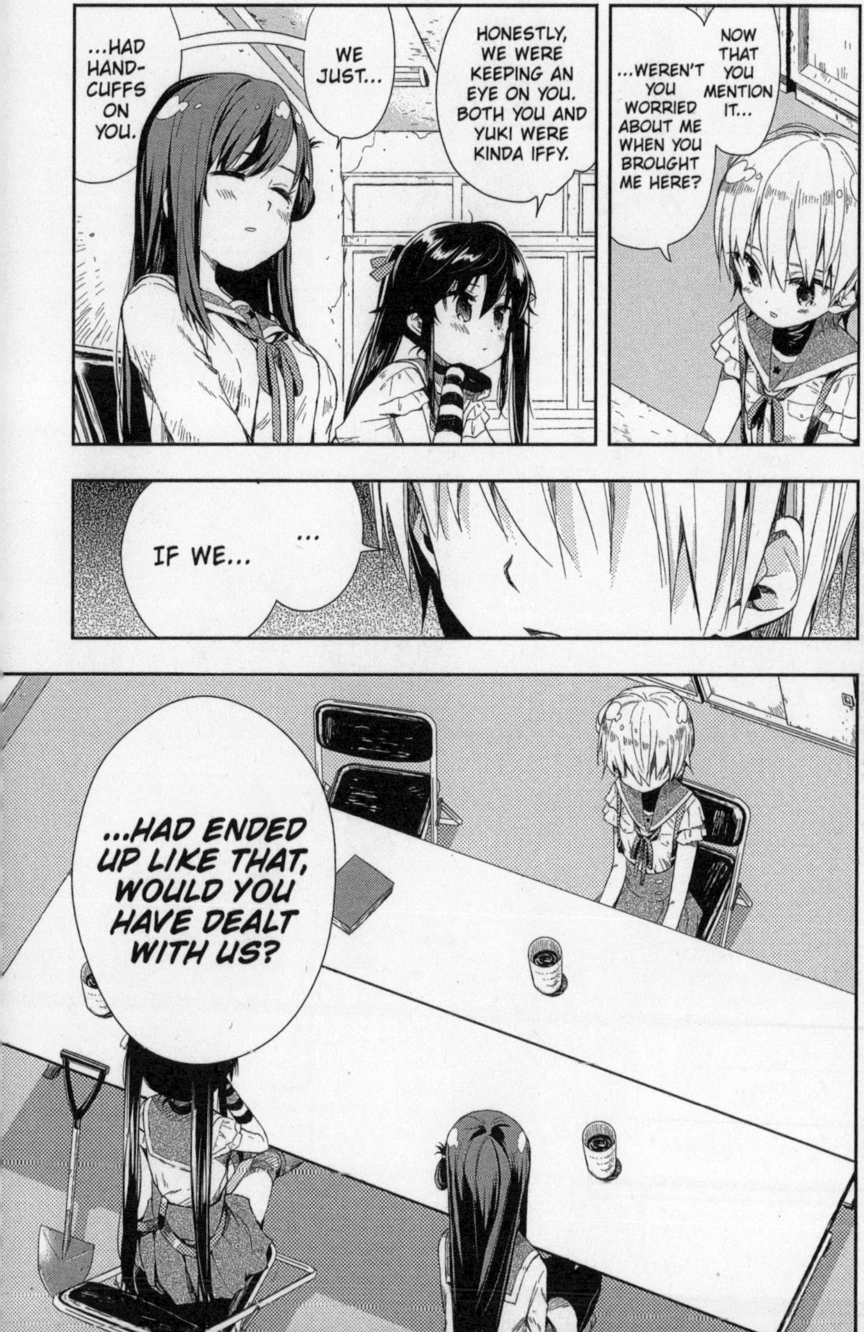
NOW THAT YOU MENTION IT...
...WEREN'T YOU WORRIED ABOUT ME WHEN YOU BROUGHT ME HERE?
HONESTLY, WE WERE KEEPING AN EYE ON YOU. BOTH YOU AND YUKI WERE KINDA IFFY.
WE JUST...
...HAD HAND-CUFFS ON YOU.
...
IF WE...
...HAD ENDED UP LIKE THAT, WOULD YOU HAVE DEALT WITH US?

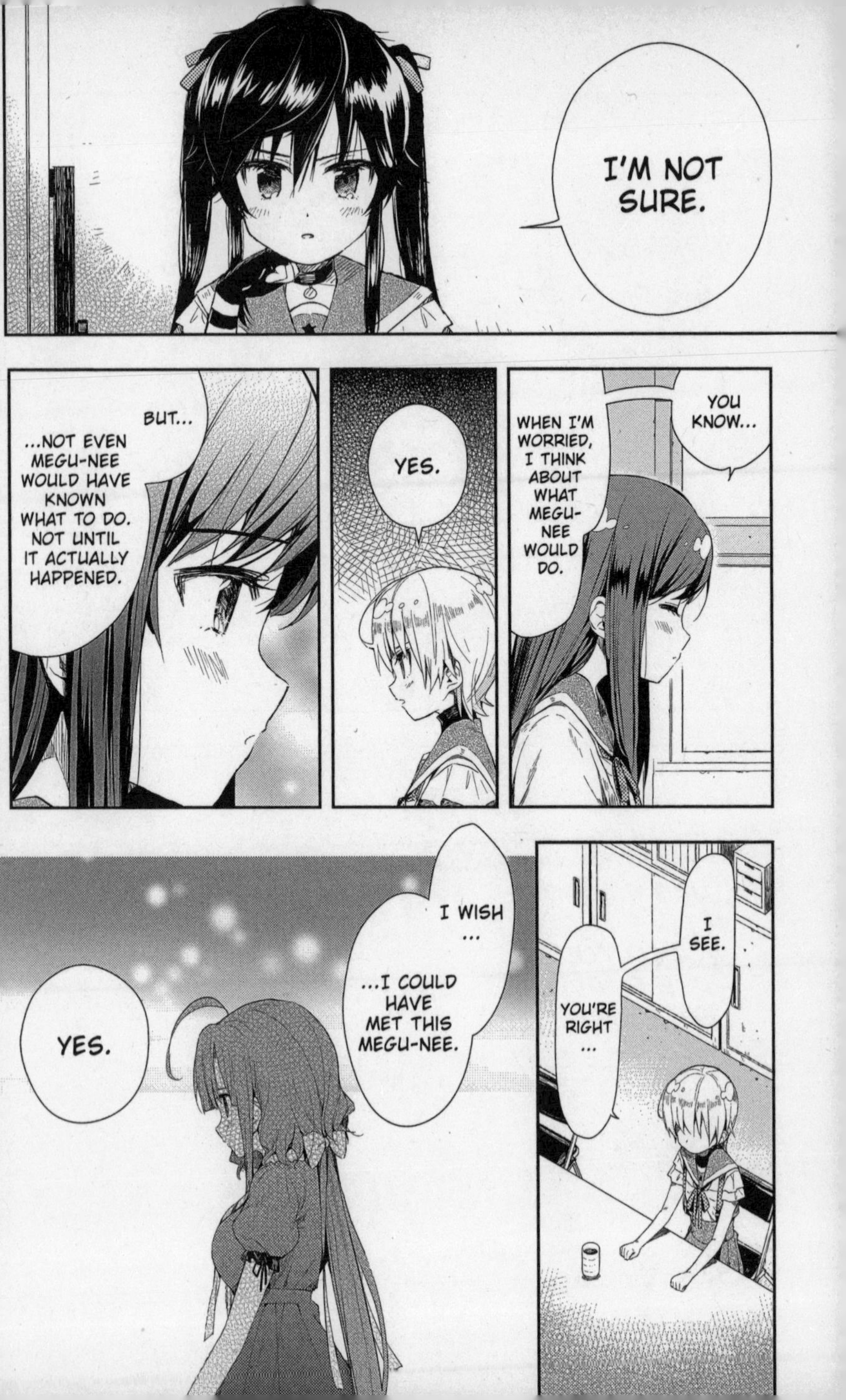
I'M NOT SURE.
YOU KNOW...
WHEN I'M WORRIED, I THINK ABOUT WHAT MEGU-NEE WOULD DO.
YES.
BUT...
...NOT EVEN MEGU-NEE WOULD HAVE KNOWN WHAT TO DO. NOT UNTIL IT ACTUALLY HAPPENED.
I SEE.
YOU'RE RIGHT...
I WISH...
...I COULD HAVE MET THIS MEGU-NEE.
YES.

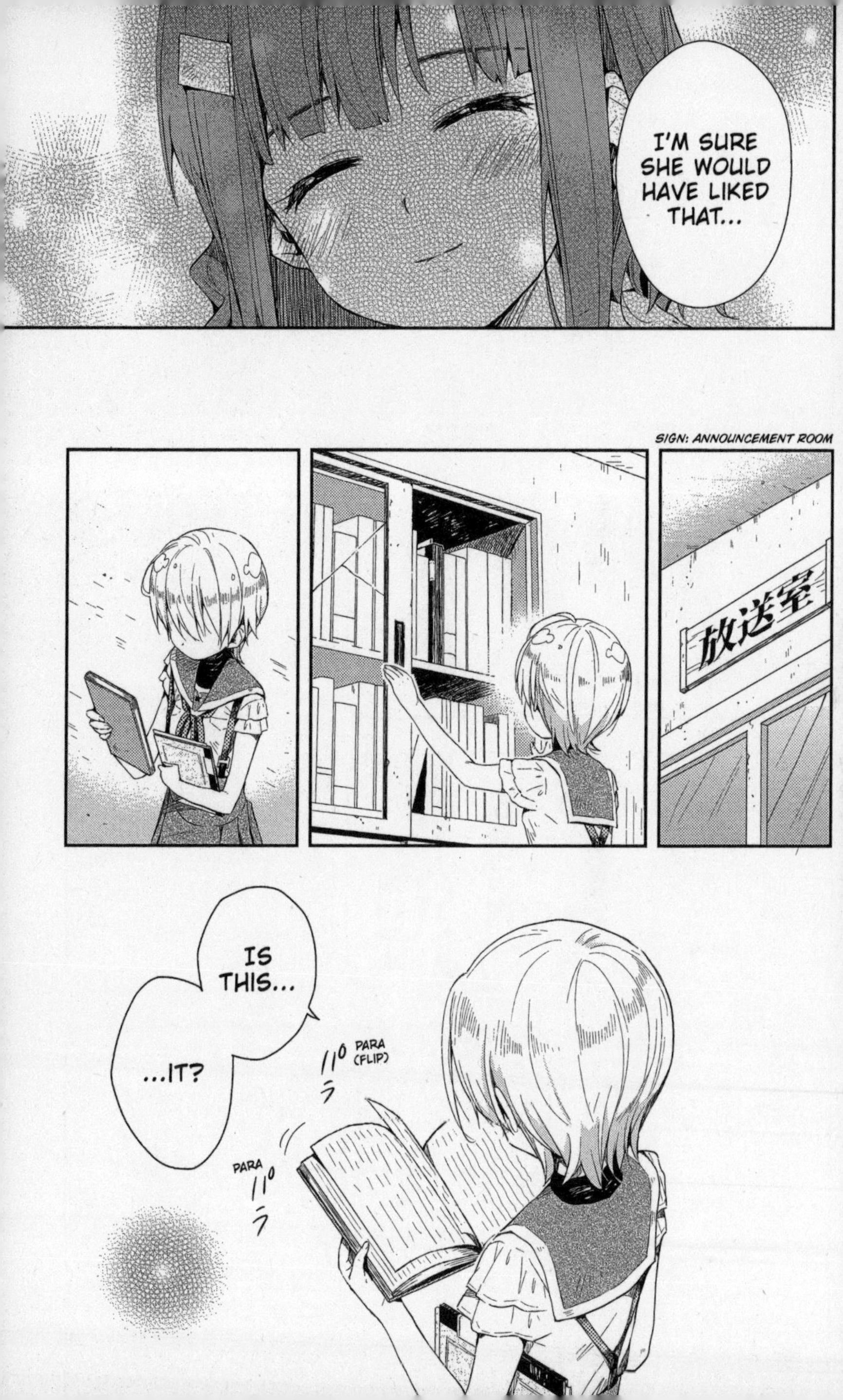
I'M SURE SHE WOULD HAVE LIKED THAT...
SIGN: ANNOUNCEMENT ROOM
放送室
IS THIS...
...IT?
PARA (FLIP)
PARA

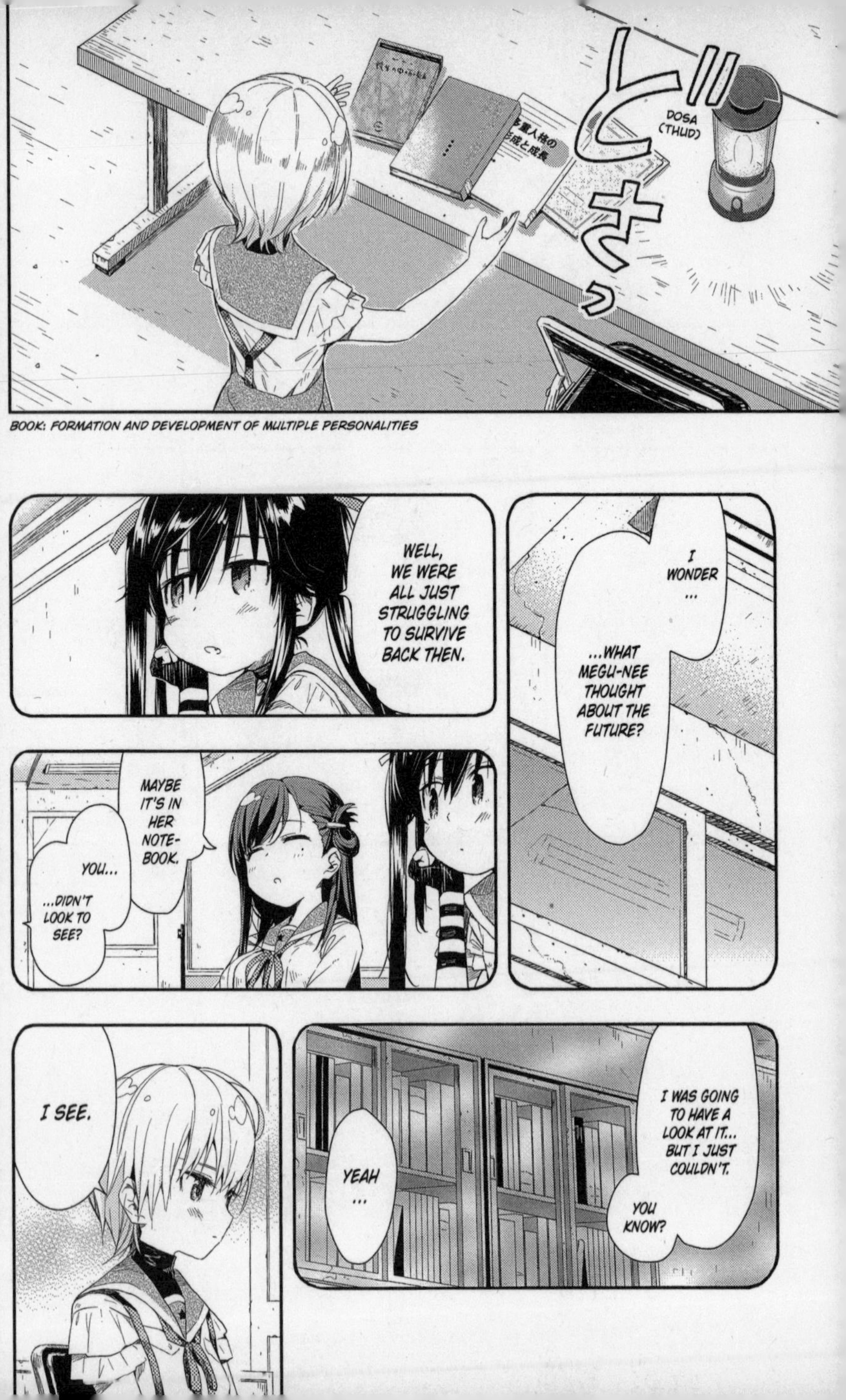
DOSA (THUD)
BOOK: FORMATION AND DEVELOPMENT OF MULTIPLE PERSONALITIES
I WONDER...
...WHAT MEGU-NEE THOUGHT ABOUT THE FUTURE?
WELL, WE WERE ALL JUST STRUGGLING TO SURVIVE BACK THEN.
MAYBE IT'S IN HER NOTEBOOK.
YOU...
...DIDN'T LOOK TO SEE?
I WAS GOING TO HAVE A LOOK AT IT... BUT I JUST COULDN'T.
YOU KNOW?
YEAH...
I SEE.

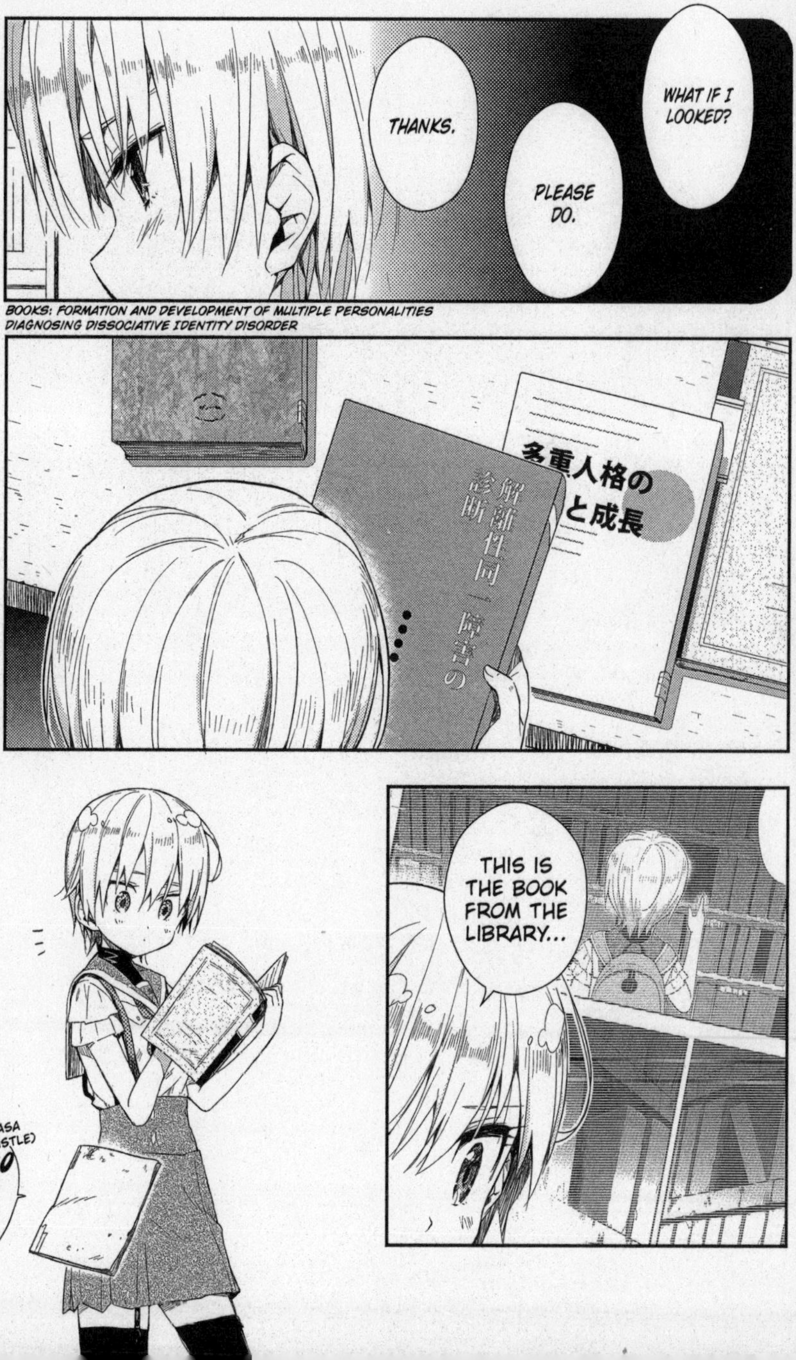
WHAT IF I LOOKED?
PLEASE DO.
THANKS.
BOOKS: FORMATION AND DEVELOPMENT OF MULTIPLE PERSONALITIES
DIAGNOSING DISSOCIATIVE IDENTITY DISORDER
多重人格の
と成長
解離性同一障害の
診断
....
THIS IS THE BOOK FROM THE LIBRARY...
PASA (RUSTLE)
パサッ

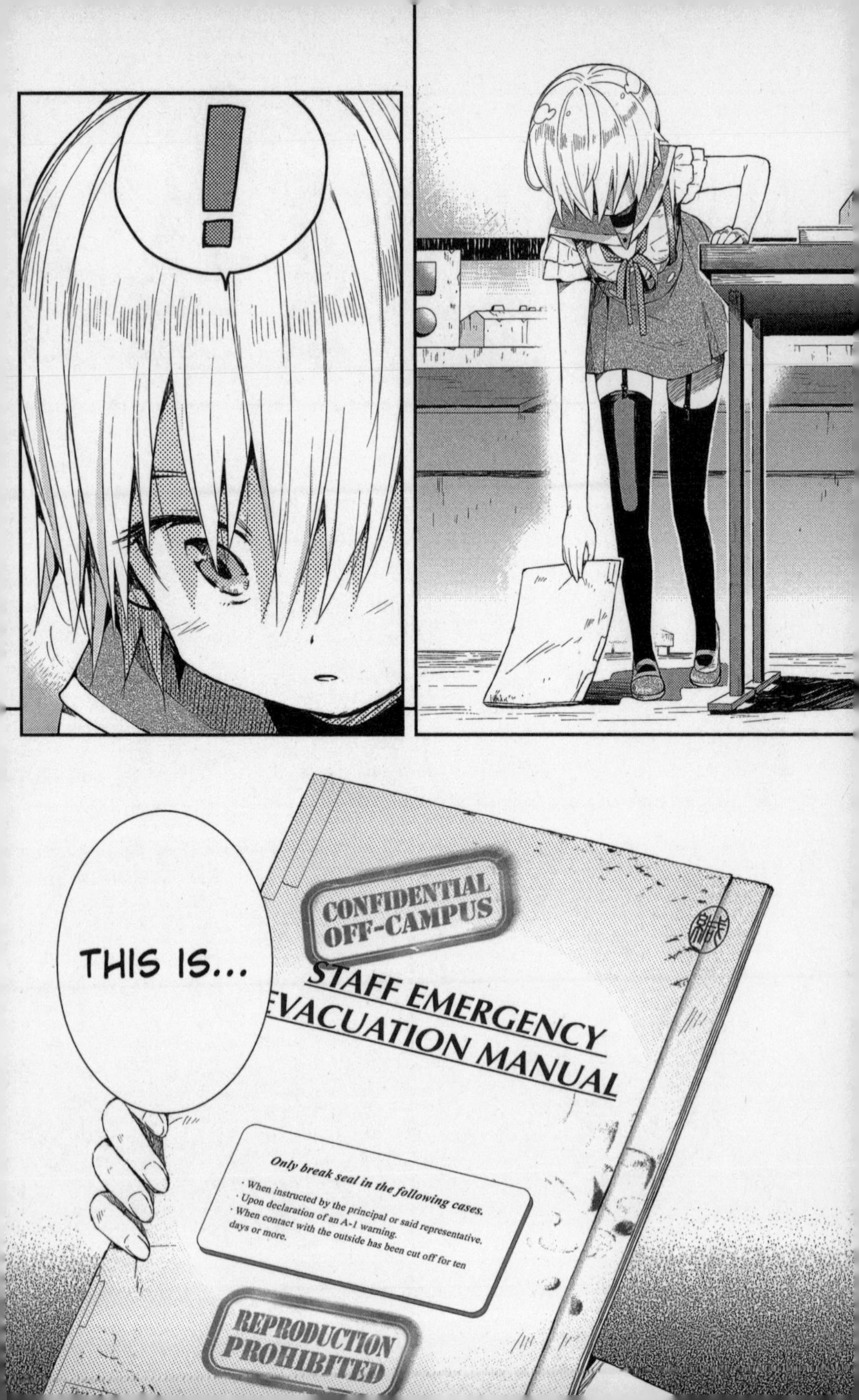
!
THIS IS...
CONFIDENTIAL OFF-CAMPUS
STAFF EMERGENCY EVACUATION MANUAL
Only break seal in the following cases.
· When instructed by the principal or said representative.
· Upon declaration of an A-1 warning.
· When contact with the outside has been cut off for ten days or more.
REPRODUCTION PROHIBITED

SCHOOL-LIVE! ❸

SADORU CHIBA
NORIMITSU KAIHOU
(NITROPLUS)

Translation: Leighann Harvey

Lettering: Alexis Eckerman

GAKKOU GURASHI! Vol. 3
©Nitroplus / Norimitsu Kaihou, Sadoru Chiba, Houbunsha. All rights reserved. First published in Japan in 2013 by HOUBUNSHA CO., LTD., Tokyo. English translation rights in United States, Canada, and United Kingdom arranged with HOUBUNSHA CO., LTD through Tuttle-Mori Agency, Inc., Tokyo.

Translation © 2016 by Hachette Book Group, Inc.

Yen Press
Hachette Book Group
1290 Avenue of the Americas, New York, NY 10104

www.HachetteBookGroup.com
www.YenPress.com

Yen Press is an imprint of Hachette Book Group, Inc. The Yen Press name and logo are trademarks of Hachette Book Group, Inc.

The publisher is not responsible for websites (or their content) that are not owned by the publisher.

Library of Congress Control Number: 2016931006

First Yen Press Edition: May 2016

ISBN: 978-0-316-30992-9

10 9 8 7 6 5 4 3 2 1

BVG

Printed in the United States of America

Translation Notes

Common Honorifics:
no honorific: Indicates familiarity or closeness; if used without permission or reason, addressing someone in this manner would constitute an insult.
-san: The Japanese equivalent of Mr./Mrs./Miss. If a situation calls for politeness, this is the fail-safe honorific.
-chan: An affectionate honorific indicating familiarity used mostly in reference to girls; also used in reference to cute persons or animals of either gender.
-senpai: A suffix used to address upperclassmen or more experienced coworkers.
-sensei: A respectful term for teachers, artists, or high-level professionals.
-nee: Honorific derived from onee-san/-sama ("big sister"). When used alone after a name, *-nee* can mean closeness.

Page 103
Mike: The Japanese word for calico cat.

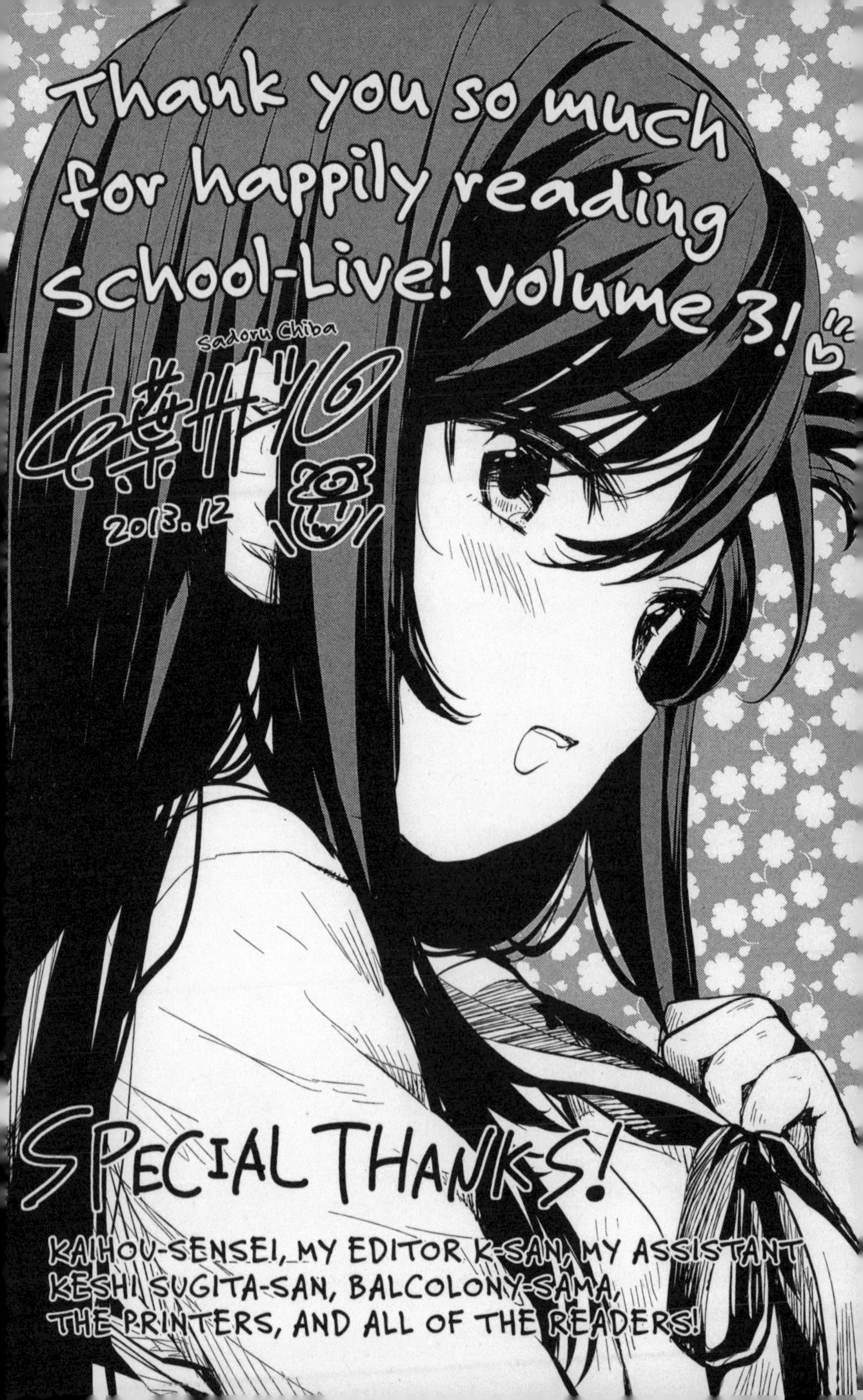
Thank you so much for happily reading School-Live! volume 3!♡
Sadoru Chiba
2013.12
SPECIAL THANKS!
KAIHOU-SENSEI, MY EDITOR K-SAN, MY ASSISTANT KESHI SUGITA-SAN, BALCOLONY-SAMA, THE PRINTERS, AND ALL OF THE READERS!

Introducing the new club member, Mii-kun.

Stuff like new members in a club, changing classes, or transfer students; when you're welcoming in a new person; or when you're joining a new group. These sorts of things can be rough, and you can end up butting heads over the slightest things.

It's wonderful when you can get everything settled properly when things like that happen.

But still, sometimes things just don't go right.

When that happens, it's best not to get too worked up and just look at it as the way things go. If things don't go well at school, I think it's best to just take a step back and focus on the outside world.

...Of course, this is assuming that the outside world is still all right.

Anyway, what do you think will become of the School Living Club now that Mii-kun is here? Do look forward to it next time in volume four.

Thank you.

Norimitsu Kaihou

Look forward to
the Sturm und
Drang of the
next volume!!

~Special Thanks~
Ryou Morise, Shouko Iwahori (creation of the school blueprint)
Itsuka Yamada (creation of the evacuation manual)

CONFIDENTIAL
OFF-CAMPUS

STAFF EMERGENCY EVACUATION MANUAL

Only break seal in the following cases.

- When instructed by the principal or said representative.
- Upon declaration of an A-1 warning.
- When contact with the outside has been cut off for ten days or more.

REPRODUCTION
PROHIBITED

Text 15-10286 Last Revision 10/1/[redacted]

Non-disclosure Clause

By opening this document, <u>you agree to abide by non-disclosure agreement #16432.</u> (See the main body of the agreement for information on the penalties.) In the event of an unauthorized opening or disclosure to or discovery by an unqualified third party, <u>contact the ████ auditing department immediately.</u> Readers of this document must keep the information gained from this document (regardless of whether gained from the text, orally, or through sight) strictly confidential.

Should a public institution or media outlet of any sort come seeking information, do not even mention the existence of this document, let alone its contents, <u>no matter the situation.</u>

1. Introduction

This document should be opened upon the declaration of an A-1 warning or when such conditions are suspected. (In other cases, see the stipulations included with the non-disclosure agreement and contact the ▓▓▓▓ auditing department immediately.)

This document covers methods of response in such an emergency situation.

In a unique situation such as this, decisions and actions must be made to fit the particular situation.

The many guaranteed freedoms and safeties of typical everyday life represent choices that are difficult to come by in a situation such as this, so keep in mind that typical common sense may lead to harm.

Many lives will depend on your ability to adapt to the situation and take appropriate action.

2. First Response

Start by contacting the authorities and waiting for a disposal team to arrive. However, the disposal team may take a while to arrive, and conditions may complicate the team's arrival.

It is important to secure and quarantine the area. After taking steps to protect yourself, secure all individuals present who have not been protected, not just the infected. You must not allow them to travel. After doing this, seal off the area completely.

You must adapt to the circumstances in order to secure and quarantine the area. The authorities in the area (such as police or teachers at the school) may be able to convince everyone. If this fails, you could consider using force or weapons, but this may also cause chaos and panic.

You should overlook the sacrifices caused by the use of force. Should you fail in quarantining the area, there is a good chance you could lose dozens of lives.

3. Responding to an Unexpected Situation

Confining the infection in the early stages is vital to dealing with the infection. Should you fail in this, the infection will multiply at a tremendous rate, and the situation could approach that of a pandemic. This could be the case if you have failed in the aforementioned confinement or if you have opened this document once the situation has already proceeded to that stage.

Even in such cases, securing and quarantining is still important. However, you must secure people and materials and quarantine anyone not infected.

You may be limited in the resources and people you can handle. Keep in mind the need to use force and be sure to secure sufficient materials.

The securing of people must be done with strict selection and a general policy of quarantine. You would be best to keep in mind the use of force when doing this as well.

4. Finally

Throughout the ages, there have been various ideas of morality, but every set of morals has shared one idea: that human life should be prioritized above all else. Therefore, you must not balk at the loss of a few lives when faced with a threat to many.

In the event that this booklet has been opened, the spirit of tolerance and kindness is no longer a virtue.

Prepare yourself.

The weight of thousands or millions of lives rests on your shoulders.

Varieties and Details of Infection

An important part of dealing with weapons is doing the required amount of damage to the required area. Biological weapons are no exception to this rule.

When used on a wide scale on the battlefield, the main aim is to lock down manpower through use of the outbreak. In such cases, increasing the number of individuals requiring care is to be desired. In other words, the vector must be designed to have a high infection rate and low mortality rate.

Conversely, when used to destroy on a small scale, a high mortality rate with a low infection rate to avoid the proliferation of victims is to be desired.

Paying close attention to the differences in these varieties of infection should allow for calm, effective action in the event of an emergency.

2. Exceptions

The more infectious strain has a low mortality rate, and the less lethal strain has a high infection rate.

These are the desired specifications of the completed products, but should strains still in development escape, this will not necessarily be the case. Also, should the product be allowed to multiply on a large scale, mutation may occur and cause the product to take on different qualities from its original state.

In light of this possibility, care must be taken when dealing with the product.

3. Categories

The following are the current research categories as of [redacted] of [redacted] These are broad classifications and may change with time.

Category α:

Wide scale infectious agent. Based off the [redacted] bacterium, this strain is particularly infectious and has unusually strong routes of infection. General symptoms include fever, sweating, and nausea.

The incubation period is 3-6 days. Routes of infection include contact, droplet, and blood borne infections.

The mortality rate is low, but without proper medical treatment, after effects such as death due to emaciation may occur.

Given the length of the incubation period, a quarantine period of ten days should be imposed.

After taking precautions to avoid infection (preferably by wearing a hazmat suit), the first-aid kit marked α should be used.

Category β:

Lethal infectious agent. Based off the [redacted] virus, this strain is particularly resistant to existing vaccines. General symptoms include vomiting, diarrhea, vomiting blood, and bleeding. The infection is blood borne.

The incubation period is approximately 2 hours. The mortality rate is more or less 100%.

Individuals exposed to Category β strains should be avoided. The virus in the blood will expire approximately seven hours after death.

Category Ω:

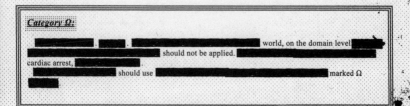

[redacted]. [redacted]. [redacted] world, on the domain level [redacted] should not be applied. [redacted] cardiac arrest, [redacted].

[redacted] should use [redacted] marked Ω [redacted].

School Map 1st Floor (left) Basement 1 (bottom right) Basement 2 (top right)

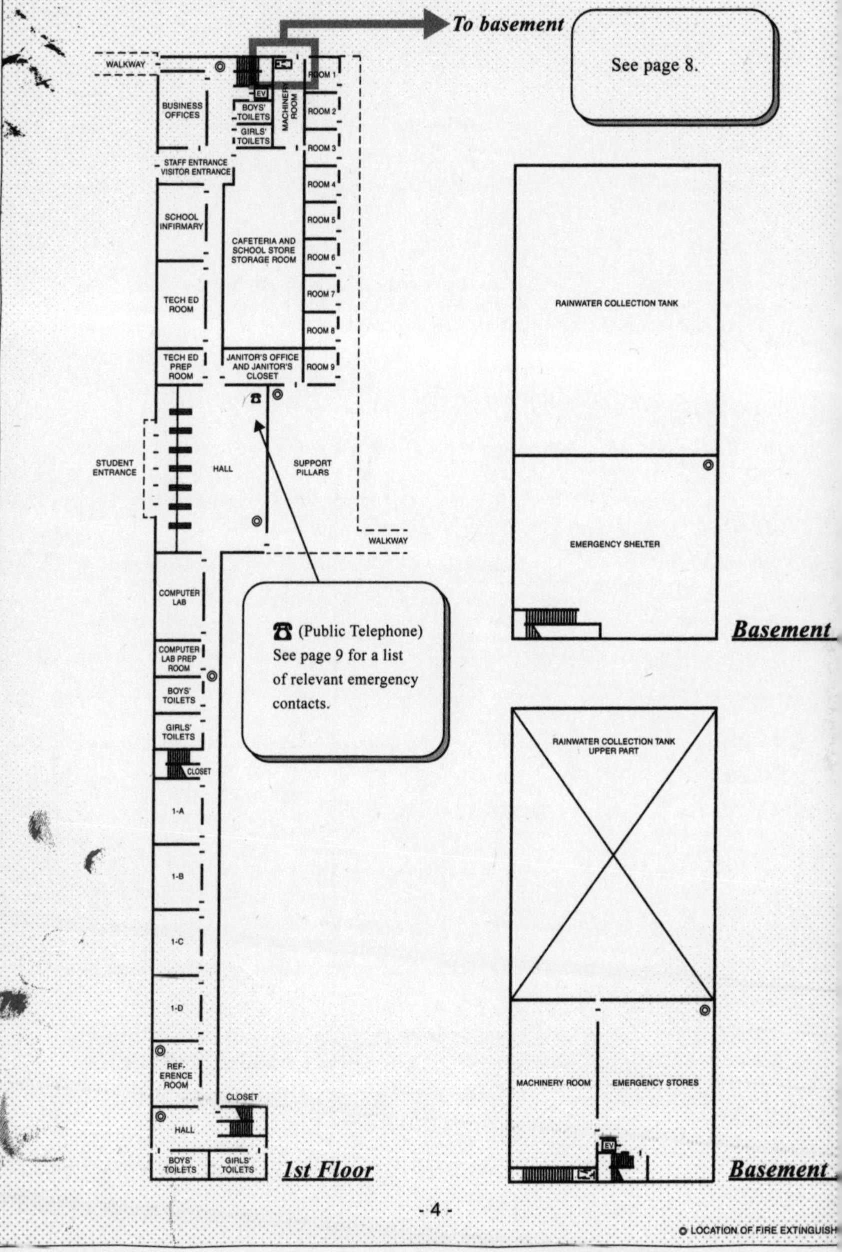

To basement
See page 8.
WALKWAY
EV
ROOM 1
BUSINESS OFFICES
BOYS' TOILETS
MACHINERY ROOM
ROOM 2
GIRLS' TOILETS
ROOM 3
STAFF ENTRANCE VISITOR ENTRANCE
ROOM 4
SCHOOL INFIRMARY
ROOM 5
CAFETERIA AND SCHOOL STORE STORAGE ROOM
ROOM 6
TECH ED ROOM
ROOM 7
ROOM 8
TECH ED PREP ROOM
JANITOR'S OFFICE AND JANITOR'S CLOSET
ROOM 9
STUDENT ENTRANCE
HALL
SUPPORT PILLARS
WALKWAY
COMPUTER LAB
(Public Telephone)
See page 9 for a list of relevant emergency contacts.
COMPUTER LAB PREP ROOM
BOYS' TOILETS
GIRLS' TOILETS
CLOSET
1-A
1-B
1-C
1-D
REF-ERENCE ROOM
CLOSET
HALL
BOYS' TOILETS
GIRLS' TOILETS
1st Floor
RAINWATER COLLECTION TANK
EMERGENCY SHELTER
Basement
RAINWATER COLLECTION TANK UPPER PART
MACHINERY ROOM
EMERGENCY STORES
EV
Basement
LOCATION OF FIRE EXTINGUISH

School Map 2nd Floor

GIRLS' TOILETS
BOYS' TOILETS
HALL
REF-ERENCE ROOM
3-D
3-C
3-B
3-A
GIRLS' TOILETS
BOYS' TOILETS
ART PREP ROOM
ART ROOM
SEWING PREP ROOM
HOME EC ROOM (SEWING)
SCHOOL STORE
LIBRARIAN'S OFFICE
LIBRARY
HOME EC ROOM (COOKING) AND SCHOOL CAFETERIA
W C
TRASH
KITCHEN BREAK ROOM (KITCHEN)
GIRLS' TOILETS
BOYS' TOILETS
SCHOOL STORE BACK YARD
EV

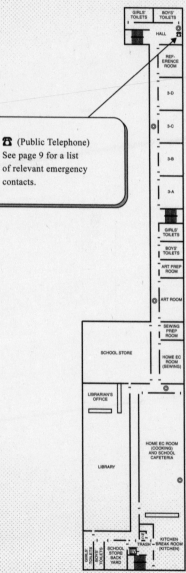

☎ (Public Telephone)
See page 9 for a list of relevant emergency contacts.

2nd Floor

◎ LOCATION OF FIRE EXTINGUISHERS

School Map 3rd Floor

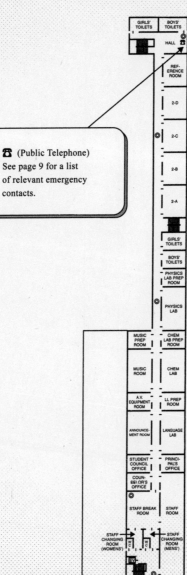

GIRLS' TOILETS
BOYS' TOILETS
HALL
REF-ERENCE ROOM
2-D
2-C
2-B
2-A
(Public Telephone)
See page 9 for a list of relevant emergency contacts.
GIRLS' TOILETS
BOYS' TOILETS
PHYSICS LAB PREP ROOM
PHYSICS LAB
MUSIC PREP ROOM
CHEM LAB PREP ROOM
MUSIC ROOM
CHEM LAB
A.V. EQUIPMENT ROOM
LL PREP ROOM
ANNOUNCE-MENT ROOM
LANGUAGE LAB
STUDENT COUNCIL OFFICE
PRINCI-PAL'S OFFICE
COUN-SELOR'S OFFICE
STAFF BREAK ROOM
STAFF ROOM
STAFF CHANGING ROOM (WOMENS')
WC
WC
STAFF CHANGING ROOM (MENS')
EV
3rd Floor

◎ LOCATION OF FIRE EXTINGUISHE

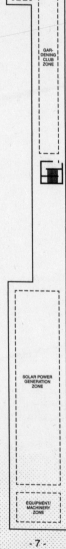

EQUIP-
MENT/
MACHIN-
ERY
ZONE

GAR-
DENING
CLUB
ZONE

SOLAR POWER
GENERATION
ZONE

EQUIPMENT/
MACHINERY
ZONE

Roof

○ LOCATION OF FIRE EXTINGUISHERS.

About this school's protective facilities

1. Basement

The first and second basements serve as the emergency shelter for this school. In the event of an emergency, use this area as a base.

. . . .

2. Supplies

Designed to support up to fifteen people. Stores contain food to last one month. Between power generation from the solar cells and the water purification system, it is possible to have unlimited use of water and power.

. . . .

3. Emergency Supplies

Stores include bandages, antipyretics, various antibiotics, and an emergency infection treatment set. Each set contains enough medicine to treat three people.

. . . .

4. Entrance

Entry is possible through the shutter in the back of the first floor storeroom.

The key to the electronic lock is the master code in the possession of the person in charge. It is also possible to enter the phone number of the school's representative (eight digits without the area code) in reverse order. It can be reset from the inside; however, the master code will take precedence over all other settings.

In case of a power outage, the shutter can be unlocked via a panel to the side and raised or lowered by hand. (The key is in the possession of the person in charge.)

Emergency Contacts

Randall Corporation Megurigaoka Branch

Phone: [redacted]-[redacted]-[redacted] (direct line)
E-mail: emergency@randall.[redacted].co.jp

Randall Corporation Main Headquarters

Phone: [redacted]-[redacted]-[redacted] (direct line)
E-mail: emergency[redacted]com

List of Locations

Megurigaoka Academy Private High School

Address: [redacted]
Phone: [redacted]-[redacted]-[redacted]

St. Isidore University

Address: [redacted]
Phone: [redacted]-[redacted]-[redacted]

[redacted] ***Garrison***

Address: [redacted]
Phone: [redacted]-[redacted]-[redacted]

[redacted] ***Air Base***

Address: [redacted]
Phone: [redacted]-[redacted]-[redacted]

[redacted] ***Central Hospital***

Address: [redacted]
Phone: [redacted]-[redacted]-[redacted]

[redacted]

SCHOOL-LIVE!

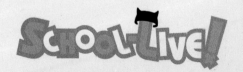

CONFIDENTIAL
OFF-CAMPUS

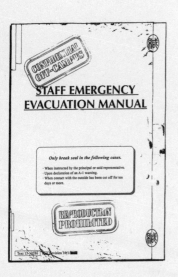

STAFF EMERGENCY
EVACUATION MANUAL

Only break seal in the following cases.

- When instructed by the principal or said representative.
- Upon declaration of an A-1 warning.
- When contact with the outside has been cut off for ten days or more.

REPRODUCTION
PROHIBITED

Text 15-10286 Revision 10/1/[redacted]

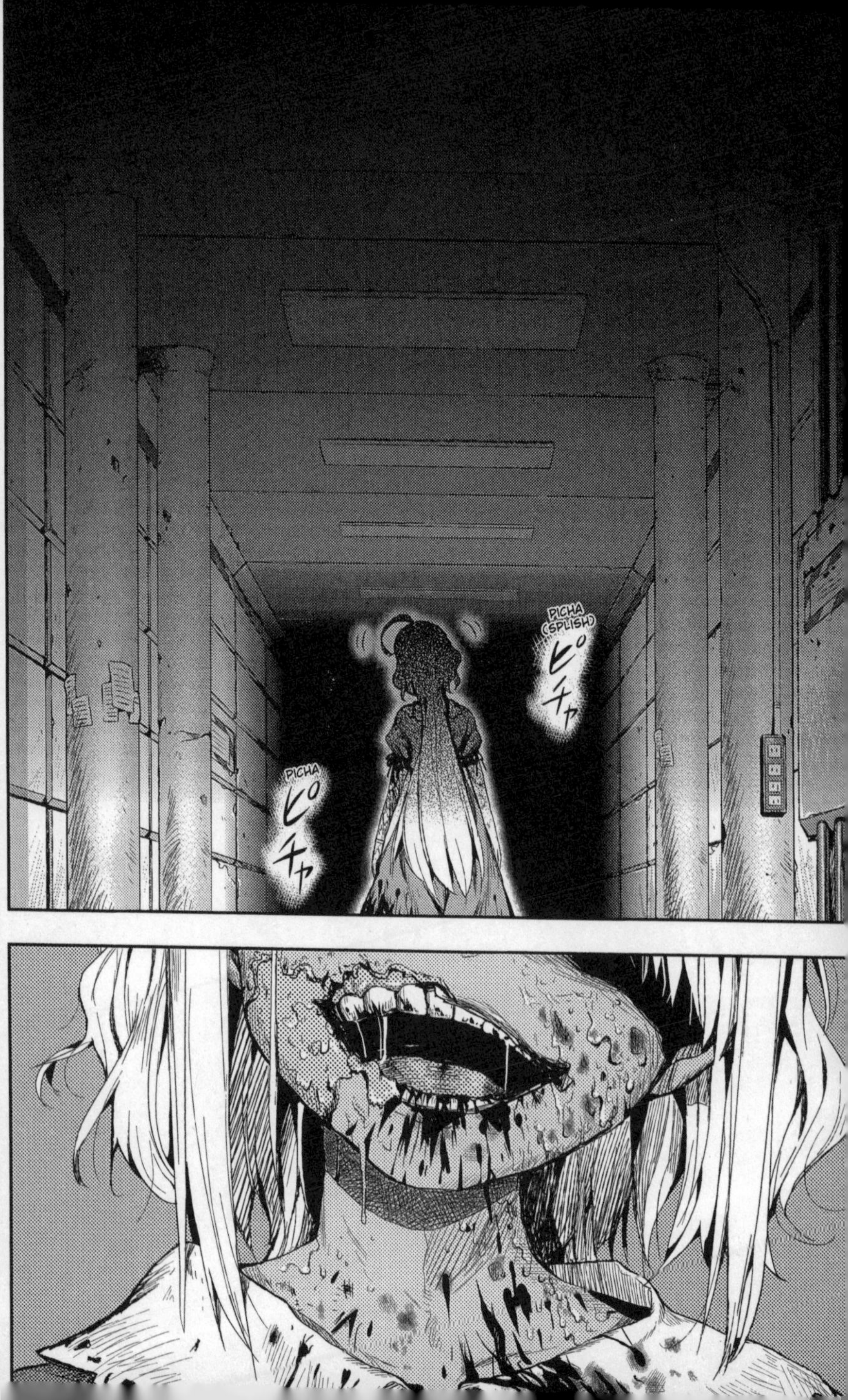
PICHA (SPLISH)
ピチャ
PICHA
ピチャ

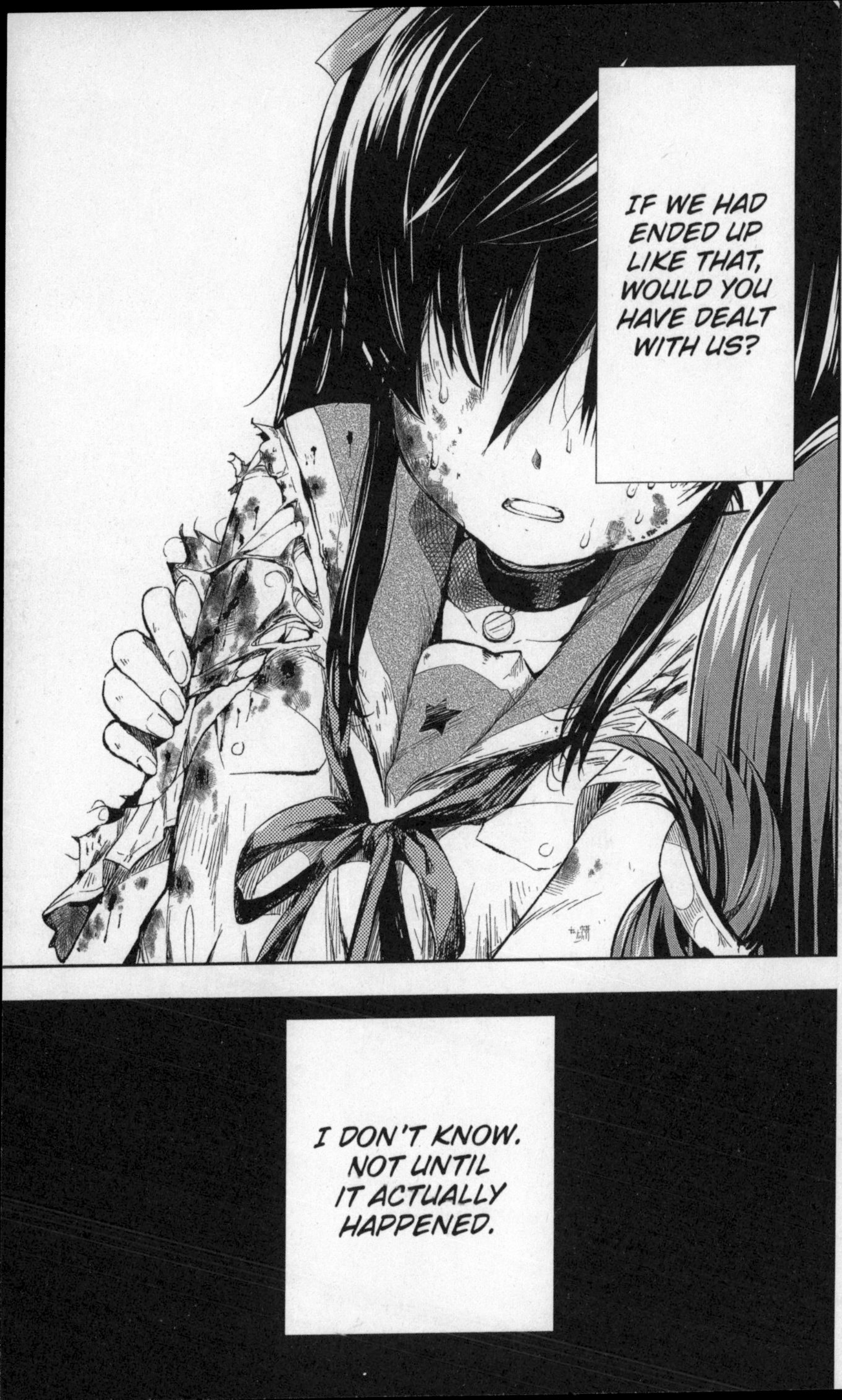
IF WE HAD ENDED UP LIKE THAT, WOULD YOU HAVE DEALT WITH US?
I DON'T KNOW. NOT UNTIL IT ACTUALLY HAPPENED.

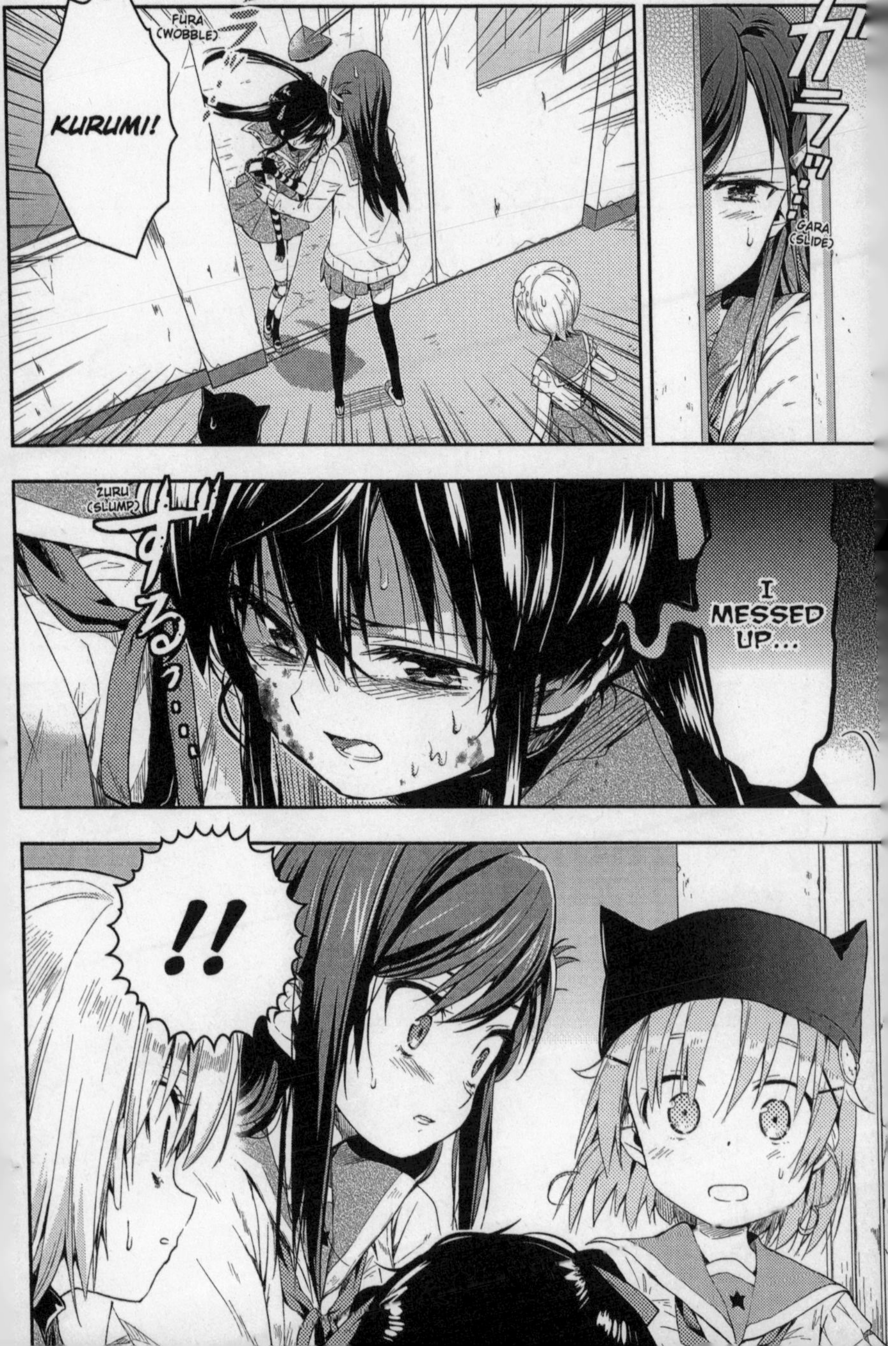
GARA (SLIDE)
KURUMI!
FURA (WOBBLE)
ZURU (SLUMP)
I MESSED UP...
!!

SIGNS: STUDENT COUNCIL / SCHOOL LIVING CLUB

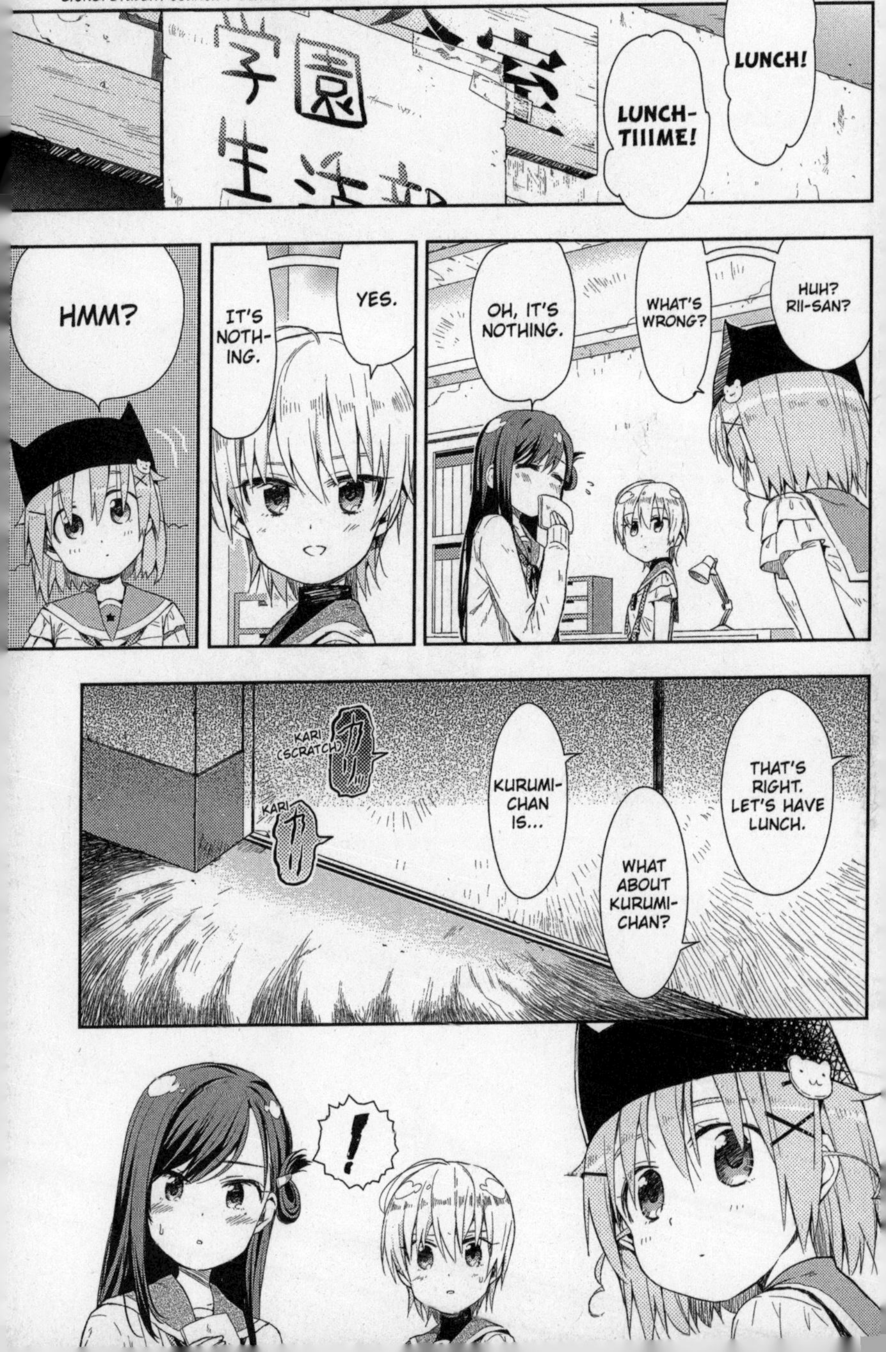
LUNCH!
LUNCH-TIIIME!
学園生活部
HUH? RII-SAN?
WHAT'S WRONG?
OH, IT'S NOTHING.
YES.
IT'S NOTHING.
HMM?
THAT'S RIGHT. LET'S HAVE LUNCH.
WHAT ABOUT KURUMI-CHAN?
KURUMI-CHAN IS...
KARI (SCRATCH)
カリ
KARI
カリ
!

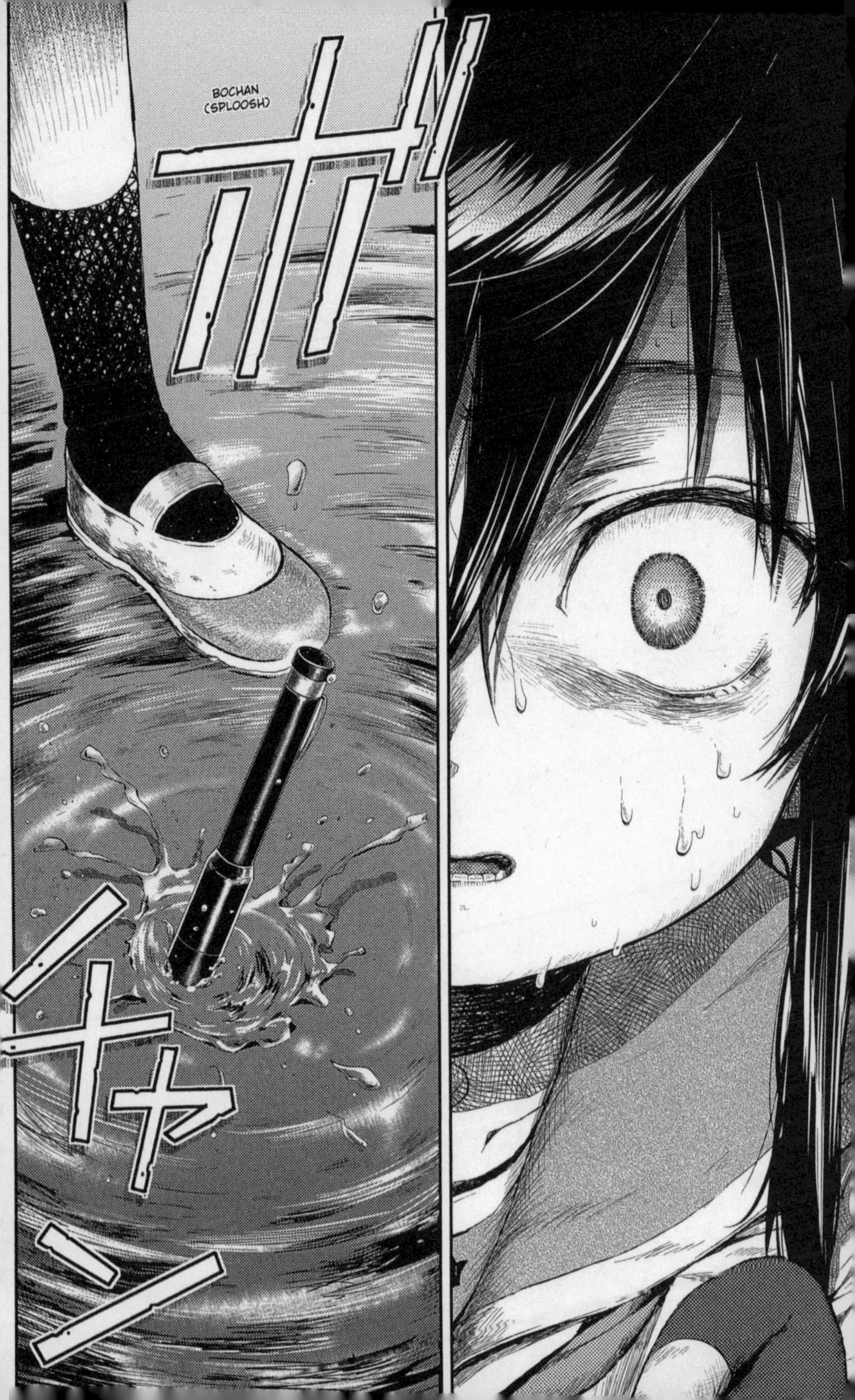
BOCHAN
(SPLOOSH)

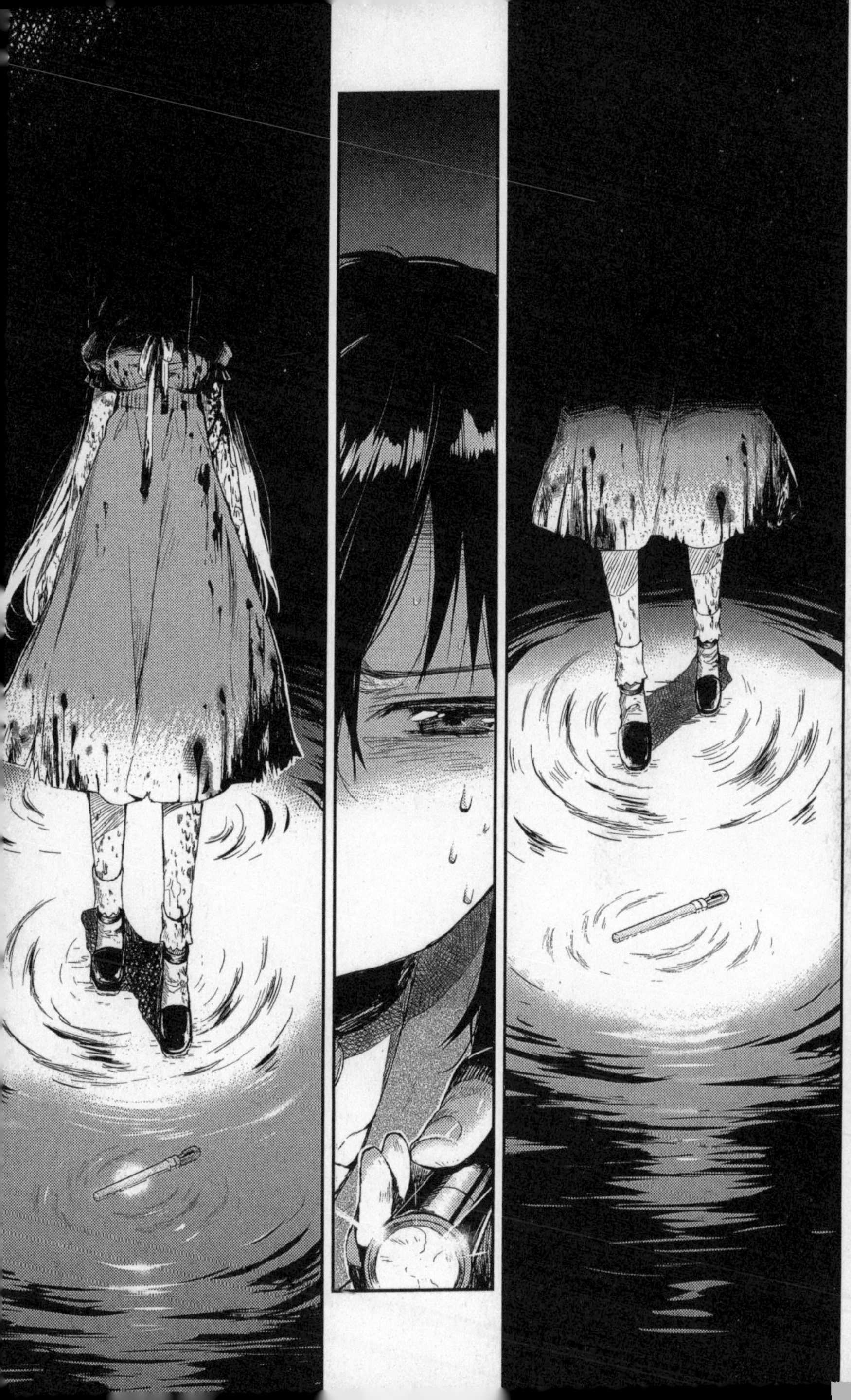

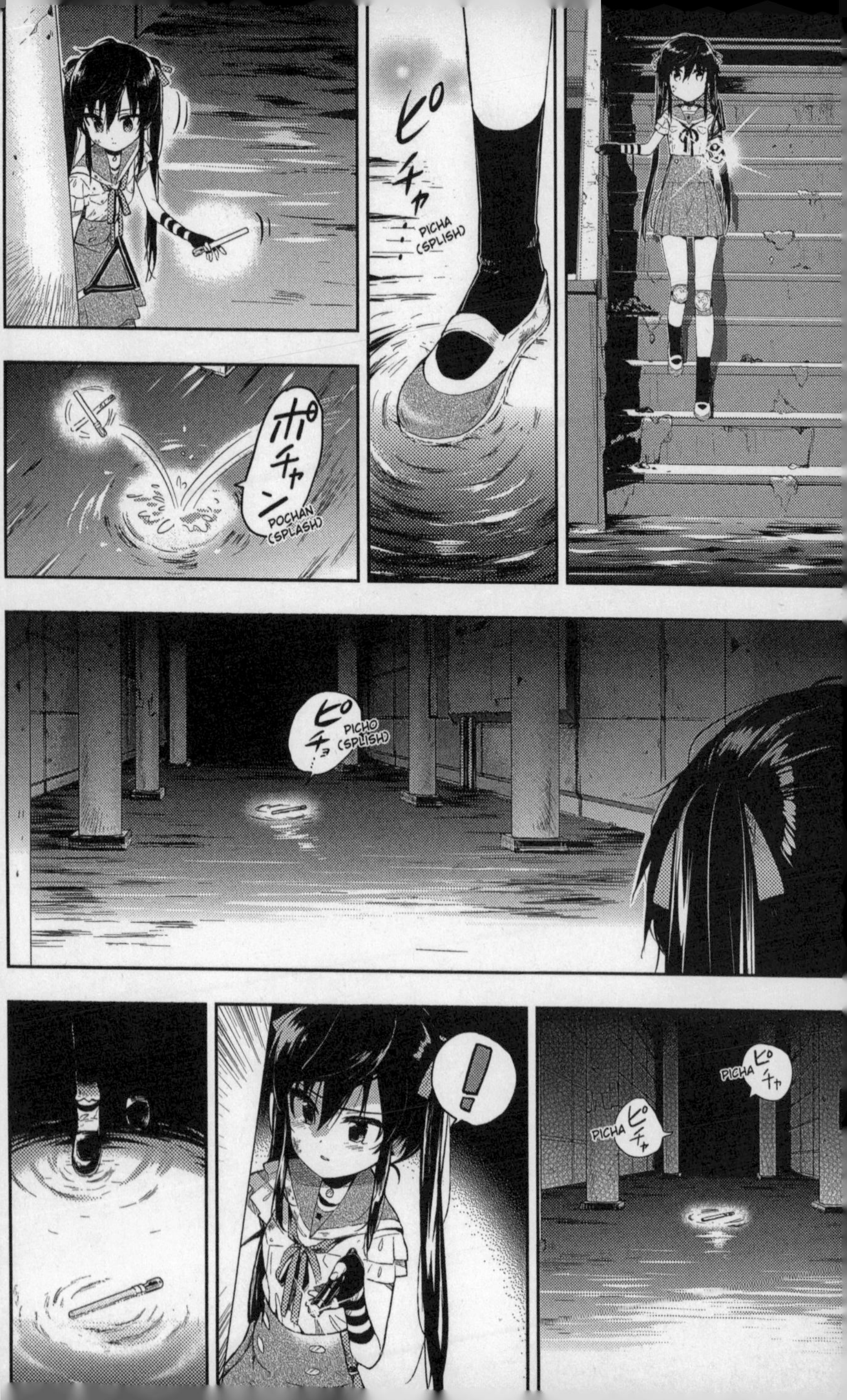

ピチャ
PICHA (SPLASH)
ポチャン
POCHAN (SPLASH)
ピチョ
PICHO (SPLASH)
ピチャ
PICHA
ピチャ
PICHA
!

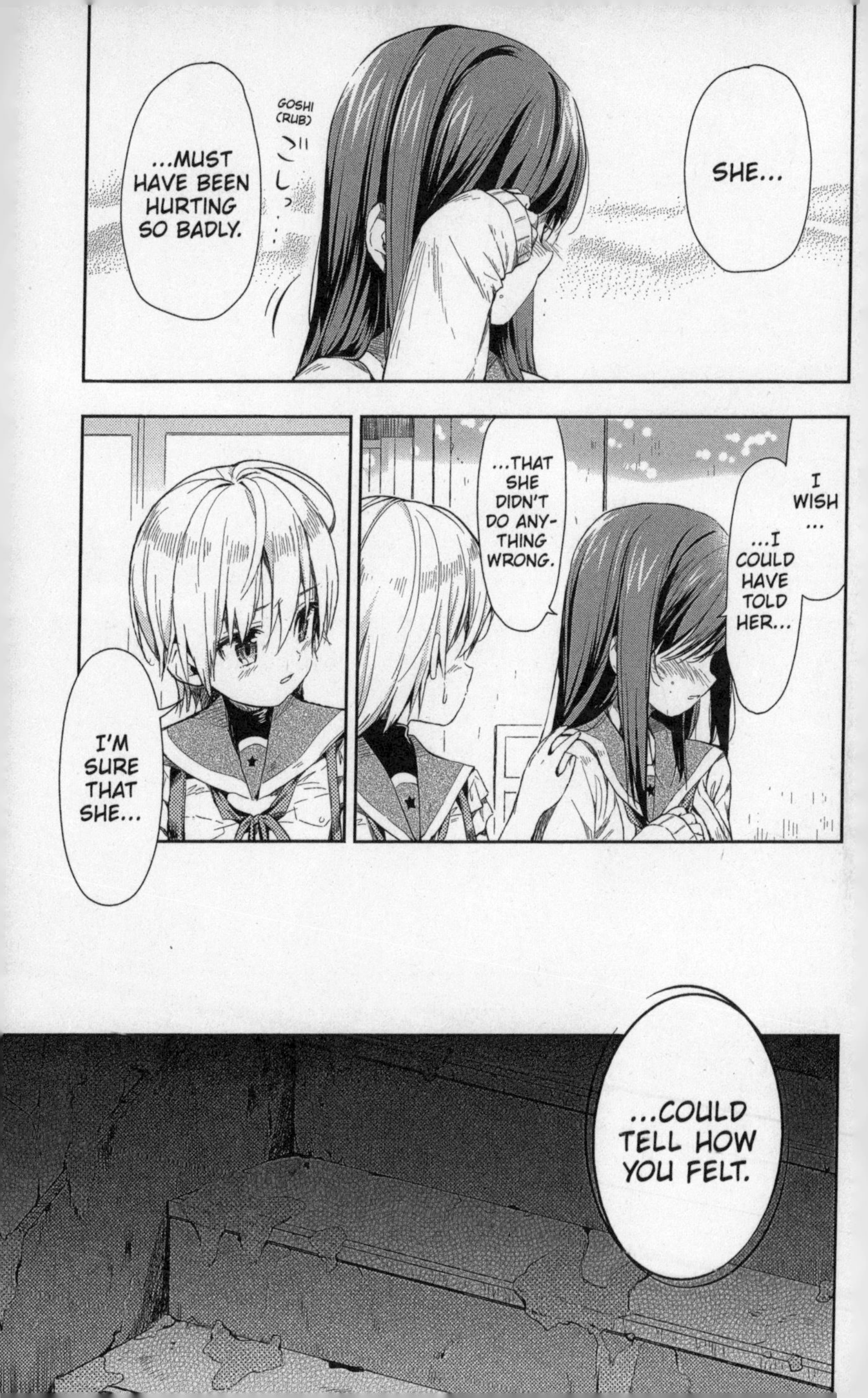
SHE...
GOSHI (RUB)
...MUST HAVE BEEN HURTING SO BADLY.
I WISH...
...I COULD HAVE TOLD HER...
...THAT SHE DIDN'T DO ANY-THING WRONG.
I'M SURE THAT SHE...
...COULD TELL HOW YOU FELT.

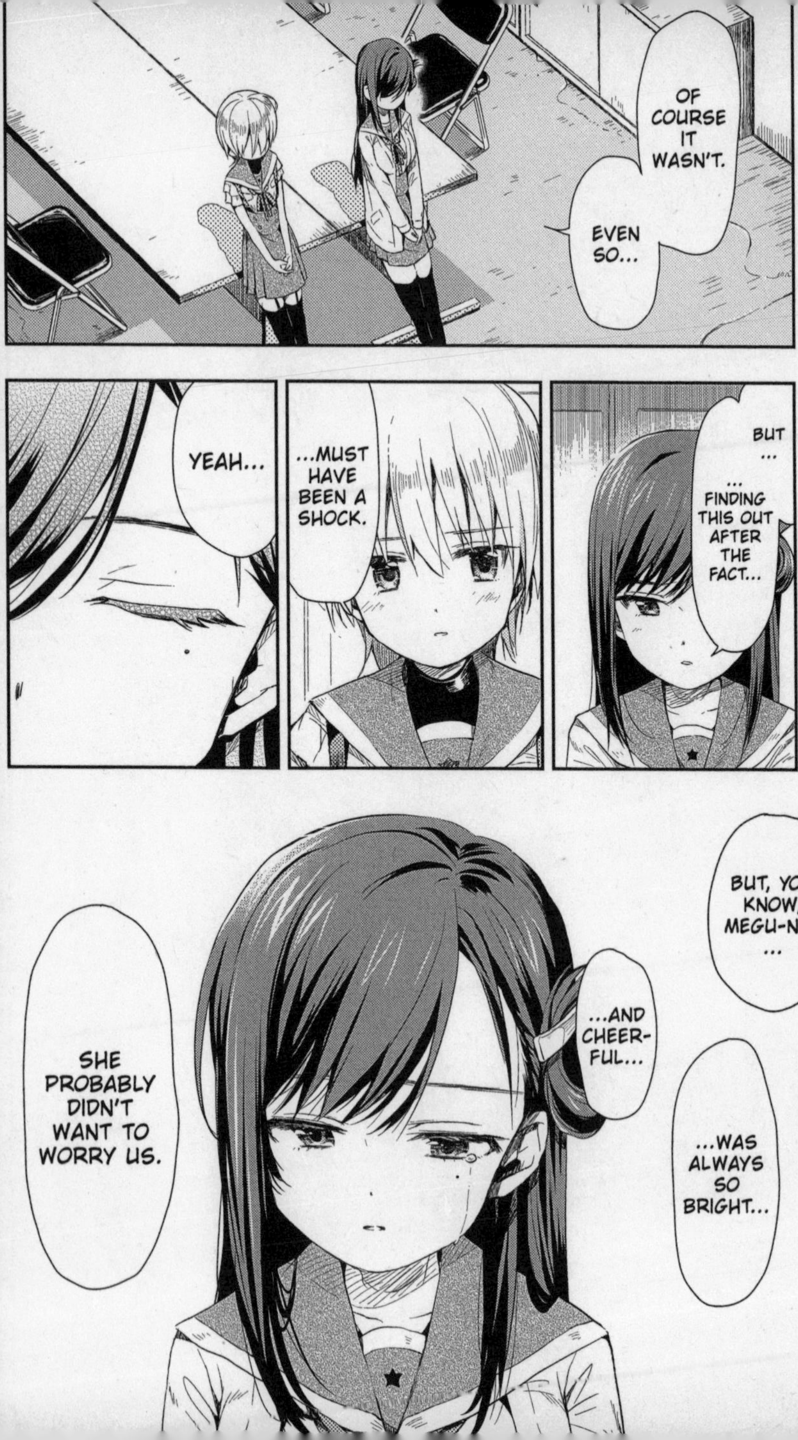
OF COURSE IT WASN'T.
EVEN SO...
BUT ...
... FINDING THIS OUT AFTER THE FACT...
...MUST HAVE BEEN A SHOCK.
YEAH...
BUT, YOU KNOW, MEGU-NEE ...
...WAS ALWAYS SO BRIGHT...
...AND CHEERFUL...
SHE PROBABLY DIDN'T WANT TO WORRY US.

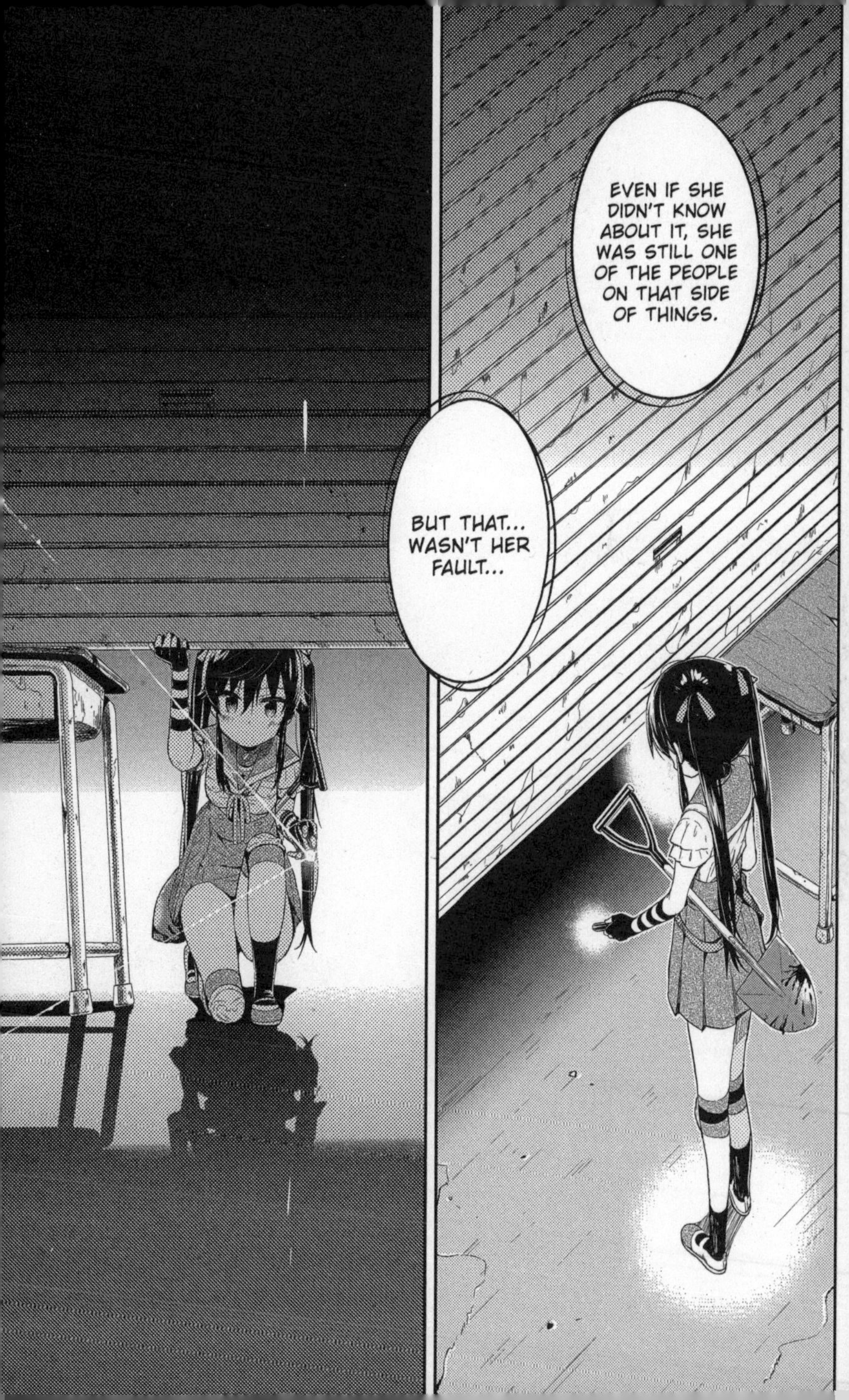
EVEN IF SHE DIDN'T KNOW ABOUT IT, SHE WAS STILL ONE OF THE PEOPLE ON THAT SIDE OF THINGS.
BUT THAT... WASN'T HER FAULT...

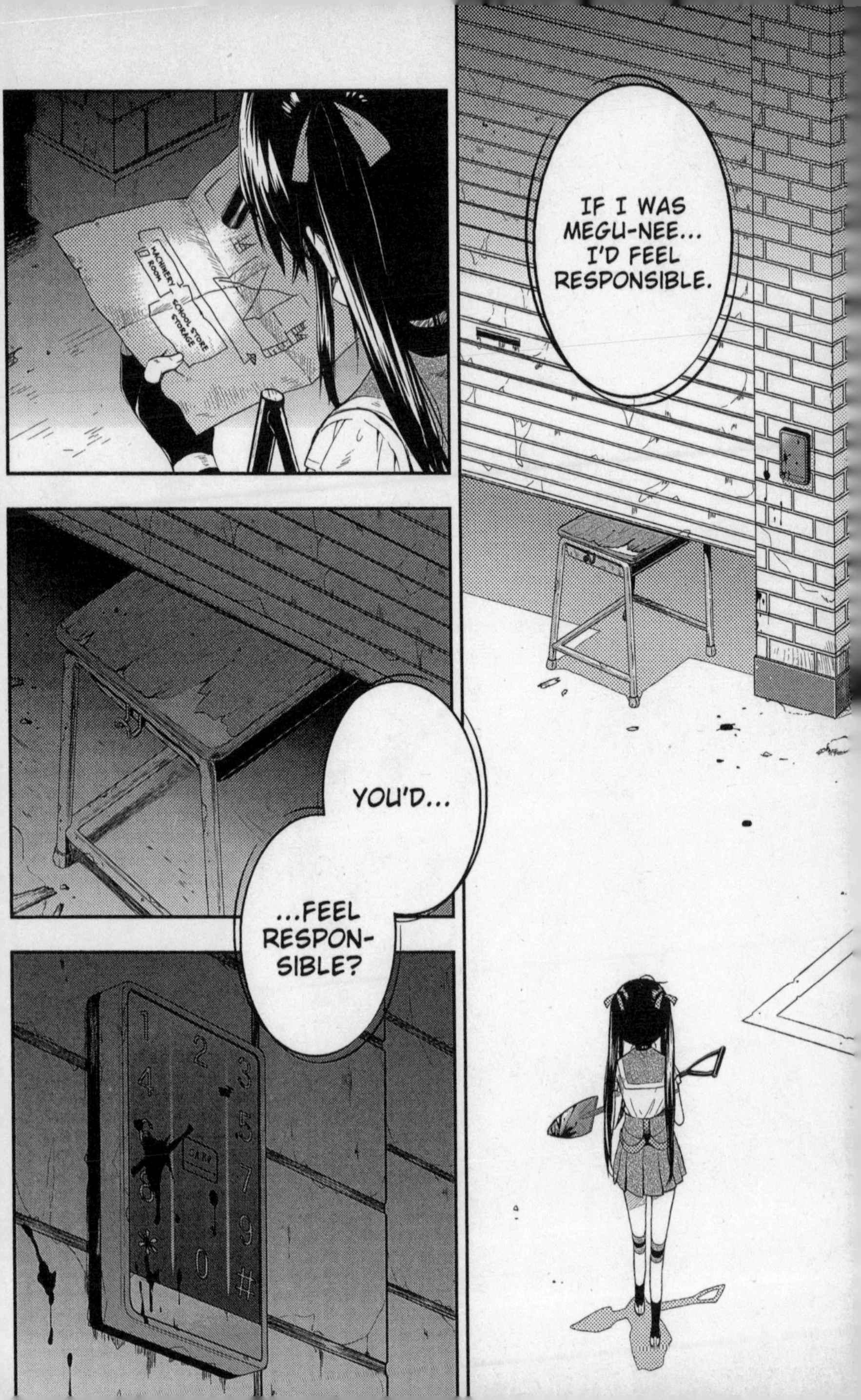
IF I WAS MEGU-NEE... I'D FEEL RESPONSIBLE.
MACHINERY ROOM
SCHOOL STORE STORAGE
YOU'D...
...FEEL RESPON-SIBLE?

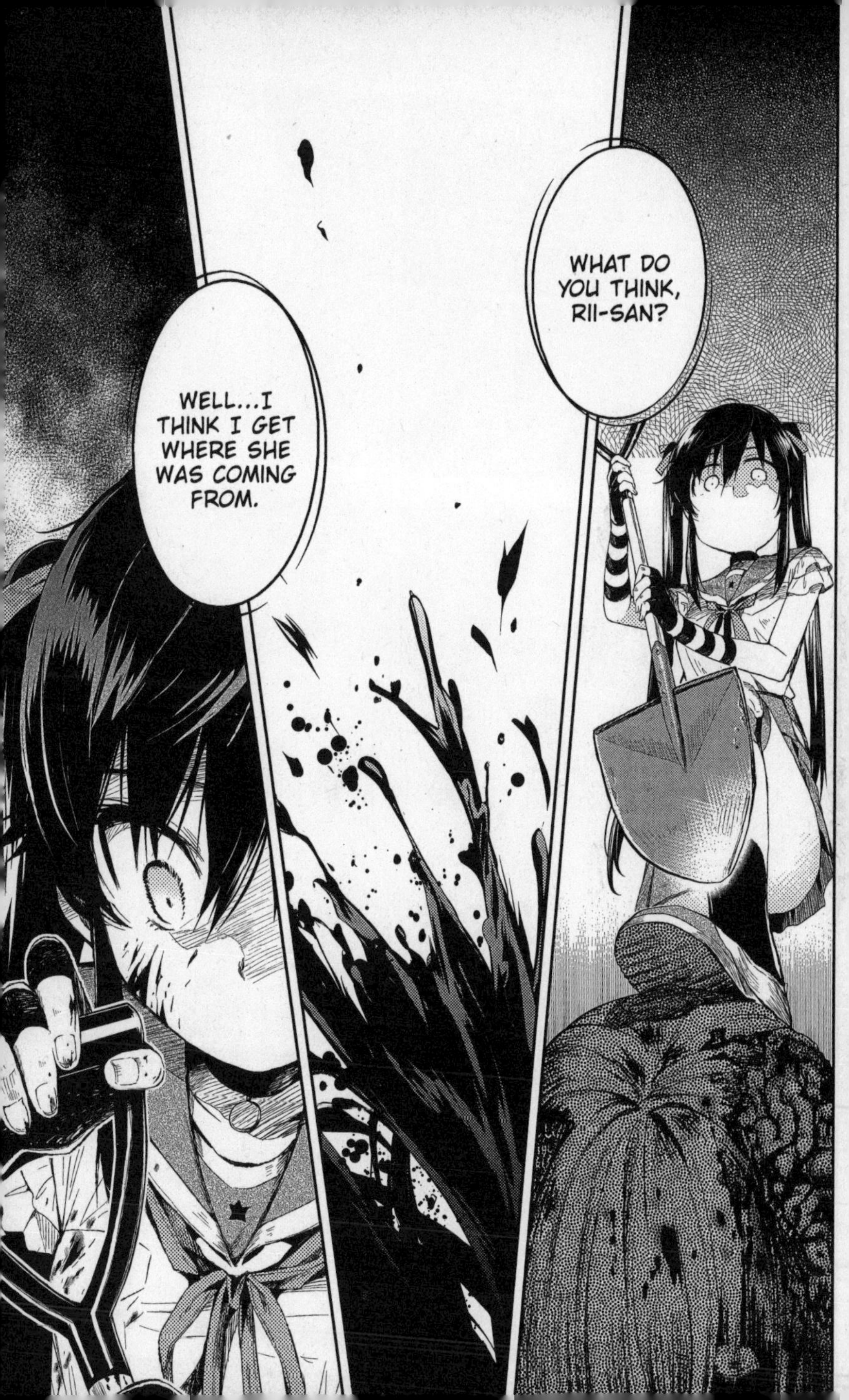
WHAT DO YOU THINK, RII-SAN?
WELL...I THINK I GET WHERE SHE WAS COMING FROM.

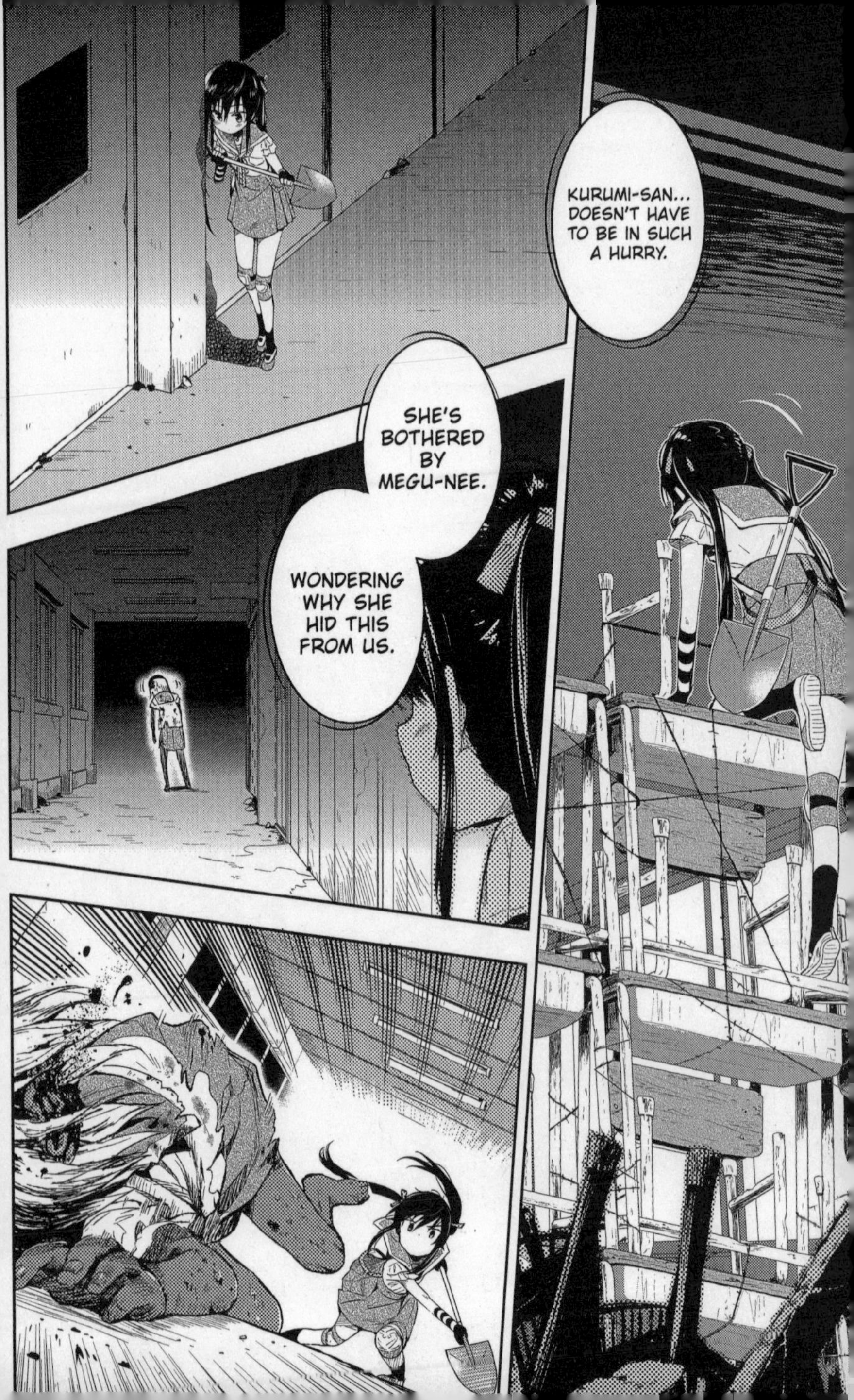
KURUMI-SAN... DOESN'T HAVE TO BE IN SUCH A HURRY.
SHE'S BOTHERED BY MEGU-NEE.
WONDERING WHY SHE HID THIS FROM US.

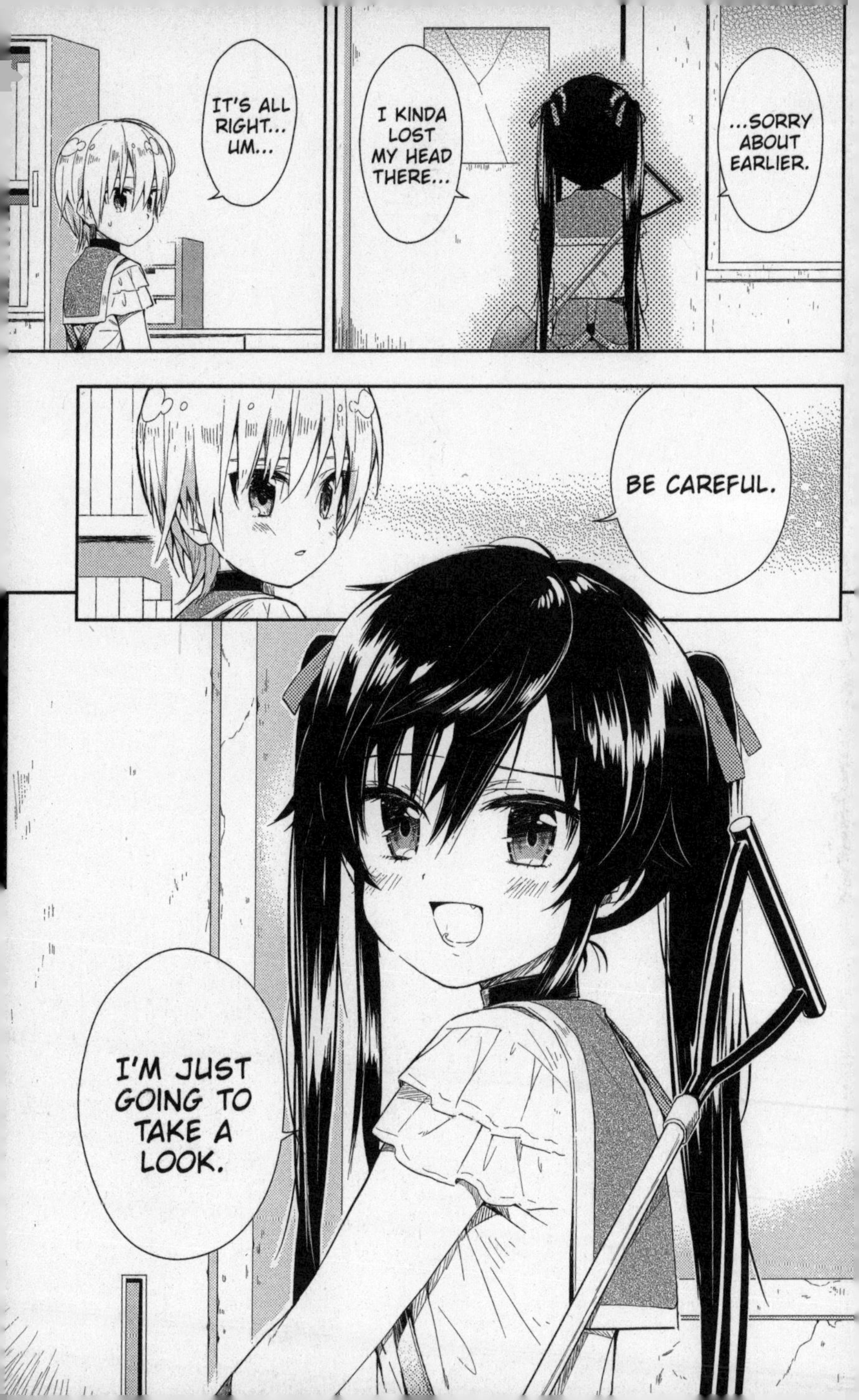
...SORRY ABOUT EARLIER.
I KINDA LOST MY HEAD THERE...
IT'S ALL RIGHT... UM...
BE CAREFUL.
I'M JUST GOING TO TAKE A LOOK.

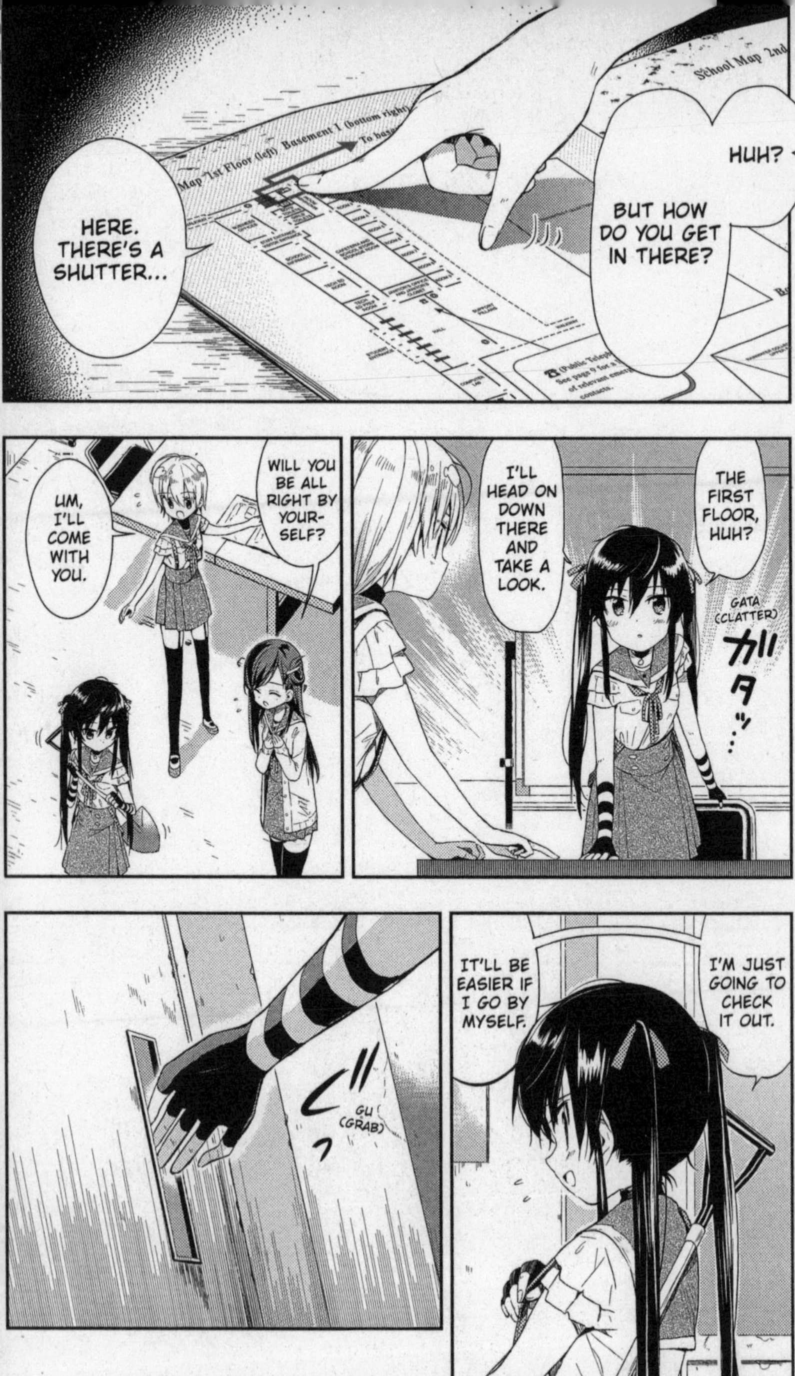
HUH?
BUT HOW DO YOU GET IN THERE?
Map 1st Floor (left) Basement 1 (bottom right)
HERE. THERE'S A SHUTTER...
THE FIRST FLOOR, HUH?
GATA (CLATTER)
ガタッ…
I'LL HEAD ON DOWN THERE AND TAKE A LOOK.
WILL YOU BE ALL RIGHT BY YOURSELF?
UM, I'LL COME WITH YOU.
I'M JUST GOING TO CHECK IT OUT.
IT'LL BE EASIER IF I GO BY MYSELF.
GU (GRAB)

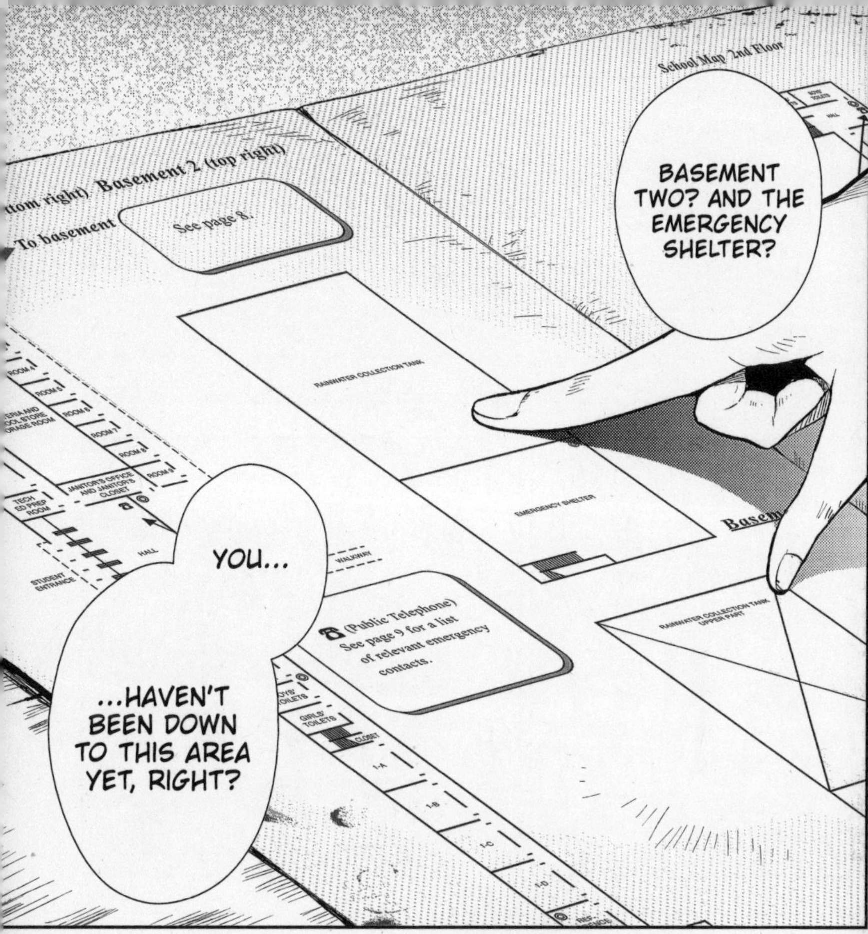
School Map 2nd Floor
Basement 2 (top right)
To basement
See page 8.
RAINWATER COLLECTION TANK
EMERGENCY SHELTER
(Public Telephone) See page 9 for a list of relevant emergency contacts.
RAINWATER COLLECTION TANK UPPER PART
ROOM 4
ROOM 5
ROOM 6
ROOM 7
ROOM 8
ROOM 9
JANITOR'S OFFICE AND JANITOR'S CLOSET
TECH ED PREP ROOM
HALL
STUDENT ENTRANCE
WALKWAY
GIRLS' TOILETS
CLOSET
1-A
1-B
1-C
1-D
BASEMENT TWO? AND THE EMERGENCY SHELTER?
YOU...
...HAVEN'T BEEN DOWN TO THIS AREA YET, RIGHT?

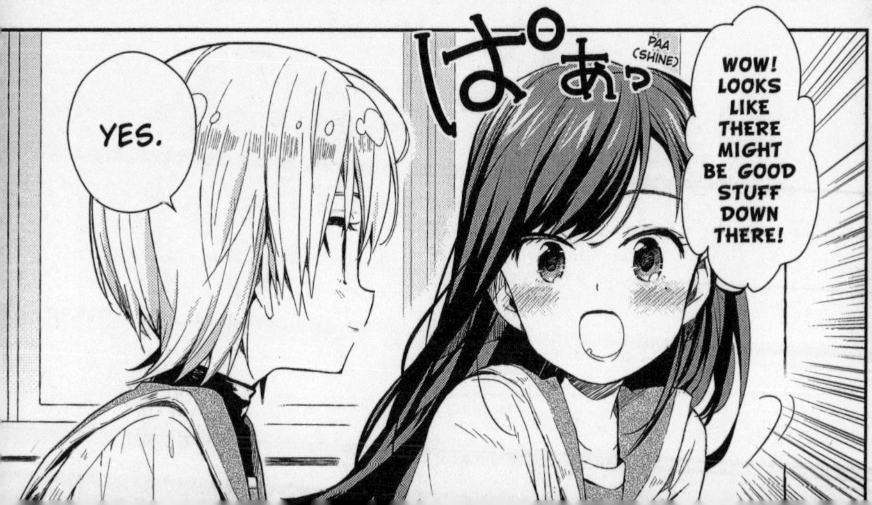
WOW! LOOKS LIKE THERE MIGHT BE GOOD STUFF DOWN THERE!
ぱあっ
PAA (SHINE)
YES.

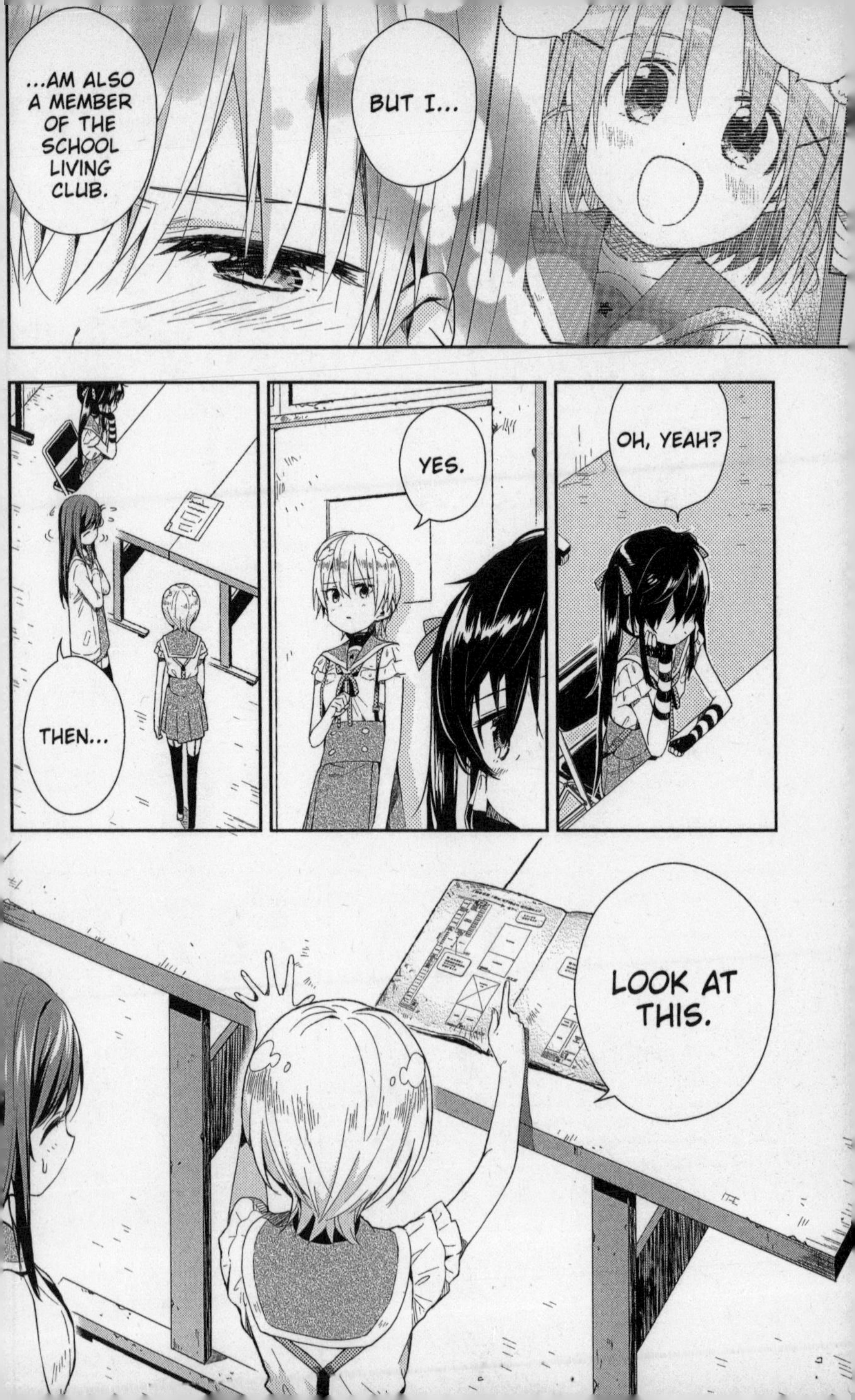
BUT I...
...AM ALSO A MEMBER OF THE SCHOOL LIVING CLUB.
OH, YEAH?
YES.
THEN...
LOOK AT THIS.

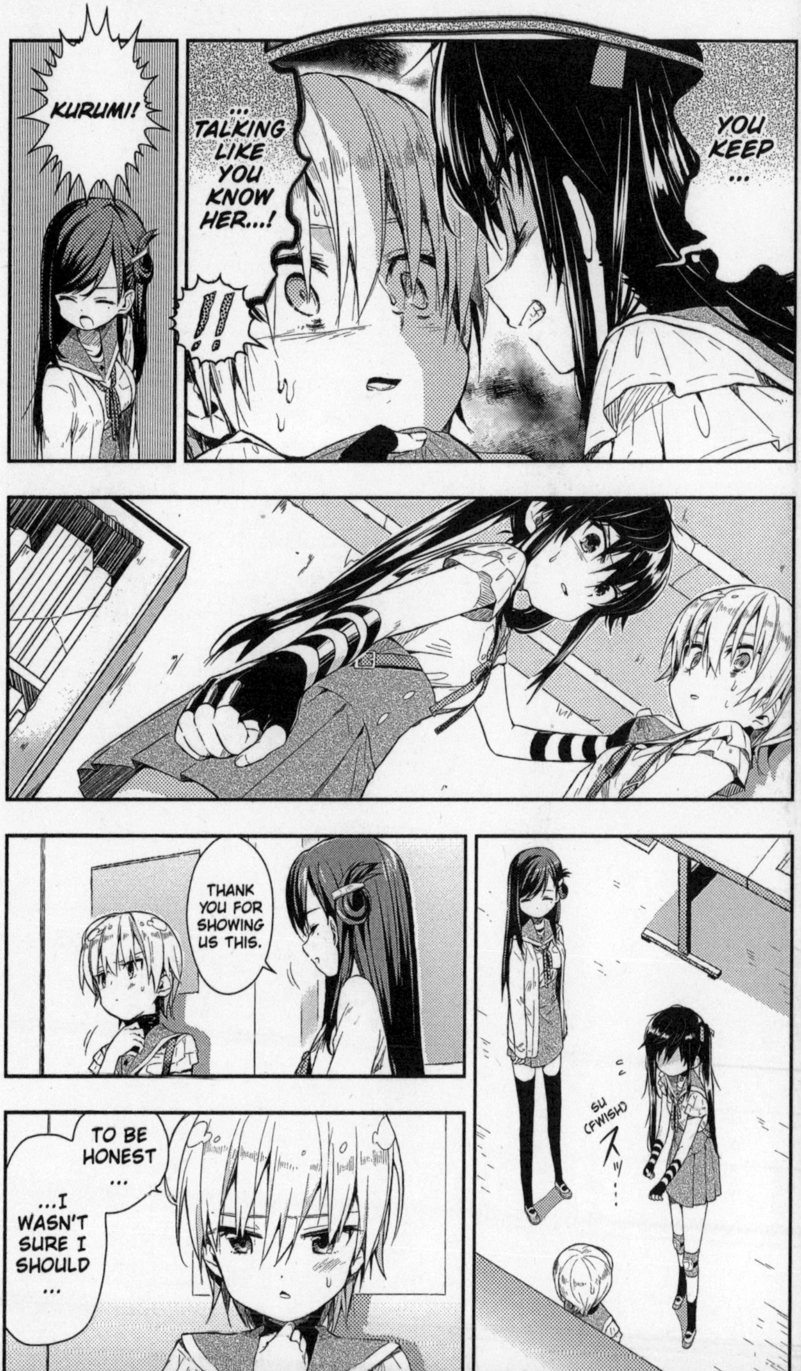
YOU KEEP ...
... TALKING LIKE YOU KNOW HER...!
!!
KURUMI!
SU (FWISH)
THANK YOU FOR SHOWING US THIS.
TO BE HONEST ...
...I WASN'T SURE I SHOULD ...

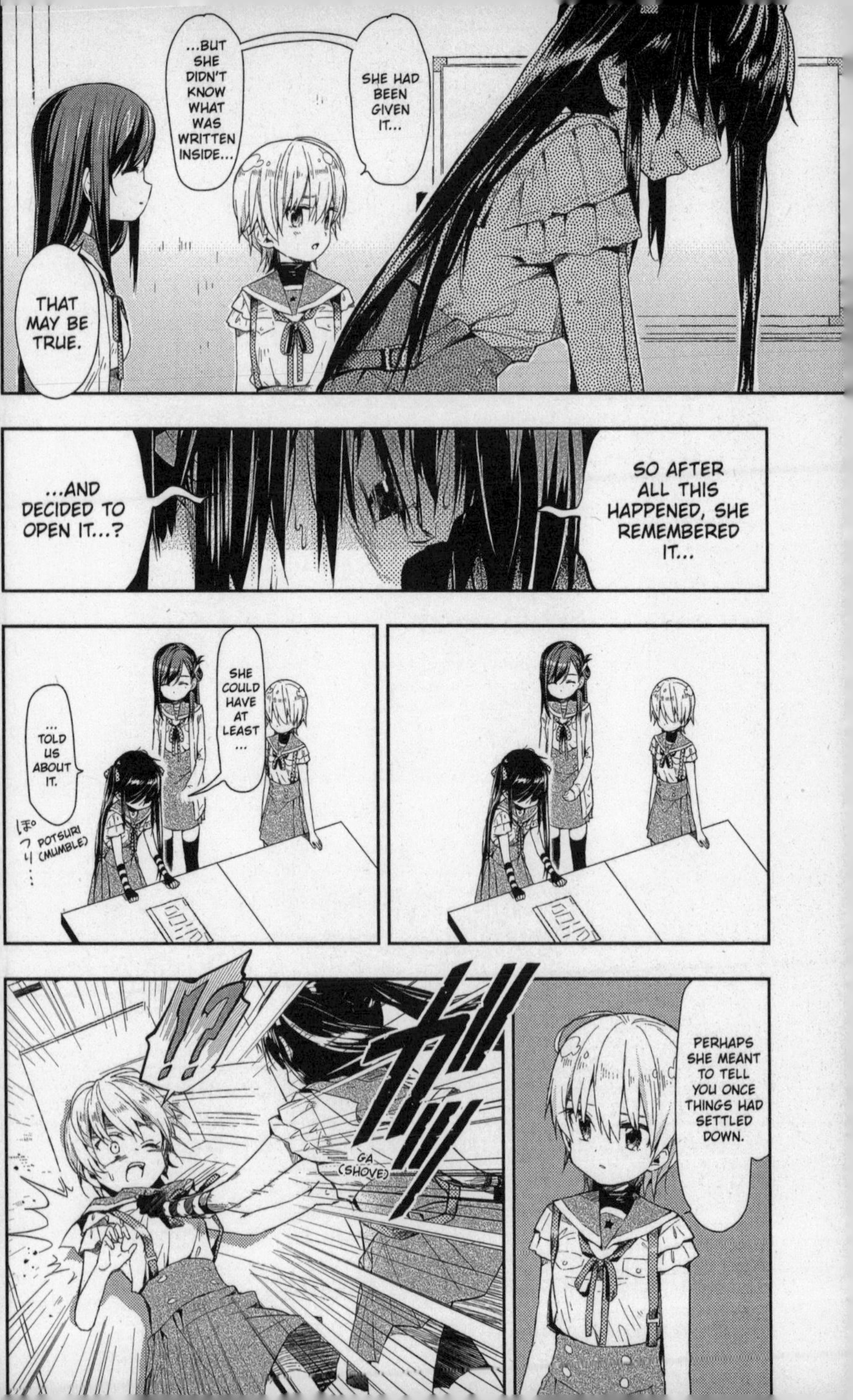
SHE HAD BEEN GIVEN IT...
...BUT SHE DIDN'T KNOW WHAT WAS WRITTEN INSIDE...
THAT MAY BE TRUE.
SO AFTER ALL THIS HAPPENED, SHE REMEMBERED IT...
...AND DECIDED TO OPEN IT...?
SHE COULD HAVE AT LEAST ...
... TOLD US ABOUT IT.
ぽつり...
POTSURI (MUMBLE)
PERHAPS SHE MEANT TO TELL YOU ONCE THINGS HAD SETTLED DOWN.
!!?
GA (SHOVE)

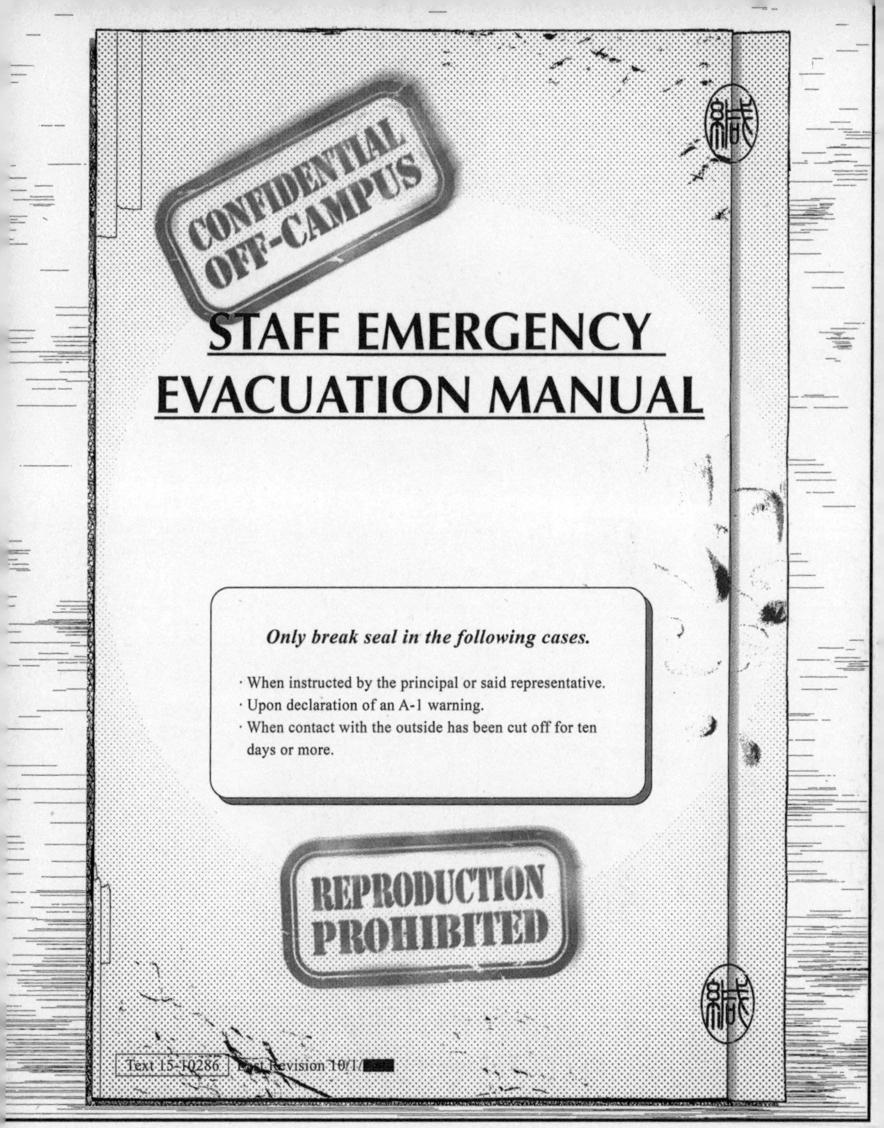
CONFIDENTIAL
OFF-CAMPUS
STAFF EMERGENCY
EVACUATION MANUAL
Only break seal in the following cases.
· When instructed by the principal or said representative.
· Upon declaration of an A-1 warning.
· When contact with the outside has been cut off for ten days or more.
REPRODUCTION
PROHIBITED
Text 15-10286
Last Revision 10/1/[redacted]

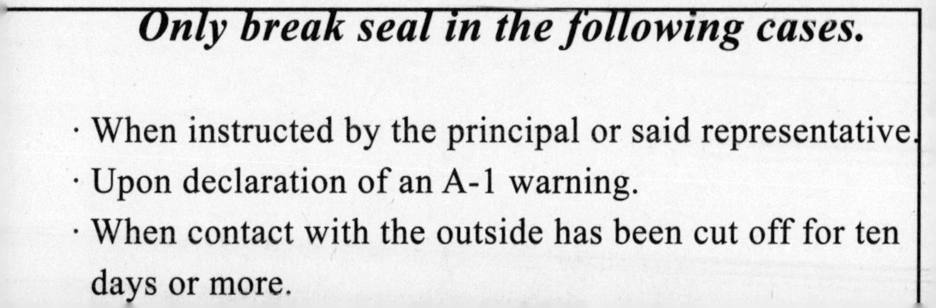
Only break seal in the following cases.
· When instructed by the principal or said representative.
· Upon declaration of an A-1 warning.
· When contact with the outside has been cut off for ten days or more.

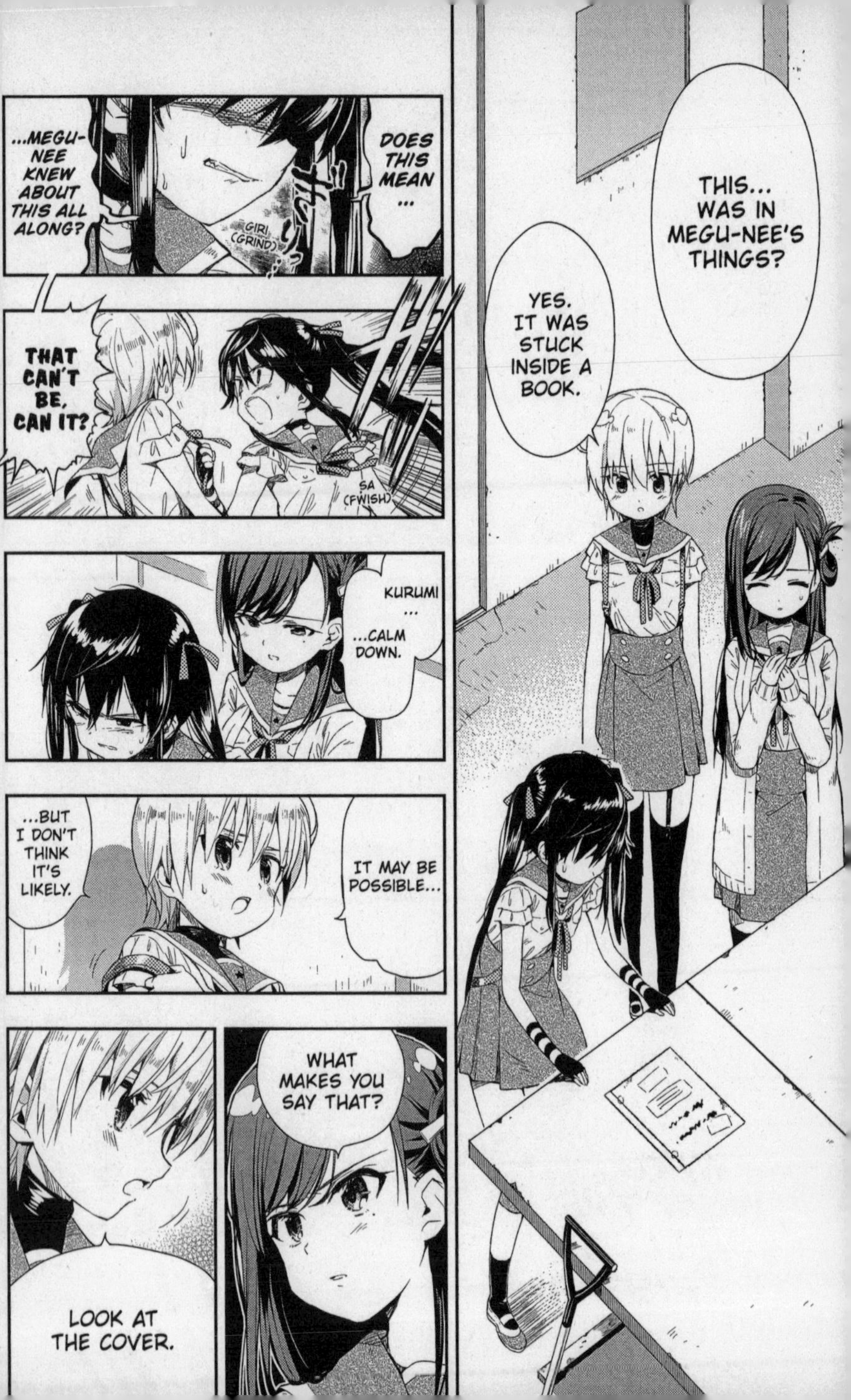
THIS... WAS IN MEGU-NEE'S THINGS?
YES. IT WAS STUCK INSIDE A BOOK.
DOES THIS MEAN ...
...MEGU-NEE KNEW ABOUT THIS ALL ALONG?
GIRI (GRIND)
THAT CAN'T BE, CAN IT?
SA (FWISH)
KURUMI ... ...CALM DOWN.
IT MAY BE POSSIBLE...
...BUT I DON'T THINK IT'S LIKELY.
WHAT MAKES YOU SAY THAT?
LOOK AT THE COVER.

BUT LET'S AT LEAST ALL THINK ABOUT IT TOGETHER, OKAY?

AND IF YOU DON'T WANNA TALK TO ME... ...YOU CAN TALK TO RII-SAN OR KURUMI-CHAN TOO, YOU KNOW.

HUH?

I JUST CAN'T WIN AGAINST HER.

...

SEE YOU!

PATAN (SHUT)

O-OKAY.

SORRY FOR SAYING ALL THOSE WEIRD THINGS.

...I'LL DO THAT.

BASA (THUMP)

CONFIDE... OFF-CAMP...

STAFF EMERGENCY EVACUATION MANUAL

WHOA. WHAT THE HELL IS THIS?

Only break seal ...
· When instructed by ... ...aid representative.
· Upon declaration of ... ...A.
· When contact with th... ...e has been cut off for ten ...ays or more.
fol...ng cas...

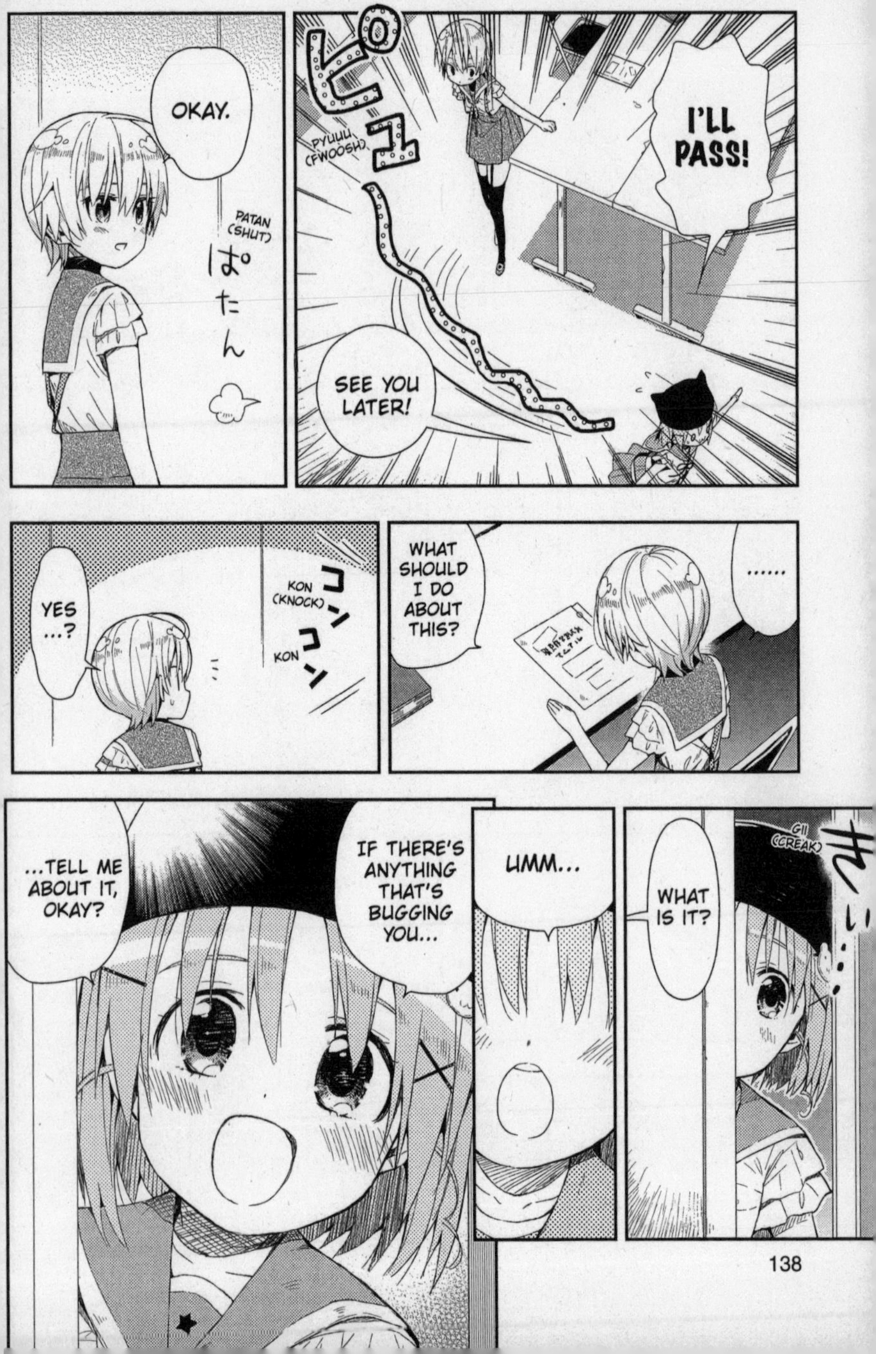
I'LL PASS!
PYUUU (FWOOSH)
ぴュ
SEE YOU LATER!
OKAY.
PATAN (SHUT)
ぱたん
......
WHAT SHOULD I DO ABOUT THIS?
KON (KNOCK)
コン
KON
コン
YES ...?
GII (CREAK)
きぃ…
WHAT IS IT?
UMM...
IF THERE'S ANYTHING THAT'S BUGGING YOU...
...TELL ME ABOUT IT, OKAY?

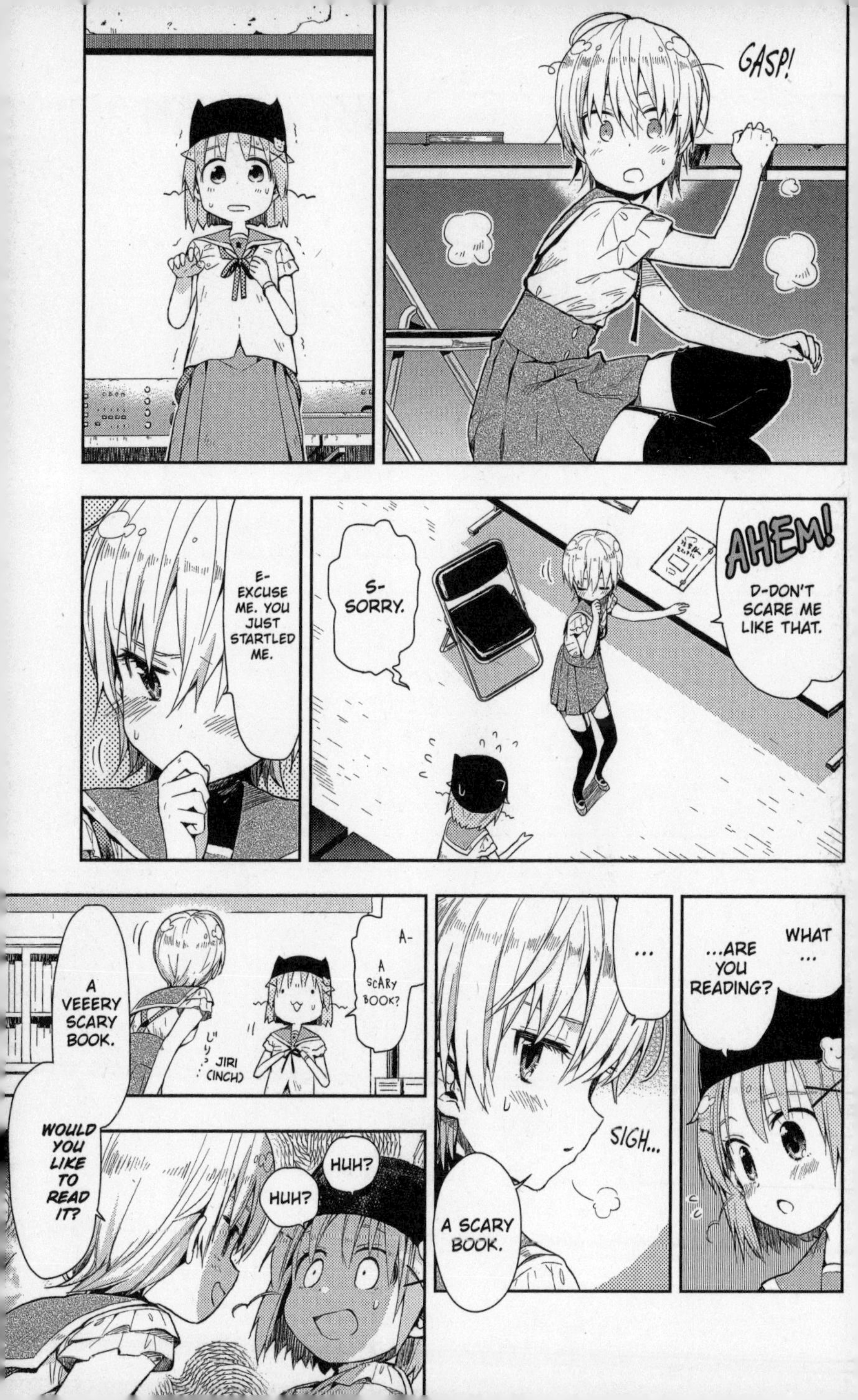
GASP!
AHEM!
D-DON'T SCARE ME LIKE THAT.
S-SORRY.
E-EXCUSE ME. YOU JUST STARTLED ME.
WHAT...
...ARE YOU READING?
...
SIGH...
A SCARY BOOK.
A-
A SCARY BOOK?
JIRI (INCH)
A VEEERY SCARY BOOK.
WOULD YOU LIKE TO READ IT?
HUH?
HUH?

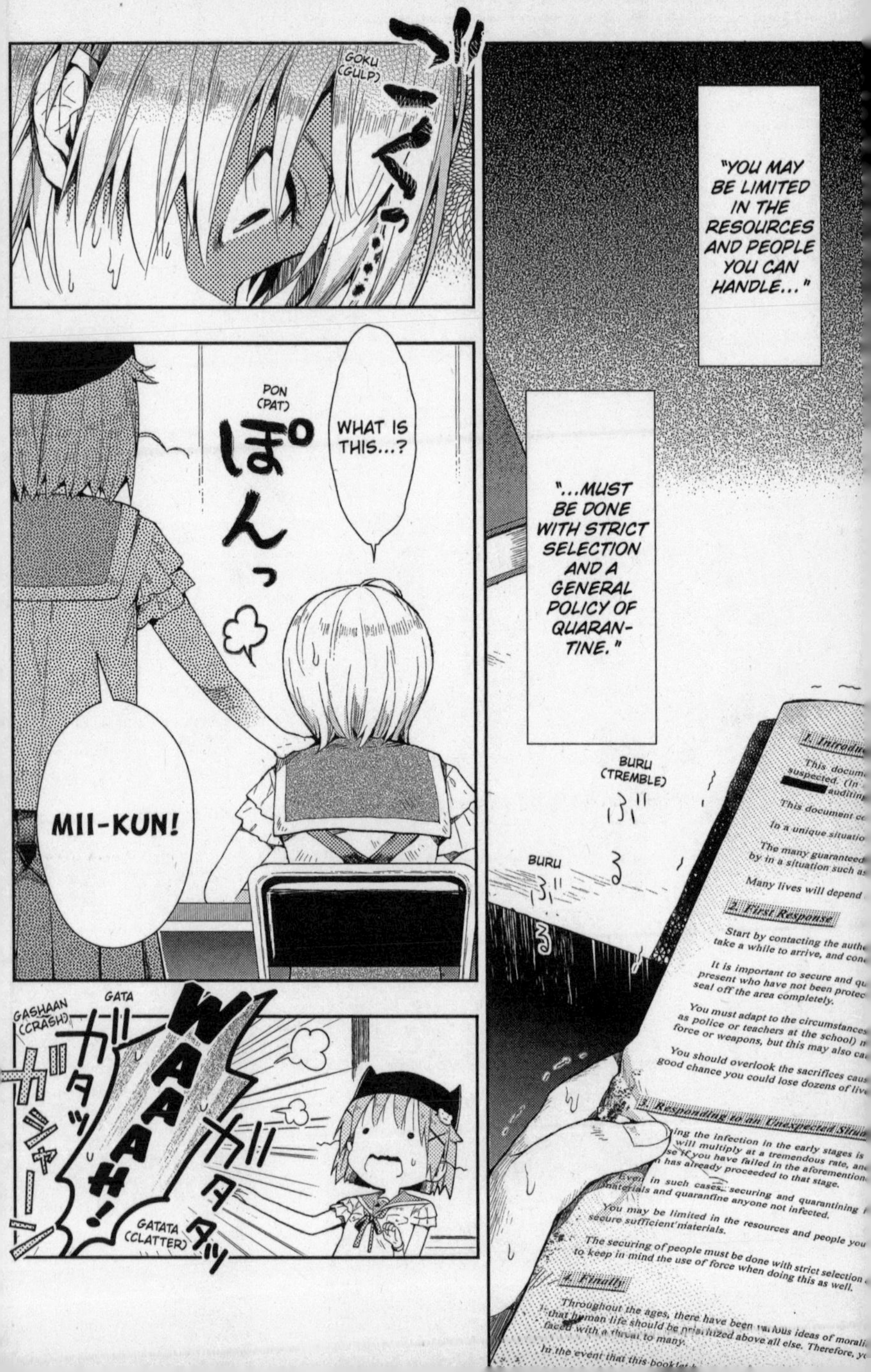
"YOU MAY BE LIMITED IN THE RESOURCES AND PEOPLE YOU CAN HANDLE..."
"...MUST BE DONE WITH STRICT SELECTION AND A GENERAL POLICY OF QUARAN-TINE."
BURU (TREMBLE)
ぶ
る
BURU
ぶ
る
1. Introdu
This docum
suspected. (In
[redacted]
auditin
This document c
In a unique situatio
The many guarantee
by in a situation such a
Many lives will depend
2. First Response
Start by contacting the auth
take a while to arrive, and con
It is important to secure and qu
present who have not been protec
seal off the area completely.
You must adapt to the circumstance
as police or teachers at the school)
force or weapons, but this may also ca
You should overlook the sacrifices cau
good chance you could lose dozens of liv
3. Responding to an Unexpected Situ
ing the infection in the early stages is
will multiply at a tremendous rate, an
se if you have failed in the aforementione
n has already proceeded to that stage.
Even in such cases, securing and quarantining
materials and quarantine anyone not infected.
You may be limited in the resources and people you
secure sufficient materials.
The securing of people must be done with strict selection
to keep in mind the use of force when doing this as well.
4. Finally
Throughout the ages, there have been various ideas of morali
that human life should be prioritized above all else. Therefore, y
faced with a threat to many.
In the event that this booklet
GOKU (GULP)
ゴクッ
WHAT IS THIS...?
PON (PAT)
ぽんっ
MII-KUN!
GASHAAN (CRASH)
ガシャーン
GATA
ガタッ
WAAAAH!
GATATA (CLATTER)
ガタタッ

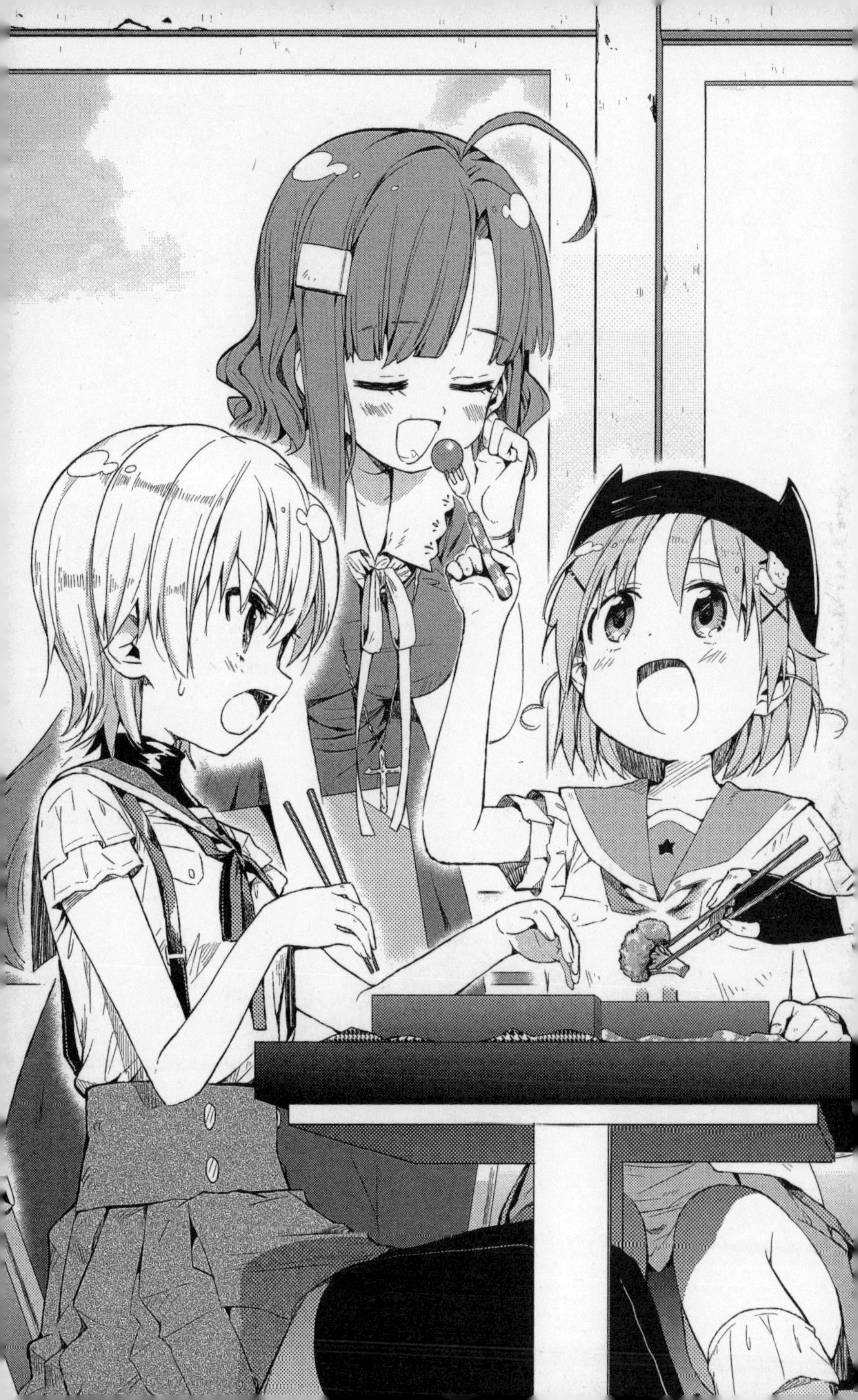

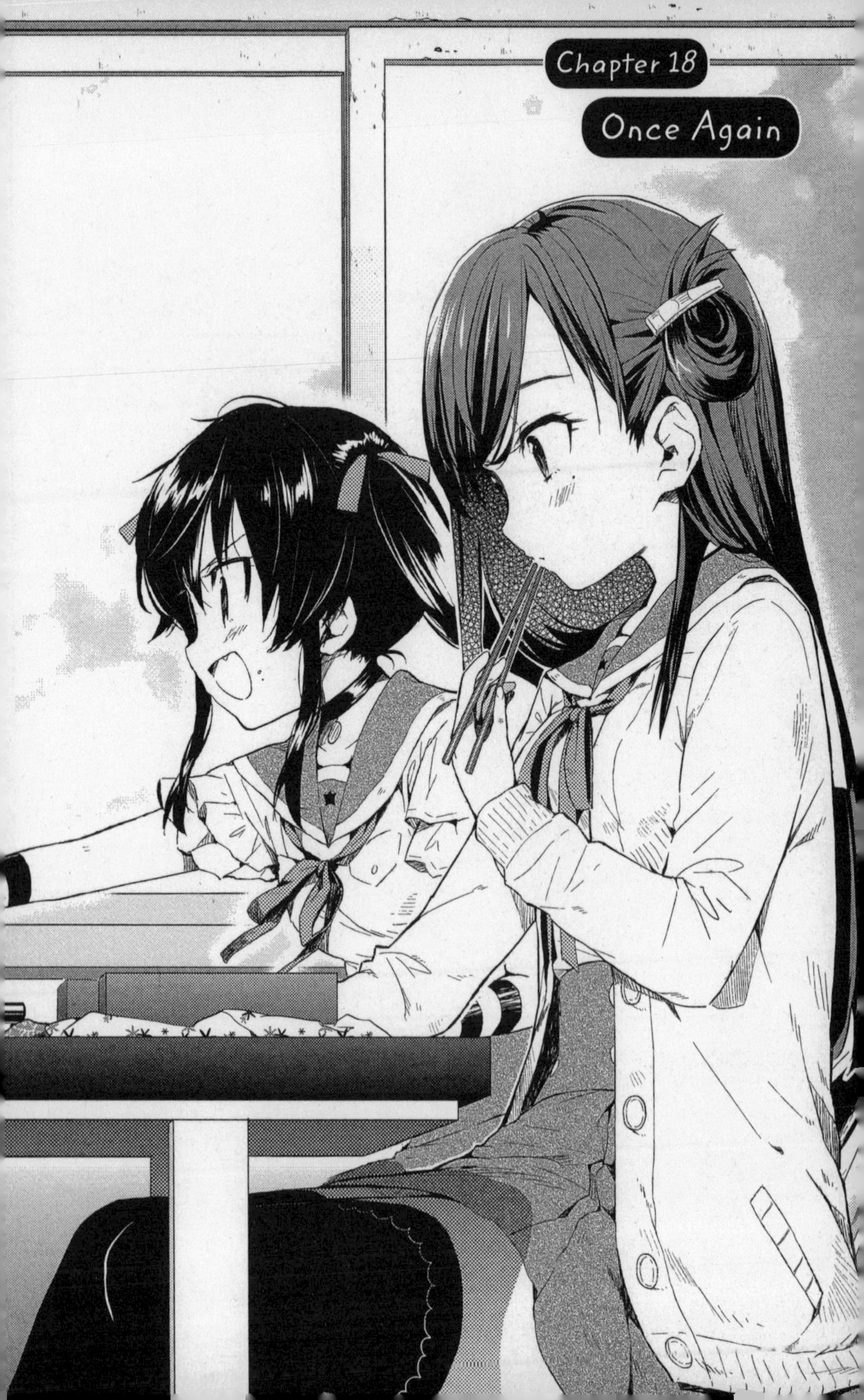
Chapter 18
Once Again

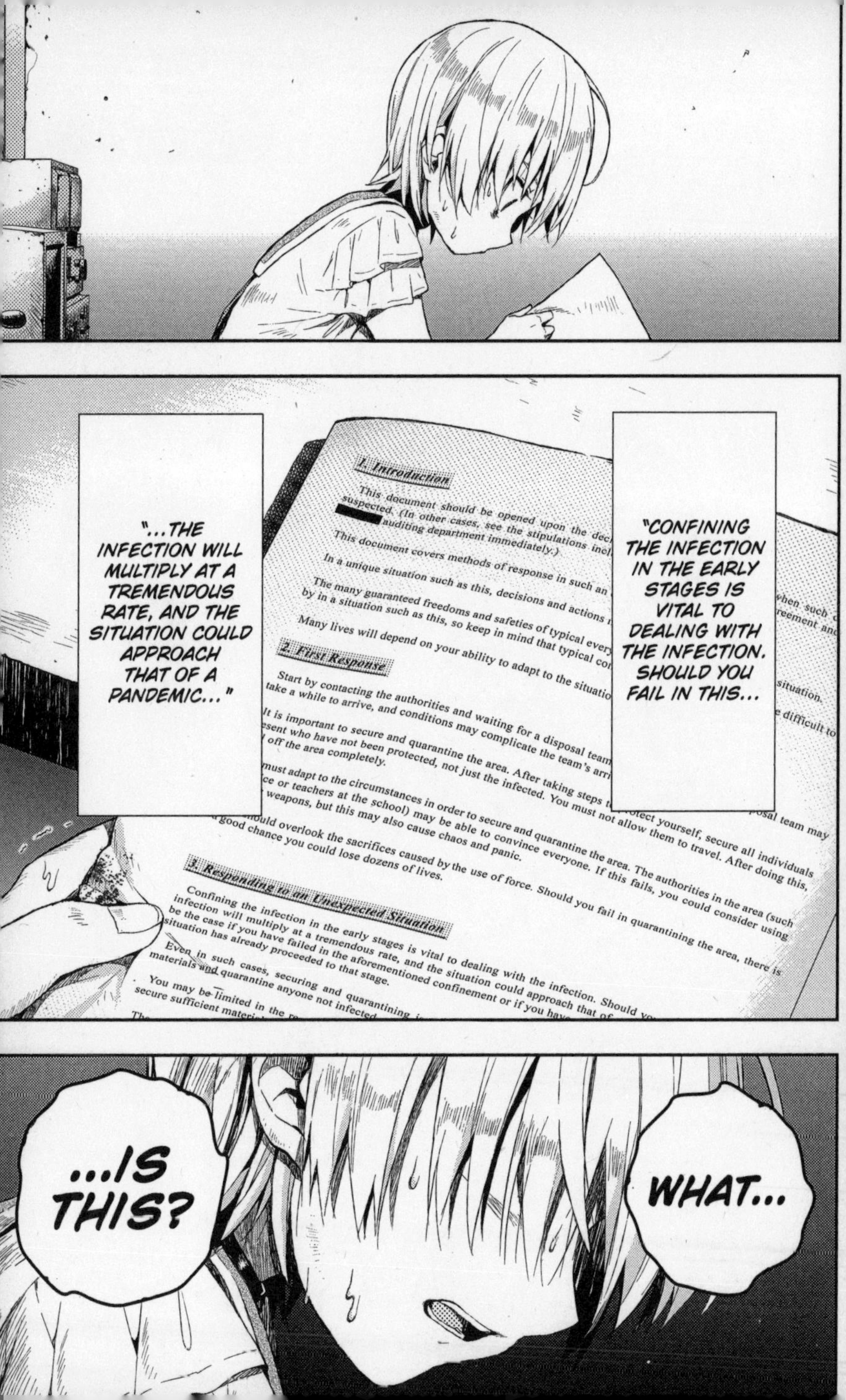
"CONFINING THE INFECTION IN THE EARLY STAGES IS VITAL TO DEALING WITH THE INFECTION. SHOULD YOU FAIL IN THIS...
"...THE INFECTION WILL MULTIPLY AT A TREMENDOUS RATE, AND THE SITUATION COULD APPROACH THAT OF A PANDEMIC..."
1. Introduction
2. First Response
3. Responding to an Unexpected Situation
WHAT...
...IS THIS?

SCHOOL-LIVE!

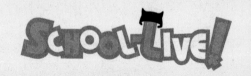